JOURNAL OF
WASHINGTON IRVING

LONDON : HUMPHREY MILFORD

OXFORD UNIVERSITY PRESS

WASHINGTON IRVING AT THE AGE OF THIRTY-SEVEN
(From the painting by Gilbert Stuart Newton, 1820)

JOURNAL OF
WASHINGTON IRVING
(1823–1824)

EDITED BY

STANLEY T. WILLIAMS

CAMBRIDGE

HARVARD UNIVERSITY PRESS

1931

PRINTED AT THE HARVARD UNIVERSITY PRESS
CAMBRIDGE, MASS., U. S. A.

ACKNOWLEDGMENT

The publication of this volume has been made possible through the kindness of Dr. Roderick Terry, of Newport, Rhode Island, in whose library is the manuscript Journal of Washington Irving, of 1823–1824.

CONTENTS

INTRODUCTION

ON THE banks of the Hudson, or in a corner of an English inn, or on a bench in an Andalusian village, Washington Irving often set down in pocket note-books the basic sentences of an essay, or sketched, not unlike Thackeray, a landscape or a castle. These "commonplace books" are filled with fragments of reading or meditation, and to the student of Irving are not without interest as originals of his finished essays, and as his reflections on the life of the nineteenth century.[1] On page [375] of the present Journal he refers to such a memorandum book; for these he reserved his more intimate thoughts. To them we must turn for revelation of that habit of his mind which he himself characterized as half-thought, half-reverie.

But Irving was an eager traveller and a penetrating observer of the ways of city and society. Thus he was so deeply interested in the drama that he endeavoured during the months of this Journal to make it his avocation; and whether at the theatre, or on the Seine between Rouen and Havre, or in the New Forest, or with Tom Moore at Sloperton cottage, he recorded minutely each incident of his daily life. This Journal (July 12, 1823–August 11, 1824), now printed entire for the first time, is such a chronicle. Without the in-

[1] See *Notes While Preparing Sketch Book &c.*, ed. S. T. Williams, New Haven, 1927.

trospection of Irving's other notebooks, it is an encyclopedic narrative of his external life during thirteen months.

For this reason, and others, it has seemed wise to publish the Journal separately. One difficulty of the editor has been his recognition of the trivialities with which the Journal abounds. That Irving was fond of whitebait; that he called on a certain "old Dropsical countess"; that his lodgings over the Palais Royal had smoky chimneys — these facts can hardly be of great moment. Yet the total effect of the explicit detail of the Journal has been to reveal Washington Irving in his forty-first year. If we tire of the numerous obscure who throng these pages, we achieve, nevertheless, because of this very fidelity of the author to his Journal, an exact picture of his friendship with Thomas Moore or John Howard Payne. Had he written less of the table-talk in the English circles of Paris, he might also have curtailed the descriptions of Talma, Rogers, and Byron. If the fault of the Journal is its meticulous completeness, this is more than once its virtue.

Nor is the story of this traveller of one hundred years ago without interest. In the German inns, in the Dutch villages, during that summer of 1823, Irving writes of shepherds or noblemen; and once he is in Paris he shows us how the Englishman or the American of that day occupies himself. We see Irving reading at Galignani's; listening with delight to Pasta; or wandering in the countryside near Auteuil. In the Spring of the next year he crossed to England.

From Brighton he took coach to London, and after arriving at the White Horse Cellars, he shared lodgings with William Robert Spencer, at 4 Mount Street. Through his eyes we see Charles Robert Leslie, now attaining fame as a painter; we call with him at Murray's and learn new stories of Byron; we hear Moore and Rogers slander each other; and through him we listen to the gossip of the battle of Waterloo, not yet a decade old. Payne was now in London, and Irving was in time to witness with him at Covent Garden the second production of *Charles II*, the play which he and Payne had so arduously composed in Paris. The journey through the New Forest, the visit to Moore's friend and patron, Lord Lansdowne, and the pilgrimages north to Birmingham, Bedford, and York — all these glimpses of a by-gone age compensate for altercations with landladies or comments on the white pantaloons of an undistinguished Englishman.

Yet, above all, the value of this Journal, as in the case of his other diaries, depends upon what we learn of Irving himself. It has been said that he left Dresden on July 12, 1823, saddened by his rejection as the suitor of Emily Foster. Yet, though he writes to Mrs. Foster frequently throughout the year, though he revisits this family at Bedford, there is not one hint of an unhappy love-experience.[1] Instead this Journal includes, well hidden, a touching recollection of his youthful betrothed, Matilda Hoffman, who had died

[1] See P. M. Irving, *The Life and Letters of Washington Irving* (New York, 1862, 1864), "Appendix."

fourteen years earlier.[1] Another fact revealed is the seriousness with which at this time Irving was writing for the stage. Day after day he labours for Payne, composing verse for plays. In addition, we gain a more precise knowledge of Irving's reading, which now, as always, is romantic in temper. Or we see him hard at work on a study to be called *William the Conqueror*. Moreover, the fate of the manuscript which he had begun in Germany two years before becomes apparent.

He had then contemplated a novel, to be called *The History of an Author*. But in Paris he is depressed and uncertain until during one sleepless night the idea comes to him of enlarging *The Sketch Book* into two volumes. He talks it over with the devoted brother Peter, and writes Murray. This letter marked the inception of *Tales of a Traveller*. We learn also that it was the traveller and painter Foy who told him the anecdotes of Italy, as it was his own literary agent, Colonel Aspinwall, with his talk of Captain Kidd, who enabled him to expand the manuscript into the final form of a miscellany of stories. In brief, we learn from the Journal that major portions of *Tales of a Traveller* were derived not from his own observations in America and Italy, but from the conversation of these later friends. We also see this book take form as Irving lives in Payne's lodgings at 89 Rue Richelieu, and we observe the unlucky haste with which he brought it to a conclusion under the cudgel of William Gifford.

After all, the thick notebook or Journal records

[1] See p. 117, footnote 2.

only about a year of Irving's life, and no very significant general conclusions may be drawn from so short
a period. The impression of Irving must be rather
like one of his own sketches — that of the traveller
and man about town — the distinguished American
author living in London and Paris.[1] Here he is, in
the Paris of 1824, already well known to the French
through translations and through his own agreeable
self; mingling in the best society, besieged by Galignani to edit, and to translate; and beloved by such
friends as Payne and Thomas W. Storrow,[2] of whose
family he is virtually a member. A girl, whom Irving thinks quite mad, requests a lock of his hair; Foy
paints his portrait, and Irving views it not without
complacence. Carlyle was in Paris in the spring, and
declared himself disappointed not to have seen this
American "lion."[3] And S. G. Goodrich surveyed him:
"Strikingly mild and amiable; dress — claret coat,
rather more pigeon-tailed than the fashion at New
York; light waistcoat; tights ribbed, flesh-colored silk
stockings; shoes; polished very bright. . . He spoke
of many things, all in a quiet manner, evidently with
a fund of feeling beneath."[4]

[1] For information concerning Irving's French reputation in 1823 see
Galignani's Messenger and Paris Monthly Review, IV, 338, April, 1823.

[2] (1779–1862). An American business man living in Paris. Storrow's
son later married Irving's favourite niece, Sarah Irving. See *Letters from
Sunnyside and Spain*, ed. S. T. Williams (New Haven, 1928), *passim*. A
few additional facts concerning this life-long friend of Irving are contained in a privately published pamphlet, in the possession of Mr. E. C.
Storrow, of Boston, Massachusetts.

[3] Thomas Carlyle, *Reminiscences* (London, 1881), II, 161.

[4] *Recollections of a Lifetime* . . . (New York, 1857), II, 442.

It is so also in London. Murray flatters him, and Rogers spends days with him. And Moore, though he did not tell Irving that he trembled — and rightly — for the fortunes of *Tales of a Traveller*, cannot have enough of this American's society. This was true in spite of Irving's occasional moods: "Took him," wrote Moore in his diary, "to show him to the Starkeys, but he was sleepy and did not open his mouth; the same at Elwyn's dinner. Not strong as a lion, but delightful as a domestic animal." [1] To Thomas Campbell also in this year Irving was "half-lamb, half lion." [2] Such comment from Carlyle, Moore, and Campbell on the fame and the personal popularity of Washington Irving in 1824 may well introduce his own story of this year.

STANLEY T. WILLIAMS

[1] *Memoirs, Journals, and Correspondence of Thomas Moore*, ed. Lord John Russell (London, 1853–1856), June 17, 1824.

[2] W. Beattie, *Life and Letters of Thomas Campbell* (London, 1849), II, 159. The most interesting pen-portrait of Irving at about this time was written by John Neal, in *Blackwood's Edinburgh Magazine*, January, 1825.

NOTE ON THE MANUSCRIPT AND
TEXT OF THE JOURNAL

THIS Journal of Washington Irving is octavo in size, and has been rebound in modern bindings. It consists of one hundred and ninety-four folios, or three hundred and eighty-eight pages. Of these the following are blank or entirely rubbed out: [2], [3], [4], [9], [10], [11], [12], [49], [51], [87], [88], [90], [92], [289], [290], [291]. The Journal contains only three sketches, and these are unimportant: [37], [220], and [242]. The writing is in both pencil and ink upon unruled paper. The Journal has suffered from wear and exposure, and portions have been blotted out. This is especially true of the concluding lines of pages. There are also passages which, in the judgment of the editor, are hopelessly illegible because of rubbing and because of haste in composition.

All entries, however, in the Journal, when legible, have been reproduced, and these have been retained with their original spelling, punctuation, indentation, capitalization, and neglect of French accents. Irving's punctuation is erratic, especially in the matter of periods and dashes, and often, in this respect, indeterminable; and his spelling, as usual, is extremely faulty. His deletions are unimportant and have not been reproduced. All doubtful readings have been queried, and mistakes have been indicated by the correct spellings after the words in brackets, or in notes, but only when it has been deemed that Irving's variation might be misleading, and only upon the first appearance of an error or a mannerism in spelling. In the matter of proper names Irving is consistently inaccurate, spelling even the names of such intimate friends as the "Guestiers" in various ways. Since the Journal reveals the sources of one of Irving's important works, it has seemed proper to indicate in detail books which he was reading. Of the numerous plays which he saw no such identification has been made, but whenever possible the correct spelling of these plays and obscure afterpieces has been indicated from such authorities as Charles Brunet, *Table Des Pièces De Théâtre* (Paris, 1914).

Irving himself left many lacunae in the manuscript of names of persons and places. Each of these has been indicated by a blank space. A word which is faded out, or is blotted, or is illegible has been indicated by one long dash (——); a phrase or a short sentence by two such dashes (—— ——); and passages of greater length by two dashes and a note (—— —— [1]).

The manuscript sheets have been numbered by the editor, and the beginning of each manuscript page has been indicated by numerals in brackets.

The notes do not aim to explain persons and places of historical interest, though this has occasionally been done, or to identify all of Irving's many casual acquaintances, but to throw light upon individuals or incidents which have some importance, from the point of view of a biographer, in the life of Irving as a whole.

A few passages in this Journal have been published, with many errors and alterations, by P. M. Irving, *The Life and Letters of Washington Irving (op. cit.)*, II, 160; 161; 179–183; 183–185; 187–190; 190; 191; 195; 196; 196–198; 199; 200; 201; 204; 205. All pagination in reference to the writings of Irving is based on *The Works of Washington Irving*, Riverside Edition, G. P. Putnam's Sons, New York, 1864, 1868, 1869.

On p. [209] of the manuscript Irving alludes to his new composition, *William the Conqueror*. After stating in a footnote that this interesting document had been lost, the editor of the Journal accidentally discovered it. This essay or fragment of a book is, therefore, now published, for the first time, at the close of this volume (p. 245), as a further illustration of Irving's interests in the year 1823–1824, and as one of the few essays ever written by him upon French themes.

S. T. W.

JOURNAL

JOURNAL

[5] Saturday. July 12.[1] Left Dresden about 1/2 past nine Oclock — in company with Mrs Foster the Miss Fosters — travelled in Mrs Foster's [2] carriage — post — The morning early was cloudy with a sprinkling of rain but cleared up fine & brightly before we started — rather windy — Col Livius [3] accompanied us on horseback for two or three miles & then bade us

---

[1] The title-page of the Journal bears the inscription, in Irving's own handwriting: "Washington Irving Sunnyside Nov. 26th 1857." In an unknown hand at the bottom of the page is written: "Given me by Miss Chalmers." The reverse of this page is blank. After two fly-leaves, blank on both sides, page [1], beginning the pagination made by the editor, has merely: "No 10," apparently the designation of the notebook in Irving's series of journals, and the words "from July 12th 1823 to Aug 11–1824." Pages [2], [3], and [4] are blank. The Journal begins on page [5]. Irving's notations immediately preceding this entry may be found in *The Journals of Washington Irving* . . . ed. W. P. Trent and G. S. Hellman (Boston, 1919), I, 159–221.

[2] Mrs. John Foster of Bedford, England, and her two gifted daughters, Emily and Flora, with all of whom Irving had been intimate throughout the sojourn in Dresden. It has been said Irving was a rejected and despondent suitor for the hand of Miss Emily Foster, but no conclusive evidence exists that this is so. The fact that this Journal records only one letter from her (p. 130); that his low spirits (p. 86) are never attributed to this cause; and that he revisited and parted cheerfully from the family (p. 219), seem to argue the contrary. *Cf.* Introduction, ix, x. See also *Genealogy of the Descendants of Roger Foster*, London, 1897.

[3] Colonel Barham Livius, a dramatist, and a cousin of Mrs. Foster. He had been a director of the amateur theatricals in which Irving had borne a prominent part during his stay in Dresden (1822–1823).

adieu — Count Rumigny [1] & Mr Henry came to see us off —

We passed through Meissen — a picturesque town on the banks of the Elbe — Old castle converted into china manufacturing — the drive along the Elbe is very pleasant—agreeable scenery—The sun was very hot part of the day & we had a shower or two — but on the whole it was fine weather — some little time after leaving Meissen we get into the common place German scenery of wide plains —

[6] We amused ourselves part of the time by singing — Did not reach Leipsic [Leipzig] until 1/2 past 12 — put up at Hotel de Hamburg — newly fitted up — very clean — prettily furnished — people extremely civil

— P. S. This evening about twilight passed the Mulda [Mulde] by a ferry — beautiful quiet scene — Silvery light on water — moon silver quarter — Evening star very bright — Mrs F told how Emily when a child of one year old was struck with the beauty of the evening star & kept calling it by name — Tar [star] — to her nurse —

[7] Sunday 13 — Walked with the ladies to the observatory — from whence we had a view over all the city and Environs — Old Keeper pointed out the whole scene of the Battle of Leipsic [2] — gave some in-

---

[1] Count de Rumigny was French minister at the Court of Saxony, in Dresden. On August 30, 1827, Irving gave Longfellow a letter of introduction to this friend.

[2] "The Battle of the Nations," October 16–19, 1813. Irving's notebooks contain many reminiscences of Napoleon.

teresting personal anecdotes of Napoleon when he had to retreat upon the town & the gates were closed upon him — wanted to force the soldiers again to the field — they refused & threw their guns into the ditch of castle — pointed out the place where Poniatowski [1] was drowned — pointed out Lützen where Gustavus adolphus was killed [2] —

Said he had a daughter killed by the blowing up of a powder waggon — From thence we went to the Cellar where Mephistopheles & Faust made wine come out of the table (vide Goethe Faust [3]) took Lemonade there & bought a tongue — very rich man who [8] owns it — a wine liqueur &c cellar (italian warehouse) — old paintings on the wall of Fausts story Walk in garden of   where Poniatowski monument stands on border of Elster [4] —— has gravel walks & clipped hedges — difficulty & demur as to letting us in as there was grosse gesellschaft [5] — Large woman sailing down upon us like a goose in a millpond — we passed without buying — Elster narrow & deep Evening theatre Mad Weisserman played the Schone Mullerin —— sang charmingly

Some of the Streets in Leipsick are very picturesque [13] [6] Monday 14. Left Leipsick at 9 oclock — on the way to the Harz we had newly arranged the car-

[1] Joseph-Antoine Poniatowski (d. October 19, 1813), a Polish general, in whom Irving had long been interested. See the *Analectic Magazine*, July, 1814.

[2] November 6, 1632.

[3] *Faust*, Part I, scene in Auerbach's Keller.

[4] The river Elster.   [5] A large party.

[6] Pages [9], [10], [11], and [12] are blank.

riage despatched some luggage by dilligence [diligence] to Cassel — put some in the post carriage with the little boys[1] & their tutor & so had plenty of room in the carriage rode on the Dicky — Flora sat beside me for the morng & then Mrs F— in the morng came to the Saale — a pretty stream wandering among willows — Country open & coverd with grass — The Saale is a haunted stream — the hexe[2] or water witches haunt it. As we rode Mrs Foster read several stories of hexe out of German—Morning very Hot—passed the Boundaries & on entering the prussian state (prussian Saxony) our luggage was ex[amined] — customs house officers very civil & light in their examination — would take nothing — one of these a little waggish fellow with [14] long pipe had much pleasantry & chatted with the ladies — Arrived 12 oclock at Merseburg — very pleasantly situated on the bank of the Saale — its old wall — towers cathedral & town houses have a very picturesque appearance from the Bridge — Here change horses for Eisleben — along part of town and high walls German works — Mrs Foster gets on the Box with me — fair & warm country begins to grow more varied — See a storm gathering ahead — it advances rapidly — I see that it is a thunder gust & likely to be a severe one — get Mrs Foster into carriage — make the carriage all fast & ready — mount the Dicky with box coat & a fur mantle about my legs — & umbrella —

[1] Mrs. Foster's two sons.

[2] Irving uses the singular of hexe, witch or sorceress. He had studied old German fairy tales throughout his stay in Germany.

Gust comes on with a hurricane of wind raising clouds of dust [15] The earth seems thrown up into the air — the clouds brown with dust — The whole atmosphere thickened & darkened — gust comes more & more terrible — horses can hardly draw on the carriage — begins to rain — rain driven with incredible violence — Hail — large as hazel nuts — storm increases — one horrible blast of wind succeeds another — umbrella breaks & is whirled off into a neighbring field — mantle flies after it — Horses get frightened — I descend from coach box — fear the carriage will be blown over — The two leaders become unmanageable — postillion jumps off & tries to hold them — They turn round & go down a bank — try to keep them quiet. They continue restive — drag carriage after [16] them down a steep bank into a ditch — pole breaks — carriage over turns — rush to the place & get the ladies out — none hurt materially — bruised a little — drenched to the skin in an instant — leave them there & run to a house about 1/2 mile off — Find a smiths shop with a small country Inn beside it — send workmen to look after the carriage & order rooms to be prepared for ladies — run back to carriage — the storm is already over — find them all drenched to the skin but in good spirits & unhurt — They walk to the Inn. The carriage is with much trouble righted & dragged up the bank backward by two horses & six or 8 men — get safe to the Inn — a new pole is made — we all change our clothes & after a repast of cold tongue & wine set off in good spirits — The ladies give [17] their hats which were

(7)

quite wet to a pretty maid servant at the Inn & likewise a shawl — she will be the belle of the neighborhood —

The evening was extremely pleasant — ride in sight
of the Salziger See & Süsser See — pretty little lakes
— at nine oclock reach Eisleben a small country town
& put up at the Goldne Schiff — a poor kind of Inn
but the people extremely civil & attentive to us. After
the storm we drove thro   a little watering place
that looked pleasant — we cut a droll figure — the
ladies without hats.

at Eisleben had a good supper at least good appe-
tite & went early to bed

[18] Tuesday 15. Eisleben has some quaint old
buildings — remains of a tower — church — left there
at 8 oclock — road hilly & very bad — came on to
rain — and continued to rain till near 12 — pass by
Mansfeld — ruined castle of the family — about 12
clears up beautifully — ride thro magnificent forests
— See castle to our left — on a height rising out of a
deep woody valley — belongs to Baron Friesen —
fine distant view of hills & forests like american scenery — Pass thro Harzgerode — See Brocken at distance — great view over the Harz forest descend Hill
& arrive 1/2 past 3 at Alexisbad — In Evg take walks
in lonely forest glen [19] Hawks screaming to one another over a profile of Hill looking at me. Return for
Ladies & take a walk towards the same valley — the
return thro woods — take tea in my little room &
chat till near 12 oclock

[20] Wednesday 16 — Fine morning — we Break-

fasted under a tree on terrace near the Inn Walked to
Mägdes sprung [Mägdesprung] — road winds thro
beautiful valley with high rocky Hills covered with
magnificent forests — Stream runs thro valley —
pluck wildflowers of various kinds — perfume of
forest — workman from the Eisenhammer [1] who
directs us on our way — a remarkably fine head —
His profile not unlike napoleons — fine black eyes —
remarkable suavity in his manner — a sweet smile
and pleasing voice — one of natures gentlemen — the
Ladies were all struck with his looks & address —
Indeed we have been generally pleased with the looks
of the people among the mountains — a fine race of
men — walked up to the maidspring — or maidens
leap — so called from little legend (See fine view over
woody mountains) [21] a stream far below us A large
Iron Cross marks the place of the maid spring — returned to dinner Little boys plucking wildflowers by
the way — few singing birds — many Hawks sailing
among the mountains — at dinner we were amused
by the ceremonies of the repast — summoned by
three blasts of trumpet — comp[an]y assembled in
salon the Duke of   Anhalt there. One old gentleman
with short leg & trunk [?] the Duke of   & the Duke
of   Duchess of   a very lady like looking personage — Dinner pleasant & decorous — we chat with
several of the company — after returning to the Inn
receive an invitation from the Duke of   to a Ball
tomorrow evg — the ladies determine to accept & to
remain over tomorrow   [22] About 1/2 past five

[1] Forge.

(9)

took a walk with the ladies — up the valley road along some beautiful mountain glens — very still & lonely — the babbling of a small stream the scream of a crow or Hawk — saw two deer stalking up a hill side — Evening symphonies — cattle returning home — tinkling of bells &c — every thing weary & pensive — ev[enin]g — every thing tending to repose the song & the whistle become pensive — birds cease to sing — see large drove of cows returning down diff.[t] valleys — their bells make suitable music to the scene — Shepherd with large flock of sheep — a tall dog haunted fellow — arms folded — crook athwart them — wallet — the belt ornamented with brass rings &c which he said was for a little State.[1] [23] His two dogs — one he called Fuchs a Fox — a yellow dog with an evil eye — came by us & I was about to pat him on the head when he gave a malicious growl — the other dog was a dirty grey — and a head like a wolf — they were very active in driving in the sheep little old cow herd with a large slouched three cornered hat and a ragged & patched blue great coat — In the evening after supper there were tableaus presented in the Dining saloon by some of the ducal court people — the word to be represented was Schutz gheist [2] — first scene — a lady & child — defended by one knight from the assault of another — 2.[d] a lady seated at a harp — musing — but not play[in]g — a female figure in white behind — with extended arms — gheist — 3 — Schutz gheist a child asleep — a Dragon about to attack it — protected by a guardian

---

[1] *I. e.,* decoration.   [2] Guardian spirit.

[24] spirit — a beautiful girl in white — hair hanging over shoulders — crown of flowers — holding a bunch in hand — the whole was represented within a door that had a gauze stretched across it — at supper met with Mr   attached to General —— The General at Harzgerode in the neighborhood —

[25] Thursday July 17 — a rainy morning — fete in honor of the Duke of Anhalt —— same day — Large assembly gathers in course of the day — strenuous assemblage at dinner — Duke of hartz at head of table — songs sung on printed card [?] — Grand chamberlain large pompous personage — director of the revels — Little singer like St Anthony — Sings on the temptation of St Anthony — Old gentleman — Large body red face white hair — great singer and Drinker — Insists upon singing very often — After dinner walk a while with the ladies — at 6 oclock a ball given by the Dukes Brother — go there with the ladies but in consequence of some gaucherie on the part of the chamberlain in not introducing me I retired — Fireworks in evening — grand effect of rockets among the mountains — two fell firing at each other comet light that illumines all the forest. Inn kept in uproar until 2 oclock After having bathed [?] slept [?] evg about 8 oclock walk among the Hills [26] & woods. Walked at dusk find myself far from home in lonely part of the forest — my alarm from the merriment of two ill looking fellows by lonely house in forest — Friday July 18 Leave Alexisbad at 1/2 past   very hot & humid but clouds over — Beautiful drive thro mountain woodland scenery —

(11)

pass Jäger[1] huts — Woods remarkably rich, strong &
generous. ground clothed with herbage and great
variety of flowers — Beautiful large ash trees — Bal-
lenstedt — castle with an old part and a very tame
new part — neat little town — horses for Hilfleute[2] —

[27] From Ballenstadt with post Horses to —— by
Thaale [Thale], a half station where we have the privi-
lege of stopping a couple of hours to see the Ross
Trap[3] — A wild scene in the Bodethal among rocky
precipices with the Bode traveling through — Our
guide tells us legends — spouts poetry & sings songs
— From thence to Blankenburg — where we put up
at the Weisse Adler

[28] Saturday 19 — Blankenburg — little old town
on the border of the Harz. Town houses with cannon
balls sticking in the walls from the 30 yr war — visit
the castle — portly fresh looking man shows it —
great quantity of bad pictures in bad condition —
two pictures painted by Prince   with his fingers—
which prove that a man with his fingers may paint
very bad pictures —

Picture of the Weisse Frau[4] who haunts this castle
as well as several others of the same family — a good
looking smiling old lady in long waist — white silk
gown &c gold watch by her side — little black dog
with her — fine view from the castle to Quedlinburgh

---

[1] Huntsmen's.   [2] Servants.

[3] Rosstrappe, the huge granite rock of Thale.

[4] One of Irving's many references in manuscript to " The White
Woman." He had been since 1816 an interested student of German tales
of the supernatural. See "The Spectre Bridegroom," in *The Sketch Book*,
pp. 206–228, and *Tales of a Traveller*, Part I.

— in fine weather to Magdeburg — Devils Mauer [1]
— Ross trapp &c

[29] Leave Blankenburg 1/2 past ten — hilly bad
road but thro magnificent forest scenery — Scenery
afterwards becomes bare—distant view of Brocken —
arrive at Raubeland [Rübeland] — Rainy — Forges
& Iron works, put up at the   very miserable tavern
— visit Baumans cavern — very fine — various
caverns to which we descend by ladders —

Have wine soup at Raubeland — then proceed to
Heideland— road wretched — Pine Scenery — mountain depths — weather clears up — Brocken surrounded by mist and clouds different effects of light
on it

at   little village among bare heights — houses of
wood & plaester [*sic*] windows worn with —— wild
neighing of our Horses.

[30] From   To Stolberg — fine forests of Pine &
others of oak &c — beautiful moonlight among the
forests — arrive a little after 11 at Stolberg — get
supper in the Weisses Ross — miserable Inn

[31] Sunday 20 — Stollberg — village with picturesque old houses wood & plaester — Old church
tower with curious Dial — Old castle whitewashed,
overlooking the town — Leave there 10 oclock —
drive through beautiful valley — with woody hills on
each side — weather over cast but does not rain —
valley open and at length terminates in the Goldene
Aue or Golden valley — The Kyffhauser mountains
beyond it — Arrive 1 oclock at Rossla — miserable

[1] Wall.

(13)

little town — stop at the Schwarzer Hirsch — black Hart — miserable Inn —

Golden valley finely cultivated — sloping field of grain up to the woods of Kyffhauser — Branfields in blossom — weather misty & uncertain —— —— [1]

[32] Rossla dorf [2] — of Grafschaft [3] Stolberg Rossla — Houses wood & plaester

go near church — organ & singing remind me of tunes sung in church when I was a child [4] —

Dine at Rossla — Soup of veal — sausages — Ham eggs & wine —

From Rossla go to Nordhausen — the roads bad but the afternoon clears up beautifully — effects of Sunshine on Kyffhauser all in shade — then Rotenburg & all lighted up but Kyffhauser town — then the town & all the rest in shade that it looked like a flame — quarrel with postillions — Nordhausen very pretty little town — Houses of wood & plaester — large square Sunday-people in best clothes & dresses — pretty faces — From thence at 8 oclock to Bleicherode — road wretched — ladies in fright — did not get to Bleicherode until near 11. A small miserable town — a wedding in the place & [33]

[1] Three lines are illegible.

[2] Village.

[3] County.

[4] Irving refers occasionally in letters and journals to the strict religious training of his youth. See letter to Emily Foster, Paris, August 23, 1825, in the *Yale Review*, January, 1926. In this letter he alludes to the religious life of the Foster household, which he experienced in 1824. This letter and the passages in this Journal (pp. 221, 222), together, depict, far more accurately than the conventional estimates of his religion, Irving's real attitude towards the orthodox beliefs of his time.

people dancing at the Inns — no beds to be had wandered about seeking shelter in rain — ordered Horses & determined to proceed — Seated ourselves near midnight on steps of Post House — servant maid brought us Bread & Beer soup from inn & we ate by the light of a lantern — Put all the ladies in post waggon with 4 Horses — Mr Trappaneger [1] in carriage two Horses — with luggage — travelled all night — terrible roads — changed horses at works — as the post waggon was small the ladies & children in that. Mr. Trap. & I in carriage — beautiful drive thro fine scenery to Heiligenstadt — where we breakfast & dress &c — then as it was cheaper [?] resumed our several seats & drove thro lovely scenery — at   came in sight of Hesse — one of the most splendid views I have beheld — before us the chateau of Arnstein on mound dividing the view of rich valley [34] to left on height the ruins of Castle of Hahnstein — to right peeps towards Hartz — descend into lovely scenery — arrive at Heiligenstadt — beautifully situated on the Werra — bridge — rocks &c — Stopped at post House — civil landlady — daughter of a captain that had served in the American war — we went just out of the town on a Hill that overlooked the country & dined under a noble lime tree — on cold meats that we had brought in the carriage —

From Werra we had a succession of lovely scenery — nothing can surpass the richness & fertility of the Hessian valleys — the Day was hot but fine — Flora rode on box by me — It was a lovely evening as we

[1] The tutor of Mrs. Foster's two sons.

drove thro the fine valley of Cassel & arrived at the town where we put up at the König von Preuss[en] — a spacious & fine Hotel — appartments [apartments] looking out on a circular public place — Balcony — Moonlight — supped in the saloon — Interesting evg [35] E[mily?] very gentle & amiable

— Tuesday 22. Cassel — rainy day — In morn-[in]g accompy ladies to the picture gallery — very pretty collection — in good appartments — Dine at Table dHote — after dinner drive to Augarten & walk about there — fine garden — good trees & piece of water — visit the Fasanerie[1] — return home — pass the evening in our appartment chatting

[36][2] Wednesday 23 — Drive out to Williams Hohe [Wilhelmshöhe] a beautiful seat of the Electors about a league from town — fine avenues leading to it — stroll thro the grounds to Löwenburg a minia-ture Rittersburg[3] — Old furniture & painted glass — Portraits of various persons among them a beautiful Picture of the Princess of Hesse — Vansomer [?] painted in 16 century — one of the prettiest things I have seen in great while — Saw the waterworks play — the best pieces are a fall from a broken aqueduct & a jet of water 180 feet high — Dine at Table D Hote — returned home — went to play & saw Das Unter-brockene Opferfest — music by Winter — Mad^{me} Arnold played in it. [37] beautiful theatre — Scenery — dresses & numerous chorus — returned home &

---

[1] Pheasant preserves.

[2] A brief note on a painting precedes the entry.

[3] *i. e.*, mediaeval castle.

remained chatting and readg ms. to ladies till near 12 oclock[1]

Thursday 24 — while preparations were making for departure strolled about the old part of the town — Houses gable end — very old & quaint — Music — military — Hessian soldiers short jackets & long pantaloons — market women with little caps[2] and cloth jackets — arsenal with burley burgo-master Making bust of warrior in stone — Public squares of Cassel are very handsome — [38] called with Mrs F with draft on Banker —

Leave Cassel 10 oclock fine weather but comes on to rain & blow. Stop at Waldeck — the residence of the Prince of Waldeck — neat little town — pass through beautiful scenery — travel all night — thro mountainous & lovely scenery — Pass the Prussian boundaries early in Evening — come into what was formerly Westphalia at 11 oclock stop at Post House an old dilapidated convent where we have coffee brought to carriage

[39] moonlight views of wild & beautiful country — very cold & windy night.

Friday morning 25 stop at Meschede and breakfast & dressed — Day grows mild & moderate — drive through a succession of lovely valleys — with little streams running thro them — dine at post House on cold meats & wine soup — much of scenery like English — In evening 10 oclock arrive at Schwelm — a

[1] This manuscript was probably the first draft of a section of *Tales of a Traveller*, which Irving had commenced at Mainz in 1822.

[2] At this point in the manuscript Irving drew a tiny sketch of a market-woman's head.

(17)

small watering place & get accommodations with difficulty people very civil & attentive — Sup — in morning take warm bath—mineral with iron in—Saturday 26 breakfast — pretty country round the watering place — after leaving it pass thro   a pretty, busy manufacturing town — thro Elberfeld a remarkably busy little valley alive with manufacturies — Houses of [40] opulent manufacturers — fine stream running thro — Houses with slate walls — Houses well built & clean people fresher & neater in looks than in other parts of Germany —

Heavy showers — drive into Düsseldorf at 3 oclock in a shower stop at   where we dine — walk about the town — neat streets large casernes [1] beautiful public walks & gardens in the vicinity of the town — leave there 6 oclock — pretty view of Düsseldorf & the Rhine — Uncertain moon — light night — sing in carriage — and fall asleep — travel all night — passed thro Wesel 1 oclock at night (effect of moonlight & sound of bell on the Ruhr)

Sunday 27 — Breakfast at Rees — poor Inn — continued on — Deep sandy roads — showery — crossed two or three ferries — Drove along a dyke crossed the Rhine — stopped & had [41] some refreshments at Inn on Bank of the Rhine — good raw Ham — good butter bread &c — We are now in Holland [2] — road good — at 6 oclock in shower come to

[1] Barracks.

[2] Irving's first acquaintance with Holland and Belgium was in September, 1805. See *Notes and Journal of Travel in Europe, 1804–1805*, ed. W. P. Trent, New York, 1920, 1921.

the Bank of river opposite Nim[e]guen — Inn on
bank of the river is neat & swarming with tea drinkers
from the opposite town, being Sunday evening — get
good quarters there — comfortable rooms carpeted
commanding fine view of river & opposite town —
beds with curtains — take tea in a comfortable style
— tea bottle & chafing dish — rusk — smoked beef —
cheese —

After tea as the evg was fine crossed the flying
bridge with the Miss Fosters & strolled about the
town — fine walk round it on ramparts with alleys of
trees — old walls have marks of war — streets well
paved & clean — people swarming about in sunday
dresses — the houses clean — long windows — people
on benches before the doors — cathedral   [42] with
handsome lofty porch — Belvedere fine view up &
down the river — Town whitewashed towards the
river gives it a cheerful look — lies on a stream that
branches between the Maas & the Rhine — Our landlord a Dandy & noodle [1] — a number of good looking
housewifely women bustling about the house

Monday 28 Left Nimegen 9 oclock — after driving a little way discovered that Miss F had left a
summer box behind — Trappaneger sent back after
it — ride along dike then on fine chaussees [2] —
paved with small yellow Bricks — very long port
Pass thro Utrecht where we change Horses — dutch
countryseats along the road neat — whimsical in-
scriptions [43] pass thro —

---

[1] Simpleton.   [2] Chausées, causeways, banks.

arrive at Rotterdam at 1/2 past 1 at night — beautiful effect of moonlight on streets & canals — put up at Bath Hotel.

Tuesday 29. Fair weather — walked about Rotterdam — market day — streets in bustle — dined at Table dHote — in the evening took a walk in the avenues in vicinity of Rotterdam with the young Ladies —

[44] Wednesday 30 went down to the Brille [1] on steam boat to see Mrs Foster & family off — Breakfast on board — in two hours we arrive at the Brille — go ashore in Custom House officers boat with some other persons & the Agent — Steamboat goes off finely — walk to the Brille — neat little dutch town — Van Trump [2] born here — return 1/2 past 11. cross ferry & ride in open waggon to Maaslandsluys — fine village — cod and Herring fisheries — road thro cornfield & along a dyke — 9 of us in old fashioned carriage — Comes on to rain lend my coat to lady

pass thro   Schiedam — famous for gin — immense number of women in the streets — arrive at Rotterdam time enough for Dinner — Dine at table dHote — Discussion of Spanish affairs —

[1] Briel, or Brielle. Formerly a fortified seaport, but now an unimportant town. Another account of the journey up to the time of this farewell from the Fosters may be found in the "Journal of Flora Foster," P. M. Irving (op. cit.), IV, 365–387. Irving's bare record of the parting is in marked contrast to this sentimental version.

[2] Irving may refer to the founder of the Dutch family satirized in his A History of New York (1809). He later used the name for a comic song in one of Payne's plays. See P. M. Irving (op. cit.), II, 173, footnote.

[45] *Thursday 31* Leave Rotterdam at 3 in morning in steam Boat for Antwerp — serene moonlight night — old rosy faced gentleman a board, who talks with a great sonorous voice accompd by a small spoken man — discuss the merit of my works [1] — Old gent I find is a Dutch merchant or ship Agent — His companion an Am [erican] capt —

In morng pass by Williamsstadt [Willemstad] — a fortified place once unsuccessfully attacked by Dumorier [Dumouriez] — By Tholen on the Masselkuck [2] — ran aground shortly after thro the ignorance of the Pilot — detained six hours from 1/2 past 11 to 1/2 past 5.

Mr Grant on board — of London — near 50 years of age — has been visiting a dutch village where he was at school when a boy — 39 years since — found his old schoolmaster — who was sexton — town clerk &c near 80 years of age still active & healthy — the Dominies servant woman who was there when he was a boy — a captain of a vessel — who was a little boy will go west &c

[46] Strange appearance in dutch scenery — mingled land & water & sky — ships gliding along fields & thro meadows — mist — shining effects of

[1] Irving was now at the height of his European reputation. During his stay in Dresden *The Sketch Book* and *Bracebridge Hall* were available in both French and German. See p. 34, footnote 1, and p. 132.

[2] An example of Irving's capricious spelling, and of his scribbling down obscure names. He refers to an inlet seldom mentioned on modern maps: Mosselkreek, or Mosseldijk, an arm of water in the Province of Zeeland issuing from the Eendragt River. See *Aardrijkskundig Wordenboek der Nederlanden*, 1839–1851.

water & clouds — Dinner on board plain but substantial & well cooked — with Mr Grant was a gentleman of Paderborn — a man of the law — of
pleasing look & address — guessed him about 40
years of age — talked with me of the Rhine — said it
assembled monuments of all ages — great Historical
monuments of the romans of the early Germans of the
times of chivalry — of cloisters & religious establish-
m[ents] & finally of modern warfare —

at 1/2 past 5 the tide rises sufficiently for us to
float — fine sail afterwards — pass by   the de-
fences of Antwerp — a shower — but sun held up —
magnificent view of Antwerp as we approach it —
The clouds hang over it almost to the horizon &
looked like a dark curtain — partially rained & Sun
shone on Antwerp & on old town — A rainbow like a
triumphal arch hung over it — light clouds piled to
the left [47] green strips of meadow land on west side
— on approaching see few houses more distinctly —
some with little round towers — quite spanish —
others high & pointed with dutch gabel ends — As I
saw the large old fashioned shut up houses I recalled
the rich burghers of ancient times [1] — the gold &
silver merchants — wandered about in quest of lodgings with the Paderborn gentleman — at length at
Hotel de Corona they let us have rooms; their own
hotel was full but they sent the waiter to a new one
near at hand — which was not quite finished — Here
the messagerie [2] of diligences is held — great court

[1] In *A History of New York* Irving had described in detail such Dutch
scenes and persons.   [2] Coach-office.

yard below — our waiter conducted us up great stairs thru long corridors — all silent & lifeless — opened doors & ushered us into two small bed rooms newly & beautifully furnished — in parisian taste — with turkey carpets —

Supped at Hotel — good beefsteaks — peas &c — rambled about the streets — people mostly gone to bed — streets dimly lighted — high old fashioned houses — good effects in [48] rambling about a town at night — see interiors — have ideas of inside of living of inhabitants — Antwerp has fine carillons — Paderborn [said?] that the tunes were not solemn enough for this kind of music which was to imitate that of heaven — music by bells is really a fine idea — sending forth harmony upon the winds — & playing high in air — Antwerp cathedral — tower seen in dusky night air — towering far above us — something noble & inspiring in towers & piramids — attempts to raise ourselves above this poor earth & to approach to heaven — have poetry-like effect —

[53] [1] church of St Jacques — Beautiful Altar piece — The Ballustrade of white marble exquisitely wrought Figures of St Peter & Paul Beside it fine window of Painted glass Woman at devotion with spanish mantle a religieuse

[1] Pages [49] and [51] are blank, and page [50] has merely a verse concerning the Englishman in Holland, which reads: address of an Englishman to Holland —

> Amphibian monster sudden be your fall
> May man undam you & god damn you all

Page [52] and the top of page [53] contain some illegible notes on books, and page [53] bears also brief memoranda on the Jesuits.

Grand altar of white marble with image of S^t
Jacques by Van Bruggen,[1] choir surrounded by
marble reredos Tombs of Spanish families viz Pedro
De Lapena Senores Diego De Lapena y Dona Maria
De Espinossa De la villa de Medina Del Campo
another of a rich merchant —— ——

[54] Tomb of Rubens — behind grand altar — it
lies before an altar in a chapel — the altar piece is a
painting of Rubens — Himself & his two wives
Rubens family entombed in the same chapel

Chasseur des chiens — dignitary of the church — a
tall fellow in light blue coat & broad belt over a common trousers carries a long cane with large silver knob
& tassel — walks with solempnitie [*sic*]

[55] Cathedral — beside the portal — Head of
Quintino Metsiis[2] ——

The Well of Hammerd Iron near by which he made
when smith

cathedral interior grand & simple — Paintings by
Rubens descent from the cross &c — Fine tomb &
statue of Ambrosius (Bishop)   by Van Bruggen

Visit American ship —

Brains of Police—strict with respect to passports—
cabinet of Paintings of town [?] small but select &
good — Buy silk india Hkfs — Dine at Table dHote

[56] At 3 start in Diligence for Bruxelles —my fare
to Paris 39 francs & some centimes — sit in Cabriolet —

---

[1] Irving probably refers, among the various artists of this name, to
Gaspar Pieter Verbruggen, of Antwerp (1635?–1687).

[2] Irving alludes to Quinten Matsys (d. 1530), the blacksmith who
became a painter.

Drive thro Malines old flemish town — Houses of ancient picturesque construction The road afterwards spacious — with fine avenues — canals — Chateaux gardens — large elegant Barges for Passengers on canals — at Half past 7 arrive at Bruxelles — having previously passed the Kings Palace at

Part with Mr Naton — who asks me to write my name — I was much pleased with him — seemed pretty well informed — civil and gentlemanlike

Lose my way in a stroll at Bruxelles & in danger of losing my passage — set off at [57] a little after nine in Dilligence — travel all night — nearly nod myself out of cabriolet

Saturday 2 Aug — at 5 oclock stop at Mons at 9 at Vallenciennes [*sic*] where I breakfast have to go to police about passport — which interrupts me in the midst of a discussion of a fine Beefsteak.

This day we pass thro Cambray —
travel all night —

Sunday 3 Aug arrive at 11 oclock at Paris get a room at the Hotel de Suisse Rue De Bailly — drive out in Cabriolet to Mr Storrows [1] — find the girls much grown & improved — dine there a Mr & Mrs Sennett there with their little son & daughter — Walk in not being able to get places in carriage — roads thronged with carriages — water works play at St Cloud

[58] *Monday 4.* Visit Mr Butels school — rue de

[1] Irving's most intimate friends in Paris. A large collection of Irving's letters to the Storrows is in the possession of Harvard University. *Cf.* Introduction, xi, footnote 2.

Clichy — to see Henry & Irving[1] — find them much
grown & improved — large school good play ground
— Dormitory bad not kept clean — bugs — take lodgings at Hotel de Yorck — Boulevard Montmartre[2]
two rooms in Entresol.[3] 110 fr pr month — dine in
Panorama passage — Evg to the variety — but
theatre so hot & I so sleepy that I could not enjoy it
— the piece [s] were

> *L Infant de Paris*
> *L'Aveugle de Montmorenci*
> *Precepteur dans L'Embarras*
> *Cuisinier*[4]

called on Mr Welles this morng

Tuesday 5 Took possession of my new lodgings —
wrote to Sally[5] & to Peter[6] — Dined en famille with
Mr & Mrs Welles at their new quarters in a beautiful
little Hotel — Rue Taitbout, 24 — formerly belonging to Talleyrand —

[1] Irving's nephews, the two sons of Henry Van Wart, Irving's
brother-in-law, of Birmingham. These boys were at school in Paris and
were partly under Irving's care.

[2] Irving's home in Paris until he moved to the quarters of John
Howard Payne. See p. 52.

[3] Suite of rooms between the ground floor and the first floor.

[4] *L'Enfant de Paris; L'Aveugle de Montmorency; Le Précepteur dans
l'embarras; Le Cuisinier.*

[5] Sarah Irving Van Wart, Irving's youngest sister, and the wife of
Henry Van Wart.

[6] Peter Irving (1771–1838), Washington Irving's best-loved brother,
who came abroad in 1808 and remained until 1836. Although by profession a physician, his talents were chiefly literary, and he aided Washington in the creation of *Salmagundi* (1807–1808), *A History of New York*,
and *A History of the Life and Voyages of Christopher Columbus* (1828).

Wednesday 6 called on Sheldon [1] — Texier — saw
Miss Texier — Mr Texier gone out — has the gout —
ordered white pantaloons — at 6 oclock accompd Mr
& Mrs Storrow into the country [2] to dine with them
found the little ladies in distress on the death of a
bird, killed by its unnatural parents — In evg read
the Loves of the Angels [3] to them — slept there —
returned in morning *Thursday* 7 with Mr Storrow —
called on Bradish, [4] not at home — Mad Bonet rue
d'Astorg faub[our]g St Honoré—not at home—Went
to school & took the boys out walk[in]g. called on
Wiggins not at home   [60] Bradish called & sat
some time with me In Evg went with Mr Storrow to
Gymnase Dramatic pieces

L'Avare en goguettes

— — — —

Le Precepteur
L Interieur d'un Bureau (excellent)

Took supper of six au lait — retd home —
Friday 8 Call on Bradish — talk with him about
Decatur [5] — Mr Patterson &c &c call with him on
Young Cooper of N York who is lame — call at
Tomasaint Tailleur & order blue dress coat — go

---

[1] An attaché of the American Embassy in Paris.

[2] The Storrows owned a cottage at Auteuil.

[3] Thomas Moore's new poem, published in this year.

[4] Luther Bradish (1783–1863), a member of a New York family with
which Irving had been intimate in 1814, was a diplomat and statesman.

[5] Irving had known Commodore Decatur in New York, and in 1815
had planned to sail with him to Tripoli.

home — then walk with Bradish to call on Colden [1]
— where we visit with his wife & his sister — Mrs
& Miss Garnet Capt Caldwell & Mr Greenough —
go with Bradish Friday to Bath in Seine — take
Bath complete 3 Livres 10 — and dine there — return
to his house take coffee go to Theatre Francais & see
Dissipateur & Valerie—. Ma[de]m[oi]selle Mars [2] in
each — see the colden family at theatre — take sup[per]
au lait at caffe [café] & return home 1/2 past 11

[61] Saturday 9 — Breakfast with Mr Colden —
present Mr Colden, Mrs. C. Miss Ann Wilkes — Mr
Livingston — Wilkes — Dr Greenough — Dejeuner
a la fourchette [3] — the Miss Garnets came in —
called on Sheldon — Bradish — returned home found
letter from Peter — went to Thuilleries [Tuileries]
with Bradish — met the Coldens &c these had ad-
mission to see the private appartments of the King —
Grand Salon de Flores — golden tapestry —
painted ceiling grand vases — Chamber where the
King receives foreign ambassadors — Throne &c.
Bed room Splendid Bed & ornaments in the purest
taste — deep blue with rich gold — The Bed in which
the King actually sleeps is brot in every night —
low — of iron — Splendid room where the [62] King
receives the ladies of the Court magnificent Throne
— richly gilt & with richly gilt trophys each side —
hangings silk richly embroiderd — Audience chamber

---

[1] Of the New York family of Cadwallader Colden, with which the Irvings had long been intimate.

[2] The famous actress, Anne Francoise-Hippolyte Boutet Monvel
Mars (1779–1847).

[3] Lunch.

for men larger but less magnificent — Ante chamber — gallery of Marshall — Theatre — some of the gents give trifles to guide — the genteel thing is to give nothing —

returning thru palais royal met with Payne [1] —

Found at home card & invitation from Kenney [2] — Bot silk stockings — dined at Welles — present Mr & Mrs Hinckley Mr & Mrs Appleton Mr. & Mrs Low — Mr & Mrs Everett & family — Misses Paul — Mr Sheldon &c &c —

[63] Sunday 10 — after breakfast took a cabriolet to the Barrier of Passy — walked from thence to Mr Storrows Auteuil — fine weather — cool & bright — passed the day there — between 12 & 1 Mr Everetts family paid a visit — after they were gone we accompanied a young Italian son of the Duc de Cansano to a garden in which was formerly the house of Moliere — on our return found that Mr Storrows little son Sam had arrived from America joyful agita-

---

[1] John Howard Payne (1791–1852), the American dramatist and poet. The story of this friendship, which began about 1807, is extremely interesting. Many references to Payne's sensitive regard for Irving occur in a large collection of manuscripts of Payne, now in the possession of T. F. Madigan, of New York City. Payne during this period, as always, was both extravagant and excitable, and Irving often acted as a restraining influence. See W. T. Hanson, *The Early Life of John Howard Payne*, and, in particular, the important series of letters published as "Correspondence of Washington Irving and John Howard Payne," *Scribner's Magazine*, October and November, 1910. See Introduction of the present volume, xi.

[2] This friendship with James Kenney (1780–1849), the author of *Raising the Wind* (1803) and *Sweethearts and Wives* (1823), was a result of Irving's collaboration with John Howard Payne in writing drama.

tion of the family — passed a pleasant day & returned late in the evg.

Monday 11 — woke at 4 oclock this morng — with a strange horror on my mind [1] — a dread of future evil — of failure in future literary attempts — a dismal forboding that I could not drive off by any effort of reason — could not sleep again — read till it was time [64] to get up — dressed — breakfasted at a caffe — went to Galignanis [2] — read papers — met there the Baron Bredberg of Dresden — talked with him some time — called at Paynes not at home — ordered shoes — went to Mr Storrows to look for letters — none for me — found Mr Everett there — drive in his carriage to Hotel Montmorenci — dismal feeling still hanging about me — determined to go out to see Grattan [3] at Sevres — on my way to the Cabriolet met Payne — he accompd me out to Passy — Talked over his plans &c — Found Grattan at

[1] These fits of depression were frequent in Irving's life and are recorded in many note-books. See *Notes While Preparing Sketch Book &c.* (*op. cit.*), Introduction.

[2] G. A. Galignani, of a respected family of bookdealers, opened a new shop in the Rue Vivienne in 1800. He published English books, and his rooms were a resort for English readers. Irving went here almost daily to read the newspapers, and in 1824 made a contract with the Galignanis for editing. See p. 187, footnote 1. Irving knew the two brothers, John (1796–1873) and William Galignani (1798–1882). An account of the Galignanis may be found in *A Famous Bookstore* (Paris, 1920), privately printed by the present bookstore, in Paris.

[3] Thomas Colley Grattan (1792–1864), author of *Highways and Byways* (1823–1829). He was British Consul at Boston from 1839 to 1846. Irving disliked Grattan (*cf.* p. 130), but he continued to be a literary adviser for him. Letter of Irving to T. C. Grattan [London], July 9, 1830, in the possession of Maggs Brothers, London.

home — walked & talked with him — called at Mr
Villamils — Dined with Grattan — present his wife
her sister & his two brothers in law — In Evg returned towards paris — stoppd at Auteuil & saw Mr
Storrow & the girls [1] — very sleepy. [65] young Duke
came in — I left them all about 10 — get into cucko [2]
& returned home — found note from Madame Bonet.

Tuesday 12 awake between 3 & 4 with same horror
of mind — read & half doze at times till near 8 when
get up shave & breakfast — go to Storrows — read
american papers — find Mrs Storrow & family in
town — at 1 oclock go in voiture (gondole [3]) to Versailles 2 francs — at Versailles go to Kenneys —
prettily lodged Boulevard de la Reine 115 — two
Miss Bryants boarding with him — Stay there to
dinner Miss Holcroft at home — much improved in
appearance — Kenney in discussion about his nose &
face which are sunburnt after dinner we walk out —
visit paynes cottage — take my leave of the ladies —
Kenney reassures me about a nub on my chin

[66] Get place in victoria for Auteuil — stop there
& pass the night at Mr Storrows —

Wednesday 13 — awake with less feeling of anxiety
& get asleep again — so as to have tolerable nights
rest — walk in garden. return at 9 to paris in cuckow
with Mr S. Driver of cuckow a great man in village

---

[1] Susan and Ann Louisa (Minnie), the two daughters of Thomas W.
Storrow. Some of Irving's most charming letters, written to these little
girls, are in the possession of Harvard University.

[2] Irving spells the word in various ways, usually "cuckow." A cuckoo
was a small coach running from Paris to the suburbs.

[3] Carriage.

— good carriage good horse & good customers — vile
barking little dog — after arriving order pair shoes &
boots at Ashleys — read papers at Galignanis —
Meet Mr Wiggins & Appleton there — return home
— dress call on Mad Bonet (Courville) find her at
home — talk a great deal about the Fosters — Mad
Bonets Mother comes in — pleasant woman — call
on Bradish not at home — on payne — find him in a
sky parlour of palais royal[1] — chat and dine together
at restaurateur[2] in palais royal — go to Opera [67]
Iphigenia en Aulide[3] & Nina — then home —— excellent —

Thursday 14 — Breakfast at caffe — had caffe au
lait — pain & beurre — 21 sous — called at Galignanis returned home & read — visit from Mr Texier
— begin letter to Mrs Foster — 2 oclock papers —
walk out, find Mrs Colden &c at a music shop —
promise to breakfast with her tomorrow — call at
school, take Henry & Irving to walk — call on Bradish — find him at home — then on Tibbets, not at
home walk thro gardens of Tuilleries to Boulevard

[1] At the beginning of the year 1823 Payne lived at 156 Galerie des
Bons Enfants, above the Salon Littéraire, of the Palais Royal. Here he
wrote *Clari*, his most famous opera, with its song, "Home Sweet Home."
In March of this year he rented a cottage at Versailles, where he could
write quietly, and used his apartment as an office. Subsequently he re-
linquished this cottage and took apartments in the Rue Richelieu, No.
89. This he sub-let to Irving, reserving one room for his own use in Paris.
This building is no longer standing, but to visit its site is to see how fortunately Irving was situated in these years for access to the theatres
and the Bibliothèque Nationale.

[2] Irving uses the word as "restaurant."

[3] *Iphigénie en Aulide.*

send boys to school — return — dress & go to dinner
to Mr Welles — present Mr & Mrs Welles & Miss
Wiggins — a pretty little girl — daughter of Mr
Wiggins of Manchester — return home at 10 — P. S.
This day Mr Villamil called on [68] me — strongly
pressed me to pass some time in the little cottage in
his park.

Friday 15 Breakfast at Coldens — present Miss
Wright (sister of the authoress [1]) Dr Greenough —
The Miss Garnets — Capt Caldwell — Mr Tibbets
comes in — discussion of American pronunciation
&c —

Call at Mr Storrow — he is in the country — dine
in Panorama passage — read papers at Galignanis —
go to theater S' Martin — see L'homme Gris — Le
Cuisinier de Buffon (good — poetic) — Polichinelle
Vampire — very extraordinary —

[69] Saturday 16 — go out early — call at Galignanis — see Sheldon — call at Paynes find him in
robe de chambre — go to coffee house & breakfast &
on returning find Payne drest — a Mr Sennet with
him — translator & teacher of German — Payne ac-
companys me home with plays under his arm — call
at Storrows — payne waits below — find letter from
Mrs Van Wart dated 8th — call at Mrs Beasley —
find her & her Brother Mr —— & wife & Miss Barton
— call on Dr Greenhouse, not at home — on Mr
Coles,[2] a literary gentleman who Payne makes me

[1] The "authoress" was Frances Darusmont, or Frances Wright
(1795–1852), philanthropist and friend of Lafayette. *Cf.* p. 42.

[2] Probably Benjamin W. Coles, of New York, the friend of James

acquainted with — Dine with Payne in Palais royal
4 fr. After dinner stroll to the quais — on the way
find a Book shop where they [70] have a pretty edition
of Sketch Book in the press [1] — find a french translation of Bracebridge Hall for sale on Quai — 4 vols —
5 francs — call on D[r] Paul — Rue Odeon 21 Bis —
not at home — take coffee in caffy close by — stroll
homeward along the Quay Payne accompanies me &
sits a little while with me — find a letter from Messrs
Plummer London, with order on Lafittes [2] for 20£ for
Mrs Foster

Sunday 17 — Taylor sends home coat and pantaloons — Read mss play by Payne write a little —
Breakfast at home — go out in coucou to Mr Storrows — fine mild day — Henry & Irving come out
there also Mr Steele — Mr Richards of Boston &c.

Fete at the village — Bourgeoisie and [71] peas-
antry dancing — the latter in silk tabliers [3] of difft
colours — walk in Bois de Boulogne — read Italian

Fenimore Cooper. See letter of Cooper to Irving, New York, July 30,
1822, quoted by P. M. Irving (*op. cit*), II, 74, 75.

[1] This was presumably an edition published in 1823 by Baudry and
Didot. The only known copy extant is in the Bibliothèque Nationale,
Paris. Baudry published an eighteenth edition of *The Sketch Book* in 1831.
The following versions of Irving's writings had already appeared: *Voyage
d'un Américain à Londres, ou Esquisses sur les moeurs Anglaises et
Américaines* . . . Paris, 1822; *Esquisses morales et littéraires, ou Observa-
tions sur les moeurs, les usages, et la littérature des Anglais* . . . Paris,
1822; *Le Château de Bracebridge* . . . Paris, 1822. For a brief summary of
Irving's French reputation between 1819 and 1833, see S. T. Williams,
"The First Version of the Writings of Washington Irving in Spanish," in
Modern Philology, November, 1930.

[2] Irving's banker in Paris.
[3] Aprons.

— return in Evg with Mr Steele &c in a coach — 5 francs — Find dinner invitations from Mr Guestier [1] — & Mr Villamil — which I accept.

Monday, 18th. Breakfast at Caffe — Coffee au lait & bread & Butter — 18 sous — return home & write to Mrs F & to Sullivan. Payne calls on me —

go at 1/2 past 2 to Mr Storrows — find letter from Newton [2] dated 14th

Dine at Mr Guestiers — Present Mr & Mrs Guestier Mad. Beasley Miss Barton Mrs Douglass & Daughters Mr Douglas (son) Mr & Mrs Myers very abundant & clever dinner — In evening more [72] company came in Mr   American consul at Bordeaux with his daughter & wife Mr Welles &c &c Music — Mad. Guestier sings & plays charmingly — return home 1/2 past 11.

Tuesday 19. Awoke triste,[3] while dressing the porter brot me a long & most friendly letter from Mrs F. giving account of their arrival at home &c. Wrote a

---

[1] Daniel Guestier (1755–1847), a prominent wine-merchant of Bordeaux, with whom Irving maintained a long friendship, staying for a time in 1825 at the various chateaux of the family. The Guestiers still recall this friendship, but Irving's letters have been destroyed by fire. An account of this interesting family, whom Irving now met for the first time, in Paris, is contained in a privately printed pamphlet given to me by M. Faure, a member of the family, *Bi-Centenaire de la maison Barton & Guestier* (Bordeaux, 1925). Irving was with the Guestiers in Bordeaux when called by A. H. Everett to Spain, in 1826. He spells the name in three ways.

[2] Gilbert Stuart Newton (1794–1835), for many years an intimate friend of Irving. Newton, with C. R. Leslie, designed the illustrations for the third edition of *A History of New York* (1818).

[3] A favourite word of Irving's to describe his low spirits.

reply — & dressed to dine at Villamils — Cabriolet
charged 6 francs — so determined to take my chance
for gondole — walked mile to Barrier of passy Gondole passed & I got Place — arrived a little before 5
— stopped at Grattans — away — at Villamils found
a Mr Dawson — a Sicilian gentleman relative of my
old chance acquaintance Baron Palmer of Turenne
&c Dinner good — company made up of difft nations
& languages & not a good ensemble — a spanish poet
in Spanish after dinner music return in Mr Dawson
carriage — Dawson & the Guestiers [73] anecdote at
dinner of the literary ignorance of King of Naples.
One day he said to gentleman But tell me whats become of a man who was here some time since qui avait
la tete un peu montée [1] Alfieri I think was his name
whats become of him The courtier shrinking at the
Kings ignorance exclaimed — hes dead sire. Dead —
ah — dead is he — he was a singular fellow — he kept
very fine horses — and hes dead is he — how long has
he been dead fifteen years sire — ah, fifteen years —
he kept very fine horses.

[74] *Wednesday 20* — Write letters &c — Send
letters to Mrs Foster & to Sullivan read at Galignanis — Dine Passage — Evg go to the Varieté —
See *Marchand Forain* — good *Stanislas* (indifferent)
Precepteur, and Les Bonnes —

Thursday 21. In the morning corrected and altered
song of the Fairy & Pilgrim for P [2]   at one oclock

[1] Who was a little exalted.

[2] Payne. A lyric in one of Payne's manuscripts. Irving wrote songs
for several of his friend's operas.

walked out to Auteuil — found the little girls at home — at 5 oclock Mr & Mrs Storrow returned — dined there & passed the night there — Beautiful full moon — In the afternoon a christening at the village church This day put my letter for Miller in the Post office

[75] *Friday 22* returned in the morning with Mr Storrow & charles [1] — Went to Mr Butels school. Took Henry & Irving & Charles S to riding school — returned home & found cards from Dr. Paul & Dr Smith — visit from Grattan — dined in Palais Royal passed the Evg at home —

Saturday 23 Occupied at home in the morning — very rainy — cleared up at midday — had mutton chop at home at 1/2 past 2 oclock — called on P. not in town — Mr Gestier called & invited me to dinner for tuesday. Passed part of Evg with Texier — a young frenchman with him who had servd with Nap-[oleon] at Dresden &c — Thinks the national energy is deadend — that the Bourbons have quelled it — on retg home find letter from Mad. Bonet — inclosing one from Mrs Foster. — N B. This day rec'd visit from Bradish & Mr Elliot —

[76] Sunday 24 — called after breakfast at the school, to take Henry & Irving to Auteuil — Extremely warm day — from Auteuil we walked to Sevres — to call on Mr. Grattan — took lunch there — Mr G informed me of my being invited to Kenneys tomorrow — sent the boys back in cuckow. Went with Mr Villamil & Mr Grattan in cuckow to Versailles — Swearing frenchman with ribbon in his

---

[1] A son of Thomas W. Storrow.

button hole — English young woman with french admirer who holds pocket Hkf on end of stick to keep the sun off her face — arrive at Versailles at 1/2 past 5 — Bother of the Kenney family about dinner — Dull deaf stupid man servt — forgets pies & tarts — Ladies scramble off to see the Water works — we remain at table. Present Mr Villamil — Grattan Payne the Miss Bryants Mr   [77] return in evg in cuckow with Mr   beautiful moonlight night

Monday 25 Fete of S' Louis — In morng breakfast a la fourchette — which makes me heavy during the day — Call & leave cards for Mr Elliott — Mr Steele — Call on Mad. Bonet — See her husband who looks very ill — go to school & take boys to see the sports in Champs Elysee[s] — intolerably hot. Dine at Caffe Francais with Kenney — Payne — met Miss Holcroft & the Bryants — go afterwards to see the fireworks &c

[78] *Tuesday 26.* Dine at Mr Guestiers — Take Henry & Irving with me — Family dinner — Mr & Mrs Guestier — Miss Barton[1] & niece of Mrs Guestier. After dinner Mr G takes the boys on drive thro Champ Elysees & leaves them at school — pass the evg very pleasantly with ladies in garden — on grass — Mrs G plays & sings delightfully

Wednesday 27. Occupied part of the day at home — Visit Mr Elliot with Mr Steele — take a walk along the Boulevard with Mr Steele dine with Mr Texier present Mr. & Miss Hendricks — French

[1] The Bartons, an Irish family, were intermarried with the Guestiers and were associated with them in the Bordeaux wine industry.

gentleman formerly in Napoleons guards & a young student at Ecole Pyrotechnick [*sic*] — Young officer gives anecdotes of campaign in Germany — Bonap[arte] falling from horse — looking around to see if any one laughed

receive letter from Peter telling me of time of Irvings [1] arrival

[79] *Thursday 28.* In morng busy looking over plays and rewriting some pages of Author [2] send letter to Peter — call on Payne — walk out with him to vicinity of Auteuil where he leaves me & returns thro Passy to town — go to Mrs Storrows pass the rest of the day with the family and return on foot at 10 oclock in the evg.

Friday 29 — Tried to write at Richelieu [3] in the morng — visited by Mr Foy [4] who brings letter from Leslie [5] — visited by Payne — Go to Mr Storrows find the family in town — Dine in Palais Royal at Chatelaines [6] with Payne — go to the Quay Voltaire & buy Biblioteque des Romans 112 vols — for 112 francs [7] — On retg home find Irving who has

---

[1] See p. 40, footnote 1.

[2] *Cf.* p. 113.

[3] Written by Payne and Irving in collaboration. *Cf.* p. 41.

[4] A painter from whom Irving evidently derived much material for *Tales of a Traveller.* Foy painted a miniature of Irving which has, unfortunately, been lost.

[5] Charles Robert Leslie (1794–1859), painter. One episode of his life probably suggested "The Wife," in *The Sketch Book.* His *Autobiographical Recollections* (Boston, 1860) contains many references to Irving.

[6] The name of a restaurant.

[7] I have been unable to identify the particular edition of this work, which had at this time a marked influence upon Irving's thinking and

eloped from school in consequence of thinking he was imprisoned unjustly — take him back and have talk with the usher — matter adjusted — go to Dilligence office to receive my nephew W^m S Irving [1] — who arrives looking very meagre & pale with a sad cough — travels in compy with Mr Kerr [80] Had room provided for him at the same Hotel with myself — receive letters from Brevoort [2] & Jack Nicholson [3]

Saturday 30 — Breakfast at lodg[in]gs with William — write to J. Irving [4] — go out with Wm to Buy him a hat — Stop in at Royal Library — call on Mr Kerr — go to Mr Storrows where we meet Mr Elliot & Mr Steel — go to Prefecture of Police about Passport — Dine at Passage — read Eng. papers at Galignanis — go to opera & see Garcia [5] in Barber of Seville — Swaggerd & was too vulgarly drunk in the tipsy scene — had a vulgar look in it.

writing. He made long excerpts from it, in a notebook which is now in the New York Public Library.

[1] The son of William Irving, Irving's brother. This nephew died within a few weeks. The New York *Commercial Advertiser* of January 15, 1824, records: "Rev. William S. Irving d[ied] at Luc[erne] Nov. 15, 1823 on his way to Nice 2nd son of Wm Irving."

[2] Henry Brevoort (1782–1848) was one of Irving's devoted friends even before the first journey to Europe in 1804. Much of the correspondence between him and Irving is extant, in the New York Public Library and in private hands.

[3] One of the less important comrades of the early days in New York. See P. M. Irving (*op. cit.*), I, 349; II, 88, 387, 397, 399, 452.

[4] John Treat Irving (1778–1838), an elder brother, and a lawyer in New York.

[5] Probably Manoel García del Popolo Vicento (1775–1832), the Spanish tenor and composer. From 1816 to 1824 he was well known as a singer in both Paris and London.

Sunday — 31 — Went out with William in coucou to Auteuil & dined there — Mr & Mrs Appleton Mr & Mrs Low Mr Eliot — Richard Steele — came in in the Evg in jarvey [1] with Mr & Mrs Low — Wm Henry & Irving

Monday Sept 1. Breakfasted at home — called with Wm on Mr Kerr saw Mr Willet & Capt called on Jones — called on Dr Berger to take advice for Wm He advises him to go south in a fortnight — Went to prefecture of police for Passport — returnd home — walked with Elliot — called at Storrows about carriage — dined at home with Wm. Went to Galignanis to read papers — retd home supped — called at Mr Gestiers & passed Evg —

*Tuesday 2*d Dined with Welles —

Wednesday 3 — In Morng called on the Garnets to apologize for not passing last evg with them — Dined at home with Wm.

The remainder of the week passed very much at home with Wm and in rewriting the Drama of R [2] — write to Peter also & send ms of author —

[82] *Sunday 7* — Had Henry & Irving with me for the day — took them to the Louvre — dined at Home — after dinner called to see Payne who is unwell — walked in the Tuilleries with the boys and returned them to school — Went to opera comique — triste

[1] A hackney-coach.
[2] John Howard Payne's *Richelieu*, produced at Covent Garden on February 11, 1826, is dedicated to Irving. This dedication acknowledges Irving's aid.

Monday 8ᵗʰ — Occupied with drama — Kenney called on me — repaid me 5£ formerly borrowed from — we dined together at trois freres provencaux walked about the Carouzel [Carrousel] &c until time for him to depart

Tuesday 9 Occupied — receive letter from Peter — In afternoon Mr Storrow calls in — go with him to the Variete. — Sheldon also calls & goes with us Marchande de Goujons — Trilby — Cuisinier

[83] *Wednesday* 10 Finish last act of Drama — call on Payne — find Chas Kemble ¹ there — accompany them to Port Sᵗ Martin — Kemble informs me of his sisters elopement —

Walk out at 3 O clock to Auteuil — dine with the Storrows — walk back in the evening —

Thursday 11 — Early in morng finish the drama — take it to P — met Chas K again — call on Jones — on Mad Bonet — Dine at Welles with Mr & Mrs W — Miss Wiggins & Jones

Friday 12 — Call on Payne then on Mr Chas Wilkes — see Miss Wright there — tall thin talking woman — Mrs Trollop & husbᵈ ² Dine at home — visit P in Evg — receive letter from Sullivan

¹ Irving had long admired Charles Kemble (1775–1854), whom he saw again in America in 1833, with his daughter, Fanny Kemble. The latter was a fervent admirer of Irving's writings.

² Frances (1780–1863) and Thomas Anthony Trollope (1774–1835), the novelist, and her husband, the barrister. The Trollopes and Irving became acquainted through the Garnetts. See Frances Eleanor Trollope, *Frances Trollope, Her Life and Literary Work* (London, 1895), I, 62. Mrs. Trollope's *Domestic Manners of the Americans* appeared in 1832, and was read in that year by Irving as he made his long journey through the West.

[84] *Saturday* 13. At work all day on farce of Married & Single [1] — call on Jones & get letters from Miller,[2] Newton, Montucci.[3] Mr Hillyard and Mr Baldwin take lodgings in hotel — In evg 7 oclock stop writing — take Ms to P find him in rotunda Caffe with Mr Sennet & Mr Raymond Jones — walk about garden of P Royal & at nine home with P

Sunday 14. Busy in morng finishing farce — P called on me & Mr Raymond — Went out at 2 oclock with Mr Jones Baldwin & Boys to S' Cloud — dined at Mr Storrows — Mr Scotch gentleman there — weather is fine moonlight evg — warm — a heavy thunder shower in the middle of the day —

[85] Monday 15. At 10 oclock William starts for Bordeaux, in compy with Mr Kerr — accompy them as far as Dr Bergers — call on Mr Jeffrey [4] — see him Mrs Jeffrey & daughter Mr Cockburn [5] Mr Richardson — Mr Wilkes Garnets &c — return home — find letter from Mrs F — call on Payne — Dine at chatelaines with Payne & Mr Raymond — am troubled with pain in face — symptoms like re-

---

[1] *Married and Single* was produced at the Haymarket Theatre, on July 16, 1824. Genest credits it to Poole, declaring that Poole adapted it from the French.

[2] John Miller, the London publisher of *The Sketch Book.*

[3] A Dresden translator of Irving's writings. See *Journal, 1822, 1823, passim,* in the New York Public Library.

[4] This is probably Francis Jeffrey (1773–1850), whom Irving met in Edinburgh in 1817. His notes for this year contain several descriptions of the famous critic. See Irving's *A Tour in Scotland,* ed. S. T. Williams (New Haven, 1927), pp. 29–31.

[5] Probably Henry Thomas Cockburn (1779–1854), Jeffrey's friend and biographer. Both he and Jeffrey were in Paris in September, 1823.

turn of complaint in my ancles[1] — In Evg Mr Payne
& Mr Bradish in my room — Payne gives me a liquid
to hold in my mouth *Elixir de Mons Layedon* which I
believe did me good by exciting the parts — lessening
pain &c —

Tuesday 16. At home all day indisposed — pain in
my face subsides towards evg but symptoms of complaint in my legs more strong — touch up farce of
married & single — Payne, Mr Raymond & Mr
Bradish in Evg — Mr & Mrs Storrow & Mr Jones
in the course of the day

[86] *Wednesday 17.* Free from Pain — but face a
little swelled — ancles inflamed — call on Raymond
— go with him to look at rooms &c call at Jeffreys
Mr Mrs Wilkes & Mr & Mrs Cockburn — call at
Storrows draw on Mr Wms [2] for 100£ get 30 naps [3] of
Mr Storrow — Take sulphur Bath — 3 francs —
Dine with Mr Storrow Jones & Baldwin at Restaura-
teur near by Theatre des Varietés — about 6 francs —
Take place in Dilly [4] for Rouen for Friday — 5 fr
arr[ière] [5] go to theatre Francais see Coquette corrigée
& Jeu de L'amour & [et] du hazard [hasard].   Mars
admirable in both —

[91] [6] Friday Sept 19th. Leave Paris at 6 oclock in

[1] A malady which, out of proportion to the brief mention here, in-
creased, and clouded later the happiness of many years of Irving's life,
especially those of his ambassadorship to Spain (1842–1846).

[2] Charles Williams, an English banker in Paris.

[3] Napoleons.   [4] Diligence.

[5] A seat in the rear of the coach.

[6] Pages [87], [88], [90], and [92] are blank, and also page [89], except for
a few illegible words and the figure "7."

(44)

Dilligence for Rouen — river road — inside passengers — two manufacturers one of Louviers — one of Paris. The latter with his wife — also a little marchand de modes who had been travelling about for 10 years — morning cool — middle of day very hot — Dine at Mantes at 1/2 past 12 — plentiful meal — great variety — 3 francs — wine included — Honest manufacturer of Pont L Arche [Pont-de-l'Arche] Eager eater & talker — intolerably hot inside during the afternoon — At Louviers several passengers leave — I get on the imperial[e][1] & have delightful evg drive. Pont L'arche beautiful — river with long bridge over it — old church on the banks — ruins of chateau of Wm the Conqueror. Fine view from top of Hill between that & Rouen — reach Rouen half past 9 — put up at Hotel de la Borde.

[93] Septr 20th Saturday — 10 oclock on Hill below Rouen. Sunny day — Seine winding through rich Valley — great flat of meadows — side hills — grain — women at work — Ploughman higher up — bells of cattle from below — crows — river glassy & still — slight Haze — smoke rising here & there Rouen with haze over it —

Mem — leave Rouen at 9 oclock in cabriolet to visit the Ruins of Jumeage [Jumièges] Abbey — fine Drive over Hills commanding glorious views — and through fine forests — Meet two horses with peddler — sheepskins — & a man following them — Servant — shortly after — old chasseur or garde de chasse[2]

[1] Top of a coach.
[2] Gamekeeper.

cocked hat — little gun — short coat — band for sword — Spurs —

red Chapel At one end of aisle Escutcheon — in rude fresco — 4 cleavers or battle axes — Support knights armour.

[94] 1 oclock — among ruins of the abbey lofty arches — remains of rude paintings on the walls — old sundial still doing its duty — chapels with rude frescoes — choked with rubbish — piles of stone overrun with weeds — two high towers — tenanted by birds — part of the abbey a hay loft — rope walk — In one of the outer parts — on abutment over cells, is a cabaret — clock strikes the hours —

Interior court — old cedar growing in center — cows grazing cock crows at distance — faint tracery of cloisters —

Dine at the little public house with a queer sign of Dragon — Dinner — 2 eggs — Bread — butter — Neufchatel cheese — coffee — 1 franc — Have a fine drive back to Rouen — where arrive a little after 6. Shortly after Steamboat arrives — go on board & meet Peter[1] — walk about town with him — Sup on bread & milk

[95] Sunday Sept 21. Breakfast — walk about town — visit beautiful church — at the Hotel here — Grecian style — take sulphur bath — 3 francs — walk to cathedral &c &c dine at Restaurateur — walk about the quay &c — embark on board steam boat at a little after 8 — nap till ten — but forced to pass night in cabin — Sleep on cushion seat in dining

[1] Peter Irving lived for several years at Rouen.

cabin — get up at 5 oclock — Moonlight — fine day
break Monday 22 pull anchor near Jumiage — beautiful sail thro fine scenery past La Malaunay gusts of
rain — pass Caudebec — fine old cathedral — Ville-
quier — come to anchor before reaching Quilleboeuf
— remain at anchor an hour — weigh & try to pass
Quilleboeuf — tide will not serve to reach Havre —
put back & come to anchor — violent gale of wind —
rain — le mistral — passengers go on shore — P & I
remain on board — cosy dinner — Ham — flounders
— mutton chop — wine — bread & butter — read —
talk — take coffee au lait — pass time very pleasantly [96] I nap for two hours, in Evg. Then talk &
read till after ten — sleep in cabin on cushion — very
sound —

Tuesday 23. Fine morng — breakfast on board —
take a long walk on shore — return on board in time
for sailing — sail a little after 11. Several passengers
come on board—passengers of yesterday a french man
& pretty little wife — pretty effect of difft vessels getting under weigh—fine view of Tankerville [Tancar-
ville] castle — Lillebonne town in distance — arrive
at Havre a little after 2 oclock — Dine at Beasleys[1]
en famille — after dinner pass Evg at Mr   number
of Ladies & gent — Mr & Mrs Palmer of N York —
formerly   Miss Delafield [?] — pretty genteel little
woman — Mr & Mrs Delleforest [?] she pretty — Mr
& Mrs Bennise — formerly Miss Rossguard — Mr

[1] The house of Reuben Beasley, American consul at Havre, was long
a refuge for Irving during holidays in France, especially while he was
minister to Spain.

Rossguard &c &c — return home at 12. Beasleys
frolick in his night cap — Just get in on time before
gates are shut —

[97] Wednesday 24 — Breakfast with Peter — sit
at Home all morng — very Bilious & out of order —
legs inflamed — walk out of town — call at Greenes
Dine at Beasleys — Mrs chancellor — Mr Taylor —
have just retd from Eng^d — return home at 9 oclock
— get lotion — solution of corros sublim [1] for legs

Thursday 25. Breakfast with Peter — legs worse
— inflamed — At 10 oclock cross on steamboat to
Honfleur [2] — beautiful mild day a little more than
one hour crossing — go up to the chapel of Notre
Dame de Grace [3] — ramble about for an hour &
quarter — N. B. while   was besieging Honfleur he heard of the death of Agnes —— women
spinning — lace making — shame follows it — look
out — peeks thro his new telescope [4] — return to
Havre & [98] arrive a little after three —

Dine at Greenes — present Mr & Mrs Beasley —
Mrs Gestier — Miss Barton Miss Palmer Miss
Mr Taylor — Mr

In the evening we had charming singing from Mrs
Guestier.

Friday 26. Read in morng — dine with Peter at his

[1] Irving's abbreviation for corrosive sublimate, mercuric chloride.

[2] Irving had already drawn from the legends of Honfleur the story of
"Annette Delarbre," in *Bracebridge Hall*, pp. 357–386.

[3] Irving describes this chapel at the opening of the story. *Idem*,
p. 358.

[4] These are apparently the notes for a story. Their meaning is not
clear.

lodgings — in Evg pay a visit to Madam Gestier — find there the Beasleys — Mr Taylor — Music from Mrs Gestier — legs bad — continue the solution of Corros sublim

Saturday 27 reading the work of Mad Campan [1] — take foot bath of sulphurated water — Walk out to Mr Gordons the Consuls — has a very pleasant place on the Cote find there a miss Gore — promise to dine with him on Monday — Dine with Beasley —

The Gestiers & Mr Taylor there — in Evg some of the neighbors (viz Delleforest & wife — Bennise &c.

Sunday 28. Rain defied — walk out along the foot of Cote.

12 Oclock — among the ruins of Graville Abbey looking over rich flat — The Seine river &c — old abbey of gothic architecture — Kitchen garden — old white court — cross before the church — Harfleur — remains of old walls — mere masses of stone & mortar — Church a fine Gothic with beautiful spire — the portal lofty and elegant — Harfleur a neat place in a beautiful valley — return along the east of the Cote — fine plain beyond — Dine at Pavé aux huitres — pass evg at Peters Mem. fair preparing in vicinity of town.

[100] Monday 29. Beautiful weather, cool & elastic — Mr Beasley sails in packet for Engd — at 4 oclock. Dine at Mr Gordons   british consul — a worthy Scot. His wife pleasant frank & intelligent — knew

[1] Jeanne Louise Henriette Genest (1752–1822). Irving was probably reading her recently published *Mémoires sur la vie privée de Marie-Antoinette*, Paris, 1823.

Walter Scott [1] — was the confidant [e] of his marriage Mrs Scott was not pretty — that the match was a little in consequence of some previous disappointment of Scott — Lady Scott had then an annuity of 500£ a year — was under the care of   an elegant woman — Did not seem to favor Scott — Said she would never marry a man with a club foot — wrote to Mrs Gordon (Miss Ponsonby) would you think it — Im to be married to Mr Scott with his club foot —

at Dinner Miss Gore — daughter of Major Gore — a nice girl — Miss Ponsonby sister of Mrs Gordon — Mr & Mrs   Scotch — pleasant — he worthy & intelligent [101] Mr Marsh who writes for Quarterly a very intelligent man — Mr Denniston a young merch[an]t Mr Gordon the son — & a young officer of marines — ret[urned] late in Evg

Tuesday 30 — Terribly stormy day — get my passport visad &c. Walked out at 12 to see Mrs Beasley, Mrs Julian &c. — Detained by the rain till near 4 — Mrs S unwell — returned home dined with Peter — In the evg went to Ball given by Mr Denniston & Mr Rossguard — at Mr Bennise's — a bel [*sic*] ball — very pleasant — a good supper — many pretty women & queer men —

[102] Wednesday Oct 1. Stormy weather — visit Mr & Mrs Green — Dine there — present Miss

---

[1] From the day when Irving borrowed from the Philadelphia publishers, Inskeep and Bradley, the English text of *The Lady of the Lake* and committed parts of it to memory (*Notebook, 1810*, in the Yale University Library), Scott's influence upon him was profound and lasting. His Journals are full of gossip about Scott, similar to that in this passage.

Palmer. In Evg Green & Peter play chess — very sleepy — return home between 9 & 10 — finish packing &c — night clear

Thursday 2d — 7 oclock in morng Leave Havre in Diligence — see Codabec [Caudebec] — distant about 7 leagues — intend to visit Lillebonne — Tankerville &c. Seated on the Banket[1] — pleasant morning — but clouds threaten showers — pass thro Harfleur Before arriving at Codabec the weather clouds up — a manufacturing town — a fair in the market place or Square — rain falls in torrents — am obliged to abandon the thought of visiting Lillebonne — continue on towards paris — stipulating to have an inside place at night —

[103] Weather holds up after a while — at one oclock we arrive at Yvetot — a village — old fashioned — in pleasant valley — Yvetot — Hotel Angel Renommé — place de Victoire — dinner 3 fr just on entering Yvetot pass equipage anglaise 4 Horses — courier riding before carriage — badge on arm — Leathers[2] &c.

Enter beautiful valley & pass thro manufacturing town before coming to Rouen — arrive at Rouen about 6 — Dilligence unpacked & repacked — take place in cabriolet — bring another horse — start about 8 oclock — Sleep all night Friday 3 — Arrive at Paris about 11 next morning — Take a breakfast at the eating house in the Messagerie passage — Dress — call at Mr Storrows — go [104] to see my

[1] Irving probably means banquette, or seat on the coach.
[2] i. e., stirrups.

new Lodgings — find Payne there Pay off old lodgings & move [1] — Dine at new lodgings with Payne — Rue Richelieu No 89 — Evg — go to French Opera with Jones Lothaire & Aline — latter beautiful —. N B find at old lodgings a letter from Mrs Foster & one from Wm Irving —

Saturday 4th — Arrange my new lodgings — the Boys call on me —

Call at the boys school with Jones about 1/2 past 2 — Dine at home — pass Evg at home & Galignanis

Visit Mrs Welles in the course of the day —

Sunday 5 a mild pleasant day — at home all the morning till past 12 — Go out with Payne to Place Louis Quinze — He takes coach for Versailles I for Auteuil. Find the Storrows at home & the boys there — great gossip in the little village — about robbery committed in Bois de Bologne Walk in the woods with Storrow & the young folks tell stories at night walk in with the Boys —

[105] *Monday* 6th at home till near 12 — Baldwin calls on me call on Jones go with Payne to see a new school for the Boys Rue Copeau — much pleased with it — walk there & back — call on Mr Storrow — find letters from Sally &c Dine at home with Payne — Nap — Evg go to Vaudeville — orchestra 3 francs & half — first piece was Vadeboncoeur — 2[d] La dame de[s] Belles Cousines — pretty — several pretty women —3[d] Chasse au Reynard — pretty — very french 4 Polichinelle aux eaux d Enghien

---

[1] From Hotel Yorck, Montmartre, to 89 Rue Richelieu.

Tuesday 7 — Begin letters to Sally & to Mrs F —
pay for boys milk 26 fr at the rate of 2 fr per qt — go
with Mr Baldwin to the Exposition — call at Galignanis — receive note from Madame Bonet — Jones
calls on me — Dine at home with Payne go to Italian
opera to see Pasta[1] in Tancredi—2d Clarissa—Dismal
rainy day ——— ——— [2]

[106] *Wednesday 8*th—Waiting great part of the day
for the Boys to go with me to the new school Call at
Mr Storrows — family just come to town (between 1
& 2) — Boys there — difficulty with the Master
about their quitting the school — Despatch them
with a letter from Mr Storrow & a fiacre to bring
their things — Letters pass between Mr S & the
Master Mr Barthelmay — Latter refuses to give up
their clothes unless he is paid for the quarter just
commenced — Call at the school with Mr Payne —
find master and his family at supper — a little glassy
eyed petulant man — Have much talk with him —
refer the matter in dispute to be adjusted between him
& Mr Storrow — get change of linen &c for the boys
& take them off to their new school—Rue Copeau
No 21.   Mr Rouet — They seem much pleased with
the change — find an old acquaintance in a watch
dog from the other school — on my way back stop
at Mr Storrows — who I find alone — Stop at Galignanis (dine this day at home, Receive letter from
Peter —

[107] *Thursday 9* — Dine at Home — Evg at Mr
Storrows — Boys clothes still in custody — receive

[1] See note on Pasta, p. 69   [2] Two lines are illegible.

(53)

parcel from Peter cont[ainin]g Ms. of Richelieu & married & single 2 frs. write to him in Evg —

Friday 10 — at home all the morning — begin Azendai [1] — Call at Mad^m Bonets — Dine at Welles — present Jones — Miss Wiggins. After dinner Mr Chase comes in. Go to comique opera — Opera of the *Neige* — very pretty music & scenic effects — intolerably sleepy — continue baths — receive note from Mr Storrow saying that he will have to give up the point with Barthelmay.

Saturday 11 — out of order — slept badly last night — could do scarcely anything with Azendai — walked out — rec^d letter from Mr Willet dated Toulouse — Williams health not so good — Dine at home — Sleep soundly for nearly 2 hours after dinner — pass the Evg at Mr Storrows — playing chess —

[108] *Sunday 12* After good nights rest was fresh — write all the morng at Azendai — write letters to Mr Willet & William — at 1 Mr Storrow & Charles call on me — go to see automaton chess Player — Mr Jones — Baldwin — Chase — Cabot — Lee Judge Jackson & sister Mr Mrs & Miss Wiggins &c — call on Capt Holdridge — Afterwards call at Mr Baldwin to take leave — find Jones — Cabot & Lee there — return home & work at Azendai till near 5. Dine at Mr Storrows *en famille*. Leave letter to be forwarded to Mrs Van Wart — go with the Storrows to Judge Jacksons — rue Rivoli — find there Mr Lee — Cabot

---

[1] The manuscript of Payne's play, *Azendai*, with corrections in Irving's handwriting, is in the possession of T. F. Madigan, of New York City. It was apparently never acted.

— Lowell — &c — Public buildings illuminated on acct of Spanish news — fine appearance of Chamber of deputies — return home at 9 — finish the 1st act of Azendai — before going to bed.

[109] *Monday 13* — write — part of 2d act of Azendai — Capt Holdridge calls — walk a little before dinner — dine at home — expect Kenney but he disappoints us — Evg call at Capt Holdridges — Mrs H just going to bed — dont stay — go to Storrows & play chess — Mr Sheldon the Mercht there

Tuesday 14. At home till 5 oclock at work upon Azendai — Kenney calls & Welles — Dine at Mr Storrows — present the Jacksons — Mr Lee — Mr Lowell — Mr Barker — take tea there — Judge Jackson says in exploring the Egyptian antiquities — in the foundations of immense ruins — are found wrought or carved stones evidently the ruins of anterior buildgs — In reading Hindoo laws — Digest — finds writings coeval with Moses which speak of writings from *antiquity* — Some Indian law writers — contemporary with the expedition of Jason when a ship was looked upon as a curiosity in Europe — speak of ships trading to foreign parts —

recd letter from Livius dated Weimar

[110] Wednesday 15 — At home till 4 — writing at Azendai — Judge Jackson called & sat some time — walk in Tuilleries till 5 — dine at home — Evg to the Fr[ench] opera Aladdin [Aladin]

Thursday 16 — write all the morning till near 12 at Azendai — Boys call on me — go with them to see

Capt Holdridge — & Jones — return home — and resume Azendai — write till 1/2 past 4 — Dine at home with payne — nap after dinner — Call at Capt Holdridge — find there Dr   & Mrs   — call at Mr Storrows — find Miss Jackson there — stop till 1/2 past 9 — Return home — write from ten till 12 at Azendai & finish it

Friday 17—Employed in the morning touching up a speech or two in Richelieu — and copying & altering some pages of Azendai. Bradish calls on me — write letter to Peter — Drive out with Jones to Mrs Welles Then with her to Judge Jacksons — leave card — Mr Wiggins & appleton — walk in Tuilleries with Jones [111] Dine at Welles — Jones & Miss Wiggins — go to variety — a benefit — Leontine Fay [1] — see 4 very stupid pieces — viz La petite Soeur — Les Vendanges de champagne — La fausse Aveugle.

Payne finishes copying Richelieu

Saturday 18 Fine morng — early touch Azendai a little — Payne determines to go to London — we go out together to Versailles — go in cuckow to St Cloud—set off to walk to Versailles thro the wood — clouds up & threaten rain — get in cuckow & ride — visit Paynes house — call at the Kenneys give Mrs K a letter for her son. Return home by myself — dine at Restaurateur—go in Evening to Storrows —flute [2] — get letter from Peter

[1] Léontine Fay, daughter of Étienne Fay (1770–1845), French actor and composer. She was distinguished in comic rôles.

[2] Irving's one musical accomplishment.

Sunday 19 work at Azendai & call at Mr S — get the boys out to walk in Tuilleries — call at Mr Texiers — Dine at Mr Storrows — pass Evg there — write at night to Peter —

Monday 20 Write songs for Freyschutz [1] &c — walk to riding schools — take tickets at one near rue Madeleine — 30 fr for 12 tickets & 15 frs entrance. Dine at home — pass evg at Storrows. The Jacksons there — send letter to Livius — send letter to Peter.

[112] *Tuesday 21* — Write Poetry of Freyschutz — Take lesson at Riding school — dine at home send letter to Livius with songs — pass evg at Mr Storrows — Mr Drury & Mr   call on me with introduction — received letter from Mr Raguet.

Wednesday 22 — copy part of Azendai for Payne to take to Eng^d — go with Mr Drury to Biblioteque royal — take riding lesson — dine at home — receive letter from Peter — pass Evg at Mr Storrows — Mr & Mrs Low — Mr Sheldon & Miss   there — fine weather

Thursday 23 — fine weather — rise at 1/2 past 6 Oclock — dressing think of subject for play [2] —

---

[1] Weber's well-known opera, *Der Freischütz*, was produced in Berlin in 1821. Five versions were offered in London in 1824. One of these was by Barham Livius. Payne's, in which Irving assisted, is said to have been a literal translation.

[2] This sketch of a play with Shakespeare as its hero was written only six years after "Stratford-on-Avon," in *The Sketch Book*, which Irving began to compose in 1817. A comparison of the essay with these romantic episodes indicates that Irving used substantially the same incidents. This manuscript has been lost.

Shakespeare as young man. Seen with Ann Hathaway — her song — Scene with roystering companions
—— at night — Deer stalking — seizure by trusty
old huntsman — prisoner Keepers lodge
Examination before country squire —
his assurance — fury of squire
Act 3. Shakespeare absconding —
[113] Adieu to Ann Hathaway who resolves to follow
him — Beautiful Scene — Adieu to Stratford — bells
at distance chime midnight — Dream — scenes of his
plays pass before his mind — His own figure in temple
of fame — wakes — feels the impulse — determines
to make for London —
Wrote to Mrs Foster — Newton — Leslie —Colburn [1] about Rio Janeiro — Miller — Mr Lee called
on me with introduction from Van Wart — Walked
out — called on Bradish. Mr Drury — walked with
Bradish on Boulevard. Return home — receive 20
Naps from Storrow which I lend to Payne — Jones
calls on me — tells me of arrival of vessel at S
America of which great fears had been entertained &
on board which he had great am[oun]t of property
uninjured — Dine at Storrows — Mr Artiquenave
there — a french girl formerly of Theatre Francais —
who has been in america 8 years past —
Moral miss but ordinary in conversation — mor-
dant but not spirituel[le] —— —— one person made
her believe that Madagascar was an isle on the top

[1] Henry Colburn (d. 1855), the London publisher. Colburn offered a
thousand guineas for *Bracebridge Hall*, but Irving was unwilling to dis-
continue relations with John Murray.

of Montmartre — Talma [1] a man distrait [2] — full of projects — wants nerve

Evg — found letter from Peter.

[114] *Friday 24.* fine weather — Payne set off for Lond early this morng — busy all the morng copying Azendai — Mr Artiquenave called on me with letter of introduction from Ritchie — went with him & his son to Rouets pension — saw the boys who are very well contented — on return home found letter from Mrs Van Wart — made more minutes [3] to day on Shakespeare at Stratford — arranged it into 3 acts — dined at home — napped — went to Galignanis — then to Storrows where I found Miss Jackson — returned home 1/2 past 10.

Pay to day 20 francs to Lamp maker on Mr. Paynes account — I owe fr 10 sous for postage of letter from Peter

Saturday 25. Busy in morng copying parts of Azendai — send it to Peter — write to him by post — call on Mr Goodsell — Lee — Artiquenave — not at home — take lesson in Riding — Visit Mrs Guestier — arrived night before last — sat there an hour — returned home found Mr Drury at gate — sat with me at home — talk of am[erican] literature [4] — he is

[1] François Joseph Talma (1763–1826), whom Irving had met through Payne on April 25, 1821. For a little-known but interesting account of Irving's impressions of Talma, see "Conversations with Talma," in *The Knickerbocker Gallery* (New York, 1855), pp. 15–22.

[2] Inattentive; absent-minded.

[3] Notes.

[4] One of the few references during Irving's stay of seventeen years abroad to the writers of his own country.

one of the Editors of the Museum — Recd letter from
Mrs Foster — who is in London — Dine at Welles —
Jones & Miss Wiggins there — very heavy — re-
turned home at 10 oclock

[115] *Sunday* 26 Misty morning—rearrange Plot of
Shakespeare — write at songs of Freyschutz — Jones
calls at 2 — Go to Pension of Boys — find them
hearty & happy — walk with them in garden of plants
— return them home call at Texiers whom we find
alone — return home — dine at Storrows — in Evg
Jones & Mr Sheldon call there — go to Galignanis —
return home at 11

Monday 27 — Tried to write songs for Freyschutz
but found feeling impossible — Mr Drury called on
me & sat for some time talking of his flax machine —
furniture arrives from Paynes cottage — pay 12 fr for
carriage — Went to Riding school for an hour. Called
on Judge Jackson who is on the point of departing —
Dined alone a little after 4. About 5 recd a visit from
Lord James Stewart — had traced me from Lafitte
the Bankers — After leaving Dresden he had crossed
Bohemia — embarked on the Danube at Lintz — descended to Vienna — visited Salzburg & Styria & the
then made for Switzerland —

Went to Vaudeville — saw a light piece —— ——
[116] called *La pauvre fille* — several pretty passages
— Madml J Colon [1] played charmingly in it — went
to Galignanis read papers & then returned home.

Tuesday 28 — In no mood to write — went to

[1] Marguerite (Jenny) Colon (1808–1842), a popular actress.

Kings library — requested permission to have books at my lodgings which was granted me.[1] took out Hartes Gustavus [2] — called at Mr Foys lodgings — not at home — called on Lord James Stewart Hotel Castiglione found him & Lady James— sat with them for some time. Mr David Morier [3] came in — Invited me to his house for Saturday Evg — Rue de Sevres 91 — went to Manege [4] for an hour — called on Jones my way home — not at home — dined alone at home — In Evg went to Gymnase — & was greatly entertained. —— —— [5]

[117] Wednesday 29 — after breakfast call at Jones, return home, write a little — take lesson at Riding school — on way home meet Mr Foy — bring him home to dinner — pleasant dinner in Evg — Mr Drury calls in — Mr Foy leaves us — get letter from Peter — Mr Storrow comes & sits for some time — Mr Kenney comes & takes Paynes bed for the night.

[1] In the Van Traet papers, in the Bibliothèque Nationale, Paris, are preserved several letters of Irving's in French to the librarian requesting certain books. *E. g.*, p. 33: "Mons Washington Irving presente ses complimens à mons. Van Traet et le prie de vouloir bien l'envoyer par la portiere [le porteur?] '*Singularità delle Guerre de Germania* . . .' Rue Richelieu No 89 8 lundi Dec^bre 1, 1823."

[2] Walter Harte (1709–1774), *History of the Life of Gustavus Adolphus, King of Sweden* . . . (London, 1759). A "wilderness," said Carlyle of this book.

[3] David Richard Morier (1784–1877), the English diplomatist, at this time consul-general for France. Irving had known the elder brother, John Philip Morier, when the latter was Secretary of the English legation in Washington in 1810. He had resumed the acquaintance in Dresden in 1823.

[4] Riding-school.

[5] Five lines are illegible.

Thursday 30. Breakfast in company with Kenney — Call on Goodsell — meet with Mr Ambler there from Richmond Va. who has a letter to me from C Nicholas [1] — talk with Mr Goodsell respecting Flax engine — wishes Peter to accept agency — write a letter to Peter by Mr Lafitte — write to Sally by Jones — call on Mr Drury — he returns & dines with me — pass evg at Mr Storrows — playing chess

[118] Friday 31. At home till 4 Oclock—part of the time employed upon the Jeunesse HV.[2] Dine at Hotel de Londres Rue de' l' Echiquier, with Mr Drury Mr Goodsell there — in Evg went to Mr Storrow found letter from Mr Van Wart & Matilda [3] — dismal rainy windy day — high wind last night —

Saturday 1 Nov. Employed upon La Jeunesse. Began letter to Mrs F. Drove to Rouets school to see the boys — they were out on Promenade — call on Sheldon — rec letter from Wm I at Toulouse — also invitation from Mad Bonet which I decline — Dine at home — Evg go to a Soiree at Mr Moriers — Rue de Sevres. Met Lord Granard [4] & Lady Adelaide Forbes — latter speaks about letter she had written to Moore — Mrs Foster [5] wife of Chaplain to Embassy

[1] Charles Nicholas married Ann Hoffman, the sister of Matilda Hoffman, Irving's betrothed, who died on April 26, 1809.

[2] *La Jeunesse de Henri V* was produced as *Charles II, or the Merry Monarch*, at Covent Garden on May 27, 1824. *Cf.* Introduction, ix.

[3] Henry Van Wart's daughter.

[4] Probably George Forbes, sixth Earl of Granard (1760–1837).

[5] It has been stated, in discussing Irving's affection for Emily Foster, that he saw her and Mrs. Foster in Paris at about this time. He met, however, as this entry suggests, a different family.

& daughter — Genl Knazervitch [?] [1] — Baron Bredberg Count de Bray — introduced to Mr Wilmot who had been attached to Mr Cannings embassy in America — Mr. Dinon — Sir Chas Stewart — Baron Humboldt [2]

[119] Sunday 2 — Employed upon La Jeunesse — rec[d] visit from Mr Ambler & Mr Snow — called at the Guestiers who had invited me to dine. Sat an hour with them — promised to dine on tuesday — Dined at Mr Storrows — the boys there — staid there till 1/2 past 9 — went to Galignanis — thence home —

Monday 3. At home till near 2 working — La Jeunesse — call on Lord Jas Stewart — not at home — went to riding school — met Garnets on Boulevard — Met Baron Bredberg on my way home — dined at home — in Evg Mr Goodsell called & sat some time with me — write a little at La Jeunesse before going to bed —

Fumiste [3] at chimneys to day —

[120] *Tuesday 4* — Work at La Jeunesse — call at Mad Bonets — sat some time with her — call at Count de Brays — Genl Knazervitch — not at home — return home — write to Peter by Mr Lafitte — Go to Mr Guestiers to dinner — find Mr Meyer there — talks abt improv[men]t in france after the treaty of

[1] This may be the Polish general, Karl Kniaziewicz (1762–1842), whom Irving had known in Dresden.

[2] Probably Frederick Henry Alexander von Humboldt (1769–1859), the naturalist and traveller, who regarded Paris as "his true home." He was there in 1823, and did not settle permanently in Berlin until 1827.

[3] Chimney-doctor.

commerce in 86 — The improvt in manufactures —
they can not equal English in Leather nor coach making — The wood of the latter various & not seasoned
— french have not patience to cure things well —
Their cabinet work beautiful, chiefly done by for-
eigners from Alsatia & Lorraine — cannot equal the
English in cot[ton] goods — more fringy — the English have improved greatly in silk goods in last 6
years. Eng have introduced the white silk worm into
India — will it is said before long make silk so cheap
in England that it will be the dress of common people
— passed the Evg at Mr Guestiers — returned home
& wrote a little at La Jeunesse — heard at Guestiers
that Peter & Mrs Beasley were to leave Havre tomorrow.

[121] *Wednesday 5* Letter from Peter who leaves
Havre today — finish letter to Mrs F — write one to
Payne — send both off — call at Mr Storrows — get
doz wine and 70 naps from Mr Storrow — Return
home & write at La Jeunesse — Lord Granard calls on
me — dine at home & finish La Jeunesse after dinner
— pass Evg at Mr Storrows

Thursday 6 —Peter arrived this morning—between
9 & 10 — about 2 call at Mr Goodsells — Rue Thery
talk with Mr Goodsell about flax machine apparatus [1]
— 6 o'clock tomorrow night to call on Peter — return
home — go with Marianne [2] — buy bedstead &c &c

---

[1] During these years in France Irving and his brother Peter were engaged in various unsuccessful business speculations. The most disastrous
investment was in a steamboat company which operated on the River
Seine.   [2] Payne's housekeeper.

— for Peters Room 4 Naps — Dine at home with Peter — In Evg go to Mr Storrows — Mr Waddington & Mr Sheldon there — return near 10

[122] *Friday* 7 — In morning Mr Goodsell called — had conversation with Peter about his Flax machine — offered Peter the agency for France for such northern parts as he might like at the rate of one half the profits — Peter required till tomorrow to think — They went out to get a wheel made — while Mr Goodsell was here Mr Cockburn[1] my bohemian fellow traveller called on me — He had left Dresden shortly after me — had put his brothers at school at Hanover — & returned to England where his father had arrived from America — He has come to stop some time in Paris. Called at Lord Granard — sat some time with Lady Granard who is in ill health. Saw Lady Adelaide Forbes. Mr   who was with Canning in America was there. Lady Sarah   we promised to dine with them en famille on Monday — called on Lord James Stewart not in — left cards — Dined at home with Peter — Evg went Galignanis & read papers

[123] *Saturday. 8* — Read a little in Dufief tried to write songs for Azendai — but could not make a rhyme — went to Menage [Manege] & rode for an hour or so — returned home — letters to day to Peter from E Irving[2] dated Sept. 30 — & from V Wart — called with Peter at Mr Welles & sat for some time — Went to Guestiers & dined en famille — came home by 10 Oclock — Dull dirty weather — mild, but

---

[1] John Cockburn, an English army officer.
[2] Ebenezer Irving, the third in age of the Irving brothers.

heavy — Peter read Letters from E. I. dated N. York
Sept. 30 —

Sunday 9 — Bright clear cool morning — call on
Cockburn, Hotel & Rue Bailiff [Baillif] — not at home
— read papers at Galignanis — call with Peter on
Sheldon — call on Morier — call on Warden — every
body out — walk to the School to see the Boys sit
some time with them — from there walk to Mr Storrows to dine — At Dinner Mr Bradish & Mr Smith —
Letters from V Wart Dated   & from Sally to the
boys dated 2ᵈ Nov — recᵈ invitation from Artiquenave to dine tomorrow which I declined —

[124] Monday 10. Fine bright cool day. Tried to
write songs but could not move my pen — read life of
Gustavus — Mr Goodsell called on us — went with
Peter to see Mr Texier — gave us some information
about patents — went to Palais de Justice — bot at
booksellers laws of court — called at Mr Storrows also
referred us to young man Mr Leroux who could get
patents out &c — returned home — called on Lord
James Stewart — not at home — on Mr Artiquenave
not at home — at Galignanis — where I met Mr
Grattan — read papers — returned home — Mr Leroux called — Mr Foy — Mr Etty [1] Mr   called.
Etty has been in Italy for upwards of a year —
Peters Trunk arrives — receive letter from Payne
dated 7ᵗʰ had been 10 days at Dieppe — and was in
storm at sea —

Dined at Lord Granard — met there with Lord

---

[1] William Etty (1787–1849), the painter. Irving used Etty's stories
and records of Italy in writing *Tales of a Traveller.*

John Russell [1] Mrs   Lady Rancliffe — In Evg Lady Thomond & Lord Thomond. &c &c Lady T asked me to her home on Wednesday. Marquis of Thomond.[2]

[125] Tuesday 11 — Bright cold weather — visits from Cockburn — Genl   Marquis of Thomond Brimner who has just returned from America — translated Goodsells patent into English — walked out with Peter & Brimner — called on Bradish — returned & dined at home — Evg Gymnase dramatique — *Freres de Lait* weak, but pleasing — Ecarté amusing — Dernier jour de Fortune, so so — Bureau de Loterie — good

Wednesday 12. Wrote to Payne & sent pamphlet of Roulier [3] — went to riding school — called on the Garnets — read at Galignanis — Bot Stocks — of Fred[eric]k. Mr Artiquenave called & gave me tickets for the Francais Lord James Stewart called — invited me to dine with him tomorrow — dined at home — went with Peter to Theatre — Saw Scylla — Talma in Scylla — saw Mr & Mrs Gordon & Miss Jones at theatre — sat with them during the last act — went to Marquis of Thomond small party — Introduced to Lady Thomonds daughters &c &c — Lord Granard & Lady Adelaide came there Lady Thomond invited me to visit them when I came to Ireland —

---

[1] (1792–1878). The friend and biographer of Thomas Moore. Irving had known Lord Russell since the beginning of his own friendship with Moore, in 1821.

[2] William O'Brien, second Marquis of Thomond (*c.* 1765–1846).

[3] *Roulier*, or *The Wagoner*. The fate of this play is unknown.

returned home before 12 At Lord Thomonds was introduced to Mr King brother to Lord Kingston — a man dissatisfied with every thing — every thing in Paris was in a state of [126] destruction — (82) [1] he had been so much at Paris that his relish was over

Thursday 13. No mood to write — went to Galignanis & read papers — took out Arab[ian] nights — paid subscription to 6 Nov[r] — went to Louvre — found there Etty Foy & Evans — walked for some time in the gallery with Foy — felt greatly excited about Shakespearean aim — My Idea is to make him a varied character beloved by his wild associates for his joyous social character — by Ann however unlike any of her acquaintances — so novel — talks so frankly—His own aspirings after something better — When in presence of nature his feelings expand — he longs for he knows not what feels as if he could embrace the landscape — The stars the moon delight him — chime of bells by midnight &c &c

from Louvre strolled thro garden of Tuilleries to Hotel Iles Britanniques called on the Gordons — whimsical scene Miss Gore & Thorntons [2] footless wine-glasses —

Called at Storrows — nobody home — ret[d] [127] home — Parcel left by Dr Kitchen letter from Mr Drury — & Mr Miller — newspapers — cards of Lord John Russell — & Mr Wilmot — Dine at Lord

---

[1] By these numerals Irving perhaps refers, as was sometimes his custom, to an amplification of his records in another notebook; or he alludes to the year 1782.

[2] Sir William Thornton (1779?–1840), distinguished for his services at the Battle of New Orleans.

James Stewarts — Hotel Castiglione — Mr & Mrs Tighe there — in Evg go to Gymnase — Grisettes — Dernier Jour de fortune — Pasta [1] —— Les filles amo[u]reuses — return home by 11. Mr Tighe lives petit Hotel de Darmstadt [?].

Friday 14 — visited by Mr Artiquenave — calls from Inn — no purchaser — to Eng — write to Murray & Newton — go to Riding school — leave card at Lord Thomonds — dine at home — Evg to Mr Storrows —

[128] Saturday 15 — No writing mood — read in Life of Adolphus Letter from Payne and from John Murray [2] — Mr Goodsell visits us — go to riding school & take exercise on horse back — leave card for Lord J Russell — dine at home with Peter — Evg call on Dr Dickerman & his wife & take tea with them — call at Galignanis — & then return home.

Sunday 16 — Read in Life of Gustavus — Henry & Irving call — receive note from Lord J Russell inviting me to dinner & Theatre (engaged) Go with Peter & the Boys to Mr Gestiers — find the family at home Mr G ambling about his garden on a Poney — the boys ride it — Lunch there — & chat till near 3 — return home Mr Gordon calls — then visit Mrs Gordon & Miss Gore — Dine at Mr Storrows — Mr Jamieson there — in Evg there Mr Sheldon & Mrs Sheldon call in — pass Evg there — stop at Galignanis on the way

[1] Madame Giuditta Pasta (1798–1865), the Italian singer, of Jewish origin.

[2] Murray had published *Bracebridge Hall*, and was to issue several other works of Irving's. From this time until his return to America (1832) Irving wrote him constantly about all his literary plans, sending to him from Spain the sheets of the *Columbus* and the *Conquest of Granada*.

home — receive letter to day from Wm Irving — dated Marseilles about to depart for Nice — health worse Letter from Van Wart & Sally

[129] Monday 17 — Read Gustavus Adolphus — Mr Artiquenave calls on me — invites me to dine on Wednesday in compy with Talma — I have to decline — being engaged — gives me admittance to theatre for this Evg — call on the Hon[oura]bl[e] Mrs Tighe — take exercise on horseback in Manege — Leave card at Brit[ish] Ministers — Meet Saml G. Ogden — call with him & leave cards at Dr Bergers (send letter to day to Wm I) Dine at home — receive letter from Mrs Foster — card from Mr Foster Evg — French theatre — see Clytemnestre by   part of Orestes by Talma — meet Ogden at theatre — return home after play without staying to after piece.

Tuesday 18 — Read Gustavus — Mr Church [1] calls on me — translate Descript[ion] of Mr Goodsells patent — call at Mr Storrows — go with Peter to Mr Le Roux about patent — call at Galignanis — Dine at Welles — present Mr & Mrs Appleton — Miss Wiggins — Mr Lewis of Petersburgh — two Misses Lewis — Lieut Levi U. S. Navy Mr Brimner &c &c Nov 17th

[130] Wednesday 19th Readg Gustavus Adolphus — Mr. Debham calls on us — invites us to pass an Evg with him — Mr Artiquenave calls — invites to dine with him & meet Talma at the Rocher de Cancale [2] on Monday next — invites to come to theatre

[1] Edward Church, a member of the steamboat company.

[2] A famous restaurant.

some evg & show the interior to Miss Gore — receive invitation from Lord & Lady Thomond to dinner next tuesday — decline it — past one — go to Mrs Storrows to meet Henry & Irving there — Henrys Birthday — 17 years old send them to Mr Guestiers — call & leave cards for Capt Sotheby,[1] Mr Church, Mr Ogden — return home. Mr Kenney calls — go to Mr Guestiers to dinner — The family only & Henry & Irving — leave there at a little after 8 — send boys to school in coach — go to Mr Storrows for an hour or so — stop at Galignanis — return home

[131] Thursday 20 — Morning reading Gustav Adolph — leave card for Dr Kitchen — Mr & Mrs Forster — call on Mad Bonet & sit some time with her also on Miss Wright — Dine at home with Peter — In Evg go to Mr Storrows & Galignanis — mild weather, but overcast —

Friday 21. Readg Gustav Adolph — Between 1 & 2 go to Manege — Return home — find 2 letters from Payne dated 14 & 18 — Note from Mrs Welles invitg to dinner tomorrow — Letter from Post master in Eng^d informg of letter in post office for me — note from Capt Sotheby inviting me to go to Lady Louisa Harveys [2] — at 9 oclock Mr Sothebys carriage comes for me & takes me to Lady Louisas Hotel de la Touraine — find Lady Louisa & the Miss Harveys — Mr

---

[1] Probably Charles Sotheby (d. 1854), son of William Sotheby, the author.

[2] Wife of Admiral John Harvey (1772–1837). Irving was deeply interested in Admiral Harvey's tales of naval adventures. Besides the allusions in the Journal, Irving made manuscript records of these narratives. One of these is in the New York Public Library.

Mackenzie & Mr Sotheby there — Sit there till 11 —
& then return home

[132] Saturday 22 — finish Gustavus — read in
Schillers 30 years war [1] — write to Payne — go to
Manege — return home & dress for Welles dinner —
Dine at Welles — present Mr Philippon of Havre —
Mr Lewis of Petersburgh Peter Miss Wiggins & Mr &
Mrs Welles — in the Evg Mrs Welles sang & she &
Miss W playd on harp & piano

Sunday 23 — write to Mrs Van Wart — called on
Lady Thomond — Then on Lady Granard who
wished me to inquire about a branch of the Hastings
in America — Then on Lady Louisa Harvey — saw
her & the Admiral — Then on Capt Barth & on Mr
Cockburn — called on Mr Leroux about the patent
— Dined at the Storrows & passed the evg with the
family — stopped & bid farewell to Debham & his
wife — gave him letter to Sally — returned home
rec[d] letter to day from Mr Kerr giving acct of W[m]
Irvings Death [2]

[133] Monday 24 — read Schillers 30 years war —
Mr Goodsell calls — receive letter from Mr Welles
dated Heyeres [Hyères] — go to Manege & ride —
return home — dine & read — Evg — go to Galignanis & thence to Mr Storrows — where take tea with
Mrs S. and the girls.

Tuesday 25 — Morning — Read Thirty years war
from 5 oclock till breakfast time — write at Azendai

---

[1] Irving probably used the German edition published in Carlsruhe in
1823.

[2] *Cf.* p. 40, footnote 1.

(72)

— copying & correcting passages — Mr Charles
Ogden of Canada called on me — went with him to
Mr Storrows — left him at Galignanis — returnd
home — sent parcel to Payne contg — *Royal Waggery* — *Le Crime d une Mere* — *Contrebandier* [1] —
wrote on Azendai till dinner — went in Evg to Mrs
Storrows — read in Wallenstein [2] — returnd home
1/2 past 10 write on Azendai — from 11 till 12

[134] Wednesday 26*th* — Morning — copyg & correcting parts of Azendai — Mr Leroux calls & reads
his acct of Patent machine — call on Mrs Gordon
whom I find at home — sit for some time & converse
walk in Tuilleries return home — receive letter from
Capt Holdridge at Hyers — Lord John Russell & Mr
Gallois call on me — go with them to Beauvilliers
to dine where we meet with Lord Lansdown[e] [3] to
whom I am presented — deserted state of Beauvilliers
rooms — pleasant dinner — on parting Lord Lansdown invites me to visit him on my coming to Eng*d* [4]
— go to Mr Storrows — find Ogden there — sit there
till past 10 — & then return home.   Lord Lansdown

---

[1] *Le Crime d'une mère.* "I yesterday forwarded by the Diligence the
Ms. of La Jeunesse and at the same time 'The mother's crime,' & 'Le
Contrebandier . . . La Jeunesse as you will perceive is altered in title to
Royal Waggery &c." Letter of Irving to J. H. Payne, Paris, November
26, 1823, in *Scribner's Magazine*, October, 1910.

[2] Irving read Schiller more assiduously than any other German author, except Goethe. See "The First Dresden Journal," in *Journals of
Washington Irving* (*op. cit.*), *passim.* He may have used the two-volume
edition in German, published in Tübingen in 1816.

[3] Sir Henry Petty-Fitzmaurice, third Marquis of Lansdowne (1780–
1863). He was the friend and patron of Thomas Moore.

[4] See p. 210.

spoke of Montaignes acct of Rome Liked it for its old style — something picturesque in his old french Moliere thot above his time & above all time — as his works are calculated to survive changes & fashions

[135] Thursday 27 — correct & finish Azendai — begin letter to E Irving — Mr Artiquenave calls on me — Pay Fudine for linen &c &c 226 fr. 11 sous — go out in diligence to Sevres — to Mr Villamils — to dine. Meet there Miss Drew — Mr Jenkins & lady — several spanish ladies — a spanish gent who plays exquisitely on Guitar — Mr & Mrs Grattan & Mrs G's brother — Music after dinner — Villamil a determined craniologist —

return home 1/2 past 8 — in cuckoo — two subalterns of the guards — one mimicking English — the other very amusing in his conversation with girl in the voiture—find at home invitations for Saturday Evg — from Lady Louisa Harvey — and the eternal Croleys.

[136] Friday 28 — Wrote letter to E Irving — rec'd letter from Payne giving acct of disappointments — visit from Mr Artiquenave — write Payne — call at Mrs Storrows to forward letters to America — call at Post office & dispatch letter to Payne — call at Galignanis — Dine at Beauvilliers with Mr Artiquenave — present Mr Talma — Mr Etienne — Mr

Talma says the English pronunciation of French is pleasant — The french dancers affect it — We talked of French character — He says the french are kind & hospitable — Difference between English & french

— If a prisoner escaped in England the com[mon]
people were ags[t] him — when at fight round paris
the austrian &c prisoners came in wounded & passed
along the boulevard the people pitied them — gave
them money — bread &c Spoke of two french prisoners that escaped in Eng[d] & made their way to a Sea
port to get over to France all their money exhausted
— none to hire boat — saw name of Bankers over a
door — went [137] in & stated their case frankly —
and asked for a little assistance promisg to refund —
He at once gave them 100£ they offerd a bill or receipt — He declined — Gent says he if you are not men
of honor such paper would be of no avail — & if you
are men of honor there is no need of it — This says
T was told me by one of the party himself. Such cases
says he are frequent among the English — none but
them would do them — but the com people have not
such liberality — says the Eng are a noble people —
but the french more amiable & agreeable to live among
— I spoke of the kindness of the french among themselves — the ties of neighborhood are next to those of
relationship & the name of neighbour has something
of kindred in it. Talma seemed struck with the ob-
servation Once when the King came to his neighborhood to walk alone & the people stared stupidly at
him, Talma advanced & addressed him first contrary
to etiquette Thinks the french at present want a
gov[t] stable when they can be free of a court [138] in-
tervention of Clergy — manufacturers — heads of
families &c — all want it

young Nap — ceases to be an object of interest

(75)

with the people — too much under the domination of a contemptible family

Talma full of warmth nature & frankness —

Recollects seeing Franklin during the revolution.

[139] *Saturday 29* — reduced Azendai to 2 acts & sent it to Payne to whom I also write — called Went to Manege & took exercise on horseback dined at home — passed the Evg at Mrs Storrows — Mr Ogden there — stopped on my way home at Galignanis —

Sunday 30 — Morning — reading German — Mr Baldwin calls — returned last Evg from Holland — at 3 — go to reading room — then to Mrs Storrows — dine there with Dr Smith — Chas Ogden — Peter — the Boys & the family — In the Evg Mr Lowel comes in — pass the evening there — receive 300 francs of Mr Storrow

[140] *Monday* — Decr 1. Morning windy — but sunshine warm & lured me out to take air & exercise after the long rainy spell — called on Ogden in Hotel de Malthus [?] — found him in a room furnished from the wrecks of fine apartments — Went to the Biblioteque du Roi & read till 1 in le soldat Suédois[1] — returned home — found a fustian letter from Mr Cardell secy of the N York Literary Society — dated Nov. 1821, having been among the rubbish in Mr Gallatins office — Letter from Livius dated Berlin Capt Butler[2] called on me & sat for some time —

---

[1] Swedish soldier. Irving perhaps alludes to the biography of Gustavus Adolphus.

[2] A friend during the months in Dresden.

Went out to call on the Harveys overtaken by a violent shower in the Rue de la paix — stop in a shop & buy Hkfs — Lady Louisa Harvey & her daughters drive up — hand her out — get into the carriage with the girls — gossip with them for half an hour — promise to dine with them on Wednesday They set me down at my lodgings — Dine at home — go to Galignanis — & thence to Mrs Storrows where I pass the evening —

[141] *Tuesday Decr 2ᵈ* Rainy morning — *wrote letter to Livius addressed to his Banker at Berlin —* near 1 oclock go to Mr Storrows where I find the boys who have holyday from school to see the Entry of the Duke of Angouleme — go with them to garden of Tuilleries — great concourse of people — See marching of the troops from Mrs Drummonds where we are invited by Lady Louisa Harvey — Hotel   Afternoon go into Tuilleries & get near enough to see the King mount — Duke & Duchess D'Angouleme — and Duchess of Duras — very slight shouting among the crowd — call at Mr Appletons — Mr & Mrs Hinckley Mr & Mrs Low — Mrs Sheldon Mrs & Miss Storrows there — return home — then call at Galignanis read papers — dine — nap & go in evg to Mr Storrows where we find Mrs Sheldon — Mr & Mrs Low & Mr Sheldon came in in course of Evg — Illumination this evg —

[142] Wednesday Dec 3 — 6 oclock in the morning — a clear star light — get out of bed & go to the window — mild weather — windy — star shoots — slight flashes of lightning in the north — like lightning

for heat read in Goetz of Berlichingen [1] — after breakfast call on Baldwin — sit for some time with him tells me of some verses he had written in America —Hillhouse [2] calls on me—call on Artiquenave—not at home — call on the Crolys — Rue Richelieu — find them at home sit some time with them — call & leave card for Dr Hyde — do [ditto] for Mr Gallois — call on Lord John Russell — find him just going out — promise to dine with him tomorrow — call at Gestiers — the family pass me in carriage just before I reach gate leave a card — call on Mrs Welles — not at home — call on Dr. Stevenson — not at home — Mr Foy do. Truttel & Wurtz books not come yet — return home — dress for Dinner — Dine at Admiral   Harveys — present Capt Sotheby Mr Mackenzy [3] & Mr   Admiral tells me of his serving in the Am States in 1776, when a midshipman — cast away in the Liverpool in month of Feby on Rockaway beach — kindness of the people to them — Quaker family of the Hicks & another family in particular — remained quartered on them several weeks — the [143] rest of the time in tents — Always hospitably & kindly treated — made great work among hearts and bosoms & with quaker girls — (no impropriety how-

[1] *Götz von Berlichingen*. *Cf.* "The First Dresden Journal" (*op. cit.*), for Irving's reading of Goethe.

[2] James A. Hillhouse (189–17841), the American poet. Hillhouse was one of the few American writers with whom Irving was in correspondence.

[3] These were probably Irving's first meetings with Alexander Slidell Mackenzie (1803–1848), with whom he was later intimate in Spain. Mackenzie's *A Year in Spain* (1829) was reviewed by Irving in the *London Quarterly Review*, February, 1831. *Cf.* p. 72.

ever) Old quakers tolerated their youthful frolicks —
when they came to pay off & expected to have a great
deal above allowance to pay for the good people would
take nothing but the Kings allowance & told them
they were people in distress — would not take any
thing out of their pockets — first night of their going
ashore & landing in boats swamped — people came
down in waggons took them up home changed &
dried their clothes & gave them supper — He has
never forgot it He has only been able to express his
gratitude in words but if he had ever met an Am. in
distress should have felt bound to befriend him —
Whenever he had met Americans or Quakers has felt
proud to acknowledge the obligation was afterward in
N York with a prize — knew Mr Kemble — Relative
of Lord Gages — prize agent — was on the delaware
in service with the flat bottomed boats — played with
infernal machines &c

[144] *Thursday—Dec 4.* Kenney breakfasted with
us — Much talk about the theatres — incredible the
rivalships & feuds between the actors — ridiculous
strifes between mediocre men for the tragic crown
which neither of them could wear — Mr Grady violent & irritable upon the subject Whenever he goes to
Lond. in a day or two he is in the midst of cabals,
complaints &c thinks Mr Grady a bad actor —
striving to do great things & pushing properties &
imagining this is character — Went with him to Bath
where Kenney was disappointed with him & so was the
audience — for it did not applaud — when they went
home at night Mr Grady would be in a rage. What a

pity a great actor would not arrive & send them all
to the right about. Young is humbug — Kean is im-
patient of having any one in same piece that has a
good part — asked Elliston[1] last season — How long
sir am I to act with that d—d jesuitical bug — r —
Young —

Kenney told story of young empty officer who
brought accounts of battle of Waterloo — invited to
Holland house — in great spirits imagining he should
make his way famously by giving accts of the battle
— Talked largely at table—Lady Holland[2] — as Luttrell[3] said Kept eyeing him with a look that seemed
to say Ill be d—d if you ever come to this house
again —

[145] After breakfast — as the day was mild and
did not rain went to Galignanis — then to Louvre —
called on Foy not at home — went to Mr S.[4] & read
Milton &c — returned & dressed for dinner — Dined
Tete a tete with Lord John Russell — at his lodgings
Bains de Tivoli — talked of Moore[5] — M has aban-

---

[1] Irving's private letters contain many detailed descriptions of actors,
English, French, and Spanish. He first knew Edmund Kean (1787–1833)
in 1815; and during his first visit to England in 1806 he had many times
been to see Robert William Elliston (1774–1831). See *Notebook, 1805–
1806*, in the New York Public Library.

[2] Elizabeth Vassall Fox, Lady Holland (1770–1845). Irving himself
had been frequently a guest at Holland House during his first fame as
author of *The Sketch Book* (1819–1820). His visits to Holland house are
mentioned frequently in Moore's *Journals. Cf.* pp. 81, 82.

[3] Irving first knew Henry Luttrell (1775?–1851), wit and poet, during
the year 1821. In 1824 Luttrell became a devoted admirer of *Tales of a
Traveller*.   [4] Storrow.

[5] The present Journal reveals more fully than any other document the

doned his great poem — the loves of the Angels was an episode of it which he enlarged — its want of success discouraged him — Lady Donegal wrote to him — it both displeases & disappoints me — this was a sore blow — Lord Lansdown who had read & liked it — just then arrived down in the country but neglected to write to Moore for three days on the subject — Moore took this as a tacit disapprobation and was very much disheartened —

Moore once undertook to tell a joke of Lambs — As L was playing whist with Hazlitt [1] which last, as usual, had remarkable dirty hands — he said what a pity dirt was not trumps — Hazlitt — you^d then be sure to have a good hand — the joke said Lord J[ohn] — was a good one but nobody seemed to take it until poor Moore was obliged to explain it — oh said Lady Holland — now I see the joke — but its one Moore that many people would not relish — now such a one would not — nor such a one — and I think Moore — I should not relish it — Moore was dashed —

[146] Sidney Smith [2] is the only one that cant

friendship of Irving and Thomas Moore (1779–1852). See Introduction, ix, xii. See also pp. 208–211.

[1] William Hazlitt (1778–1830) assured Irving in 1821 that he would endeavour to persuade the editors of the *London Magazine* to accept Payne's writings. For Hazlitt's opinions of Irving's work see "Elia — Geoffrey Crayon," in *The Spirit of the Age* (London, 1902), pp. 362–368. It is possible that Irving met Charles Lamb through their mutual friendship with Payne.

[2] Irving did not apparently meet Sidney Smith, the critic and wit, until his appointment as Secretary to the American Legation in London,

be overcome by Lady H. He jokes at breakfast about her dish of pats of butter — I wonder now says he what would be the consequence if I were to take one of my ladys pats of butter &c

Lord John [Russell] is not affraid [*sic*] of her — has been accustomed to her from infancy — & indeed is a kind of pet — Says they read nothing at Holland house except a novel or some political pamphlet — generally is selected then for its amusing qualities no matter what are politics &c

Rogers [1] at 40 years of age began to go among people of Rank — before that he was among literary people & his own family — He knew Ward — who was a man of wit & information — was with him at Holland house — was piqued & annoyed at seeing Ward so much at his ease "Aye there they go" — said R "— theyre all cousins!"

Passed Evg at Mrs. Storrows

[147] *Friday 5* Dec^r — wrote a little at Hist of an Author [2] — Mr Kenney breakfasted with us — Mr Goodsell called — is bothered about Servt &c — called at Mr Storrows — not returned yet — ret^d home — Mr Baldwin called — left cards at Mr Gordons — Met the Gestiers in their carriage — called on the Harveys — sat with the old admiral till the ladies

in 1829. Irving refers later to Sir William Sidney Smith (1764–1840), the admiral, whom he met at about this time.

[1] The beginning of Irving's lasting friendship with Samuel Rogers, the banker-poet (1763–1855), was in 1820, at Wimbledon, at the countryseat of Lord Spencer.

[2] "The Poor-Devil Author," in *Tales of a Traveller*, pp. 152–179. Irving had originally planned this sketch as the basis of a novel.

came in — dined at home with peter — In Evg went
to the Variety — Saw — Ninette (very pleasant &
pretty) & Barbe bleu — (very amusing) the Fabri-
cant (in which acting is very good) & Les Coutou-
rieres [Couturières] — very Good —

Saturday 6. Read & make extracts from Life of
Gustavus — 30 yrs war &c — Go to Manege & ride
for an hour — return & dine with Peter — Evg to Mr
Storrows — Mr S. returned this morng from Lyons —
receive & accept invitation from Mr Morier for dinner
on Tuesday

[148] *Sunday 7* — Night of troubled dreams —
light candle & read a great deal in Elia [1] — much
amused — After breakfast called on Foy — found a
Miss Collins — an artist, with him — sat with him
for some time — called on Etty — he showed me
sketches &c — called on Texier in new lodgings —
Rue de Sevres No 4 — on my way home stopped at
Galignanis — Dined at home with Peter — In Evg
went to Mr Storrows — Mr Chas Ogden there —
came home at 11 —

Monday 8th Uncomfortable dreams again — rose
early — exercised in french Dufief [2] ate & after breakfast read in literary gazette — then tried to commence work on Germany [3] but could not do any thing
— towards twelve oclock an idea of a plan dawned on
me — made it out a little & minuted down heads of it
— Felt more encouraged — Felt as if I should make

[1] *Essays of Elia*, 1823.
[2] A French grammar written by N. G. Dufief. *Cf.* p. 65.
[3] *Tales of a Traveller*, Part I.

(83)

something of it — rec[d] invitations from Brit Ambassador & Lady Thomond to evening parties — paid visit to the Gordons found them & Miss Gore at home — sat there for some time — returned home dressed for Dinner — & dined en famille with the [149] Gestiers — pleasant dinner — Mrs G. tells anecdotes of her grandfather — and his escapes from Guil[l]otine during revolution — now an old man & blind — sits in his chair & tells story over & over of his escape &c muddy walk home — slippery hill &c fog

Tuesday 9 — overcast — cold — chilly — read french exercises — Literary gazette — look over papers & try to write on Germany — but the spirit does not move — invitation to Mrs Forsters for friday evg — engaged — at one oclock go out — call at Baldwins & Perkins not at home — Welles — See him. Mrs Welles ill — Sheldon at his new lodgings 42 Rue Taitbout — pays 400 fr a month — Very pretty lodg[ings] — go to Galignanis — read papers — settle & discharge library account — Call at Ashlys & buy shoes — Dine at Mr David Moriers consul genl — pres[en]t — Genl Knazervitch — Baron Bredberg — a son of Lord Darnleys — Russian Admiral — Mr & Mrs Blackburn (a very pleasant, pretty woman) Mr Hornsby — Lady Mil[d]may sister to Lady Minto — &c. Gen Knazervitch delivered me a most kind message from the Queen [150] of Saxony & Prince Max [1] — After dinner was presented to Lady Milmay who told anecdotes of Scott — never wrote verses

[1] Irving was presented at the court of Saxony on December 22, 1822.

before 40. Once in compy doomed at forfeits to make rhyme — had to give up & be fined.

Evg to the Eng Ambassadors — Met there with Mr & Mrs Philips — David Parish — Mr Rice — Lady Thomond &c &c   came away after 1.

Wednesday 10. This morning began German work — with sketch of Heidelberg Castle [1] — Mr Artique-nave called & sat some time with me — note from Mad Bonet — to whom I sent 7 Naps to buy em-broid^d Hkfs for Mrs Foster — went out between 2 & 3 called on the Philips — sat some time with Mrs Philips until Mr P & Mr Rice came in N B Mr P has invited me to come to see him in the country in Eng^d — Walked in the Tuilleries — then ret^d home — N B — Mr P says Mr Robinson talks of decreasing as much as possible the duty on Books & prints — Speaks highly of Mr R's administration as liberal & intelligent [151] after dinner rec^d invitation to Evg Party from Lady Susan Douglas — which I decline — Pass Evg at Mr Storrows — Peter & Ogden there

Thursday 11 Decr Rise early & dress by candle light — Try this morning to write on German work — but find it impossible — go out at 1 oclock — leave card for Mr Parish — call at Mr Storrows — drive with Mrs S & the girls to Rue de la Paix where I leave them — leave card for Mr Wilmot — 10 Place Vendome — Call at Mrs Douglas' — Miss Lucy Drew still indis-posed find Mr Villamil there — Mrs V comes in so does Lady Thomond & daughters — Mr   there —

[1] Omitted in the final version.

Dine at home tete a tete with Peter — In evg go to
Gymnase Dramatique See Grisettes — Dernier jour
de Fortune — Rodolph[e] — Michel [et] Christine
highly entertained —

[152] Friday 12 Dec[r] — Try to write on German
work, but in vain — write letter to Mr Cardell [1]
Sec[re]t[ary] of N York Belles lettres Academy — at
one oclock go out — call at the Harveys & find the
admiral & Lady Louisa at home — Miss Harvey
comes in — Admiral going to convey the girls to the
Fêtes — go to Manege & ride for an hour — Dine at
home with Peter — after dinner receive note from Mr
Philips inviting me to Ambassadors Box at theater
— call at the Philips & accomp them & Mr Spring
Rice — Play the Cid — very heavy & played by
Doubles [2] — except Talma — whom I do not much
like — The afterpiece *Amour & Amant* — very neat
& pleasant & excellently played — From thence went
to March[i]oness Thomonds to a Dance — Mr
Sotheby set me down — Met there the Harveys —
Lord Granard Lady Adelaide Forbes — Lord Mil-
town with whom I engaged myself to dine tomorrow
— Capt Butler — whom I knew at Dresden — Mr
Wilmot &c &c came away at 12 [153] rec[d] letter from
Mrs Foster

Saturday 13 — Woke early — restless and anxious
— full of doubts as to literary prospects — After
breakfast tried to summon up ideas to write but in

---

[1] This long letter, describing certain literary conditions in America, is
now in the possession of E. W. Harden, of New York City.

[2] Understudies.

vain — Went out & strolled to various places — read
papers at Galignanis — called at Mr Storrows & get 40
Nap^s Drove with Mrs S & the girls to Tuilleries where
I left them — went to Manege & rode for an hour —
returned home — napped a little — dressed and went
to Lord Miltowns to dinner — neat little Hotel —
at Dinner Hon^{be} Mr Lawson (brother to Lord etc)
Mr Fox & Mr   Much talk in early part of dinner
about Germany & Germans — afterwards become
more pleasant Mr Bingham came in afterwards In
Evg — went to Lady Louisa Harveys — Met there
Lady Adelaide Forbes — Mr & Mrs Blackburn
they leave Paris tomorrow — He goes for 7 years
as Judge to the Mauritius (Isle of France) — [154]
Stories of Blunders of Mrs   & Lady. She had been
to see Mary the Magic & St Johns Latter end —
Says the Priests prostitute (prostrate) themselves —

 Sunday 14 — Mr Philips called on me — I had rec^d
an invitation last Evg to dine with him today which I
declined — Mr Foy entered at 1 — Took him to
Mr Storrows & introduced him — Mr Baldwin called
— called at Mad^m Bonets & sat some time with her —
Dined at Mr Storrows — present Mr Richards — a
Cadet from W Point — an intelligent lad — passed
Evg at Mr S — & on returning home find note from
Mrs Guestiers offering ticket for Grand Ball of to-
morrow evg —

 [155] Monday 15. Henry & Irving breakfast with
me — Send them to Mrs Gestiers with note, excusing
myself from Ball — go to Galignanis — then to Mr
Storrows — get Charles to pass the day with me re-

turn home — Mr Grattan calls — Young Dr Courville also — talk with Grattan about his ms. Mr. Sheldon calls on us & sits for some time — go to Galignanis & read papers — Dine at home early — the Boys & Chas Storrow dine with us Receive letter from Payne — In Evg go with the Boys & Peter to Theatre Port S' Martin melodrama of 2 Sergeants — La Chastete — Le Conscrit Polichinelle Vampire returned home & find Parcel from Mrs Foster — with Germ[an] Book & miniature painted by Emily [1]

[156] Tuesday 16. after a night of broken sleep — and uneasy thoughts arise a little before 8. The boys breakfast with us & then set off for school — read Goetz of Berlich[ingen] — try to write but in vain — Ogden calls to take leave — Cockburn calls (& Mr Goodsell) — Cockburns story of   when commanding fort at Dinan — came home first night late at night, in November, Drunk — lay for a while in ditch, under draw bridge — Sentinel saw him —·To put a good face on matter he called sentinel! Sir — call me in ten minutes — In ten minutes sentinel called Mr   the ten minutes are over Sir — got up & walked as well as he could into fort —

Went to Galignanis & read papers called and bade farewell to the Gordons — called & sat with the Harveys, who gave acct of the ball — called & sat some time with Mrs. Philips — Met Lord Bolingbroke there. Dined at home with Peter — In Evg to Mr Storrows. read two acts of Macbeth to the family.

---

[1] This miniature, made in the Dresden gallery, Irving prized until the end of his life. See P. M. Irving (*op. cit.*), IV, 219.

[157] *Wednesday 17* Dec^r — Woke early — felt depressed & desponding — suddenly a thot struck me how to enlarge the Mss. on hand so as to make 2 vols of Sketch Book [1] — that quite enlivend me — at Breakfast communicated it to Peter who was highly pleased with it — Sent several pamphlet plays to Payne — write to him & Newton — Mr Goodsell called — visited the Gestiers — found the ladies at home, who gave me account of their adventures at grand Ball — visited Mad^m Bonet & Mr DeCourville & sat some time with them —

Dined at Mr Welles — present Mr & Mrs Appleton — Mr Wiggins — Mr Baldwin. Miss Wiggins, Peter & Myself — In evg went to French opera to join Mrs Gestier &c — Opera aladdin — return home found message from Douglas inviting to party — tomorrow evg.

[158] *Thursday 18th* copy & correct sketch of old Frenchman [2] — Mr Goodsell & Mr Leroux call about the Patent business. Call at Lady Susan Douglas — to disengage myself from evg party — no body at home — leave note — read papers at Galignanis — Dine at home with Peter — In Evg — go to Mr Storrows — Mr & Mrs S. dining out — sit with Susan & Ann Louisa — & read from Shakespeare to them — Mr & Mrs S come home, chat for an hour with them & take leave — find at home invitation from the Thayers to dinner on Sunday — Shall decline rue de Bois — 37bis

[1] This plan was never executed.
[2] "My French Neighbor," in *Wolfert's Roost* (1855), pp. 219–221.

Friday 19. rewrite & enlarge sketch about the Tuilleries.[1] Masons at work at chimney Capt Sotheby calls & sits with us — Receive letter from Livius — Dine at Admiral Harveys — present Capt Sotheby Mr & Mrs Drummond and Miss   Mr   and a gentle man belonging to Austrian Embassy. In evg — play ecarté[2] — return home at 11 — heartily sleepy.

[159] *Saturday 20* — After a night of broken rest and scanty sleep rise at 8. After breakfast rewrite and enlarge sketch of Eng & French Character [3] — write to Livius — rewrite & correct sketch of Eng-Absentee [4] — Dine at home — go to Theatre Francais — our Billet de caisse [5] of an old date would not admit us — pass the evg at Mr Storrows — meet there old gentleman of Nismes — Mr Jamieson. Peter & Mrs Storrow play at chess —

Sunday 21 Decr. Again a watchful night — rendered more impossible by the intolerable howling of a dog in a neighboring yard — Write this morng at a couple of pages of "Literary immortality" [6] and finish sketch of Englishman — call at Galignanis to read papers. Young Galignani wishes to know if I have objection to their republishing Salmagundi[7] & upon

[1] "The Tuileries and Windsor Castle," *idem*, pp. 230–234.

[2] This game of cards was now extremely popular in Paris.

[3] "English and French Character," in *Wolfert's Roost*, pp. 226–230.

[4] Presumably "The Englishman at Paris," *idem*, pp. 222–225.

[5] Theatre-reservation.

[6] These two pages probably became the section called "Literary Life," in *Tales of a Traveller*, pp. 135–138.

[7] Irving continued to be ashamed of this early publication. It was, however, reprinted in 1824. See p. 120.

my saying I had he promises not to publish it — Says
he expects to buy the Paris edition of Sketch Book &
Bracebr[idge] Hall or else print an edition — Wishes
me to sit for a miniature to be engraved & put in
front — Decline for the present — Call on Mr Foy —
not at home — call this morng on Mr Welles — not
at home — Dine at Mr Storrows — present Mr
Jamieson — Mr Baldwin — Peter — In Evg came in
Mr & Mrs Low & Mrs Sheldon — return home about
1/2 past 10

[160] Monday 22. Night of broken Sleep — Look
over papers in the morning but do not write — wrote
to Murray & Livius & send letters. Tell Murray I
shall probably have 2 vols of Sketch Book for him in
yᵉ Spring — Mr Foy calls — about taking the Miss S.
likeness — Go to Mrs Storrow — accompany her &
the girls to Miss Collins rooms where they have a sitting till 1/2 past 3 — Dine at home — In Evg go to
Variety — pieces &c Bonnes des Enfans—Precepteur
dans Embarras — Coutourier.[1] Very sleepy come
away before last piece — stop in at Galignanis & then
return home.

Tuesday 23. Morning wrote part of essay on
French & Eng animosity & characters — Frederick
calls & explains about Theatre ticket — write note to
Mᵐᵉ Duport requesting a new billet — Cockburn
Calls & borrows 7 napoleons — note from Mrs Welles
with list of music — Mr Le Roux calls about patent.
Call on Mr Foy who I found busy with the little pic-

---

[1] *Les Bonnes d'enfants, ou une soirée aux boulevards neufs; Précepteur
dans l'embarras; La Couturière.*

ture return with Mrs S & the girls meet Mr Morier
at my door. Go to Panorama passage & order music
read papers at Galignanis — where I meet with
Grattan — Dine at home with Peter — receive invitations from Mr Welles & Mr Douglas for Xmas dinner
decline both — Evg at Mr Storrows — Capt Holdridge [161] & Mr Lowel there—

Wednesday 24. Finish letter & send it to Mrs
Foster write an article on English & French rivalship
— Mr Airey [1] calls — just arrived in Paris — Have a
long chat about Dresden — Airey stays at Hotel
Richelieu read in German work of Grimms [2] — Dine
at home — Pass Evg at Mr Storrows — The boys
there — Christmas eve — Play at games — return
home between 10 & 11 —

Thursday 25 — *Christmas* — The Boys slept at my
lodgings last night — breakfasted with us — change
bed room with Peter — receive letter from Powell [3]
& Mrs   take cabriolet — leave cards with Harveys
— Drummonds — Villamils — Airey — call on Mr
Artiquenave—find him at home in cluttered up lodgings — Cat piss smell — Our old night gown — Ill
with Rheumatism — tells me of Mr Gonpiny's going
to make a vaudeville on my story of the Fisherman
— Mr Sherman — Talma & Gonpiny going to call on
me — Finds fault with Rouets school — go from him

---

[1] Richard Airey (1803–1881), son of Sir George Airey, whom Irving
had known in Dresden. Richard Airey was later a general during the
Crimean War.

[2] Irving had been reading in Grimm's tales since the period in which
he began *The Sketch Book*.

[3] Peter Powell. See p. 192, footnote 1.

to Hotel Dusseldorf — where girls are sitting for their
likeness. Mr Foy is making a charming picture of it
— return home with them — Find Peters trunks
arrived [162] note informing me that Mad Bonet is
brot bed of a girl — Call on Mr Thayer — then on
Mr Henry — read papers at Galignanis — dine at
Storrows — present the Boys Mr Lowell & Peter —
have Xmas games in the Evening.

Friday 26. Morning — write note to Grattan
write a little at story of Wolfert Webber [1] but cannot
please myself — walk to Foys to see picture — returning — stop at Baudrys [2] & buy books — then
walk in Thuilleries Dine at home with Peter — Letter
from Newton & from Payne — after dinner & sleep go
to Crolys — not at home — Storrows — not home —
stop at Galignanis — & then return home — find invitation from Douglas for N Years day shall not
accept — card from Gen[1] Airey.[3]

[163] *Saturday 27* — Finished correcting Grattans
Mss — wrote commencement of tale of Wolfert
Webber — received letter from Ebenezer I — also
from Payne enclosing draft on Lafitte for 800 fr —
Invitation from Reed for New Years dinner which I
decline cards from Sir J Wilmot & Mr Wilmot —
Invitation from Lady L Harvey for Sunday Evg —
Walk out before dinner for 3/4 of an hour — Dine at

[1] "Wolfert Webber, or Golden Dreams," in *Tales of a Traveller*, pp.
455–486.

[2] Baudry published various English and French versions of the writings of Irving. In 1836 he issued in Paris the complete works of Irving in
one volume.

[3] Sir George Airey (1761–1833).

home with Peter — Evg go to Vaudeville See La Dame des Belles Cousin[e]s — Mort Vivant — Femmes Volantes — very pretty — Chasse au Renard — Jenny Colon very pretty and played well.

Sunday 28 — After an indifferent nights rest feel indisposed to work. Write a little at story of Wolfert Webber, but give up the attempt — & as the morng is fine, dress to go out — weather changes & begins to rain — return home — try again to write, but in vain — write letter to E. I. Mr Baldwin calls & sits for some time — go out for exercise — call on Mr Foy who I find painting at Hotel Dusseldorf — Sit some time with him — then return home — Dinner — take a sound nap after dinner — Go to Mr Storrows — find there Mr Artiquenave & son — Letter from Van Wart — Talks of sending Irving to America — return home at 10 oclock.

[164] Monday 29 — Write to Payne — write on Wolfert Webber — but get on rather slowly — 10 pages today — Receive long letter from Brevoort — call at Mr Foys — find the Storrows there — Mr Foy getting on well with the painting — Mrs S sets me down at home — Dine with Peter — Evg go to Mr Douglas but find his party is put off, having heard of the death of his mother — go to Galignanis & then return home at 1/2 10 Mr Cockburn gives me a number of Sketches of his fathers

Tuesday 30. Send letter to E. I. Write on the Story of W Webber — 15 pages — Mr Le Roux & Goodsell call — at 2 oclock dress & go out to Mr Foy's — where I find Mrs S & the girls — after sitting some time I return with them & they set me down at home. Find Mr Lowel at home — with Peter — sits some time with us — Dine at home with Peter — in the Evg go to Mr Storrows — Dr Smith there early part of the Evg — Mr Brimner the better part

This day pay Mr Paynes Bill in favour of Mr
for

[165] *Wednesday* 31. After a very indifferent nights rest, rise with feeling of exhaustion — after breakfast resume writing on Wolfert Webber. Interrupted continually this morning — visit from Baron Bredberg — another from Airey — fumiste altering chimney &c &c &c. — do not write above ten or twelve pages tho I keep at it till 3 oclock — go to Foys — nearly finished the picture — find the Storrows there who return with me — Dine at home with peter — Sleep for 2 hours after dinner — go to Storrows find Henry & Irving there — pass the evg till 10 — then return home — first stoppg to buy books for Etrennes [1] — find cards from Count Bray — Genl Knazervitch — Mr Sheldon

1824

[166] Jany 1. Henry & Irving pass the night & breakfast with us. Shocking rainy weather — Smoky chimney — I myself unstrung from a sleepless night — Give Etrennes to Marianne 2 naps — Porter 1. Send presents to the young Storrows of books & bird — write a little but very little, on W Webber — Chas & Saml Storrow come in carriage — take the boys

---

[1] New Year's gifts.

out. Send cards by them to the Ambassador — Wilmots, Villamils &c &c — go to Storrows to wish happy year. Then to Adml Harveys, where I sit some time — Then to Madam Bonets — return home & dress for dinner. Mr & Mrs Storrow call in carriage — dine with Reed. Was hot dinner — splendid. Mr & Mrs Appleton — Mr & Mrs Welles Mr & Mrs Wiggins Mr & Mrs Storrow — Miss Wiggins Mr & Mrs Frank. Dr & Mrs   2 Mrs Sheldons — dinner to me dull. Evg — Ecarté — staid till 1/4 past 10. Drive home with Storrows — & brot the boys home from Mr Storrows.

[167] *Jany 2.* Henry & Irving still with us — write a little at Wolfert W. Go to Mrs Storrows at 2 oclock arrange Tableaus — Dine there — Mr Baldwin The Miss Chaplins. Peter, Henry & Irving — In Evg. The Sheldons. Lows &c. Play at Tableaus & other games — display the little picture by Mr Foy — return home at 11 — very much out of order

Jany 3. The boys breakfasted with us.   This morng — paid note of Paynes to Lowenthals for 58 fr.[1] Finished Wolfert Webber — (rough draught) 74 pages Dressed to go out but Mr Etty called & sat with me (Mr Goodsell took leave of me this morng) After Mr Etty went, I laid down, feeling very languid, with symptoms of approaching pain in my face — At five went to Mr Gestiers to dine — Met there Mr Beasley — the family & three gents whose names I did not

[1] These endless debts of Payne's were a source of constant irritation to Irving, as demonstrated by several letters from Payne to Colonel Thomas Aspinwall, in the possession of T. F. Madigan.

know — pleasant dinner — In Evg Mrs G played & sang for us — returned home at 11 — feeling much better — took hot bath & went to bed.

[168] Sunday Jan 4 — Rather indisposed — symptoms of an inflammation in cheek & ear & throat — the Boys still with us — after breakfast write a little on various parts of Wolfert W — Go to Galignanis & read papers — promise Galignani to sit for my miniature — Return home & lie on sopha. Mr Storrow calls & sits some time with us — Dine and pass evg at home — take foot bath & go to bed at 1/4 past 10

This day pay Paynes note to Marchand for 125. fr

Monday 5. Boys Breakfast with us & return to school. Feel much better today. At work all day touching up & altering story of Wolfert W — Billet of Mr Paynes to Mr Sennet, presented — for 85 francs, which I pay. Dine at home with Peter — In Evg Mr Winslow calls & plays chess with Peter. Mr Storrow also calls & sits for some time — do not go out of the house today — go to bed about 10 —

[169] Tuesday 6th Rise much better this morning than I have been for the last three days — work at Wolft W retouching & altering, till 1 oclock — Mr Teacher of violin &c brings me music for the Harp — to send to F Foster [1] — 19 francs. Pay balance of Bill of Brinton agst Payne 10 fr 5 Sous — and the rest to Marianne, making in all 35 fr 5 sous. Mr Cockburn calls & stops a little while — go to

---

[1] Flora Foster. It was her Journal (published in 1863) which ascribed Irving's depression in 1823 and 1824 to an unhappy love affair with her sister, Emily Foster.

Lafittes & cash Bill of Exchg sent by Payne — of the —— for 800 fr. Baron de Bredberg calls — go with him to Mad Quandts — round, smooth spoken little German lady — meet there with an agreeable looking German lady & a Germ[an] gent engage myself to drive with Mad d[e] Quandt on Friday — Call at the Harveys. See the Admiral lady Louisa & the young ladies — sit there some time Dine at home with Peter — In evg Mr Winslow comes to play chess with him. Go to Mr Storrows meet there Mr Hillyard of Boston just returned from Germany. Mr Jamieson & Mr   a German — talk of German flowers &c various esquisses[1] of pictures of flowers which the young ladies have. Stop at Galignanis on my way home

[170] *Wednesday 7 Jany.* Write to H V W[2] — Payne & few lines to M^{rs} F with music — leave the letters & music at Mr Ettys to fetch in to England — call at the Louvre to see Etty but he was not there — Leave card at Mr Artiquenaves — Call this morng at Galignanis agree to correct Salmagundi for him — bot Byrons last cantos of Don Juan.[3] On returning home find Mr Beasley there who sits some time with us — Dined at home with Peter — Pass Evg at home dozing & reading part of 9th Canto of Don Juan, which I did not much relish. Go to bed a little after 10 oclock.

Thursday 8. — Awoke at 4 Oclock this morng —

[1] Sketches.
[2] Henry Van Wart, Irving's brother-in-law.
[3] Cantos VI–XIV appeared in this year.

read Don Juan till 6 — napped till 7 — rose at 8 — finish Don Juan after breakfast — Go out 1/2 past 11. call on Airey — Introduced to his family. Genl Geo Airey & Lady Airey two daughters & younger sons — sat some time with them chatting — had been to Duke of Orleans Court last evg — Weak mind & affability of the family. Promise to dine with the Aireys on Sunday at 6 oclock. Call at Mr Artiquenaves explain to him Law of copy right — Call on Grattan — meet there with Lady Vavasour and Miss Pollard former the wife of Sir   Vavasour of Hall in Yorkshire — Miss Pollard a young lady of fortune — agreeable. [171] Talk with Grattan about his new work — He is in too great haste to publish — hurries into print incorrectly — call on Villamil who has been confined some time with the Gout — find there Lord John Russell — Mr   Capt Medwin [1] a friend of Lord Byrons & author of the Wand[e]ring Jew [2] & Mr S' Albans son of L[ord]. St Albans & Sir   the Last grand Inquisitor of Spain — a fat old man tired look — with dark complex[ion] & black eyes. Dissertation by Villamil on craniology — Capt

---

[1] From Captain Thomas Medwin (1788–1869), the biographer of Shelley, and the author of *Conversations of Lord Byron*, Irving derived various suggestions for his writing. One of the most interesting is recorded in full in a notebook of 1826 (in the New York Public Library), a synopsis of a lost Spanish play, *Embozado*. This theme Irving later employed in his story, "Don Juan: A Spectral Research." Irving never met Byron. Medwin was one of the chief mediums of the influence of the poet upon him, an influence that during the years 1810–1830 is very noticeable in various essays of Irving's.

[2] Medwin's dramatic poem, *Ahasuerus the Wanderer*, appeared anonymously, in London, in 1823.

M says Byron is very abstemious & has reduced himself quite thin — Is in excellent health.

Dined at Mr Welles's — present Mr & Mrs Beasley — Mr & Mrs Appleton — Miss Wiggins Mr Baldwin, Mr Hodges Lieut Levi Mr Lowell &c. &c After dinner Mrs Bonfils & daughters came in had music & danced to the piano. Came home at 12.

[172] *Friday 9.* After Breakfast called at Mr Foys — not at home — called at Truttel & Wurtz & go Play of Partzer Wuth[1] also Bought Mullers Genl Hist.[2] 3 Vols — 24 fr. 10 sous — went to Galignanis & read papers — called at the Gestiers found them all at home — Lunched and went with them to see the Marquis Lornarivas Galleries. Several beautiful pictures — The Pygmalion — Fine statue of the Magdalen by Canova another of Terpsichore — Marquis was there & showed us several superb cameos representing his pictures — Marquis was an advocate & not a rich one in some place in Italy — appointed to some situation by Bonaparte — bought up estates &c &c thus quickly made an immense fortune — He is very polite and attentive — Went afterwards & saw writing & musical automaton very pretty —

Dined at Mad^m De Quandts Hotel Mirabeau — a German Lady — Blue Stocking — round fresh look-

[1] *Partei-Wut*, or *Party Rage.* Irving describes in detail a performance of this play in Prague. Letter of Irving to J. H. Payne, January 31, 1824, in *Scribner's Magazine*, October, 1910.

[2] Johann Müller (1752–1809), German historian. His *General History* was translated into French in 1814–1817.

ing little old lady, with tall thin dingy looking companion who seems to take charge of every thing — Meet there Mr ⁣ ⁣ ⁣ a tall frenchman with lively eye & much animation — one who has written a tour to Plombier[e]s & acc^t of nations, a work of talent and brilliance I am told — Writes & occasionally recites also Fables in verse & other morceaux, very fine gent & witty. Mons ⁣ ⁣ ⁣ Dr Galt—middle sized old gent— with bald head — hair bushy each side — round forehead. [173] wrinkled — Dry brownish chinese complexion, black eyes, — At dinner conversation turned on misers Mons ⁣ ⁣ ⁣ told how in consequence of his situation in a public office he had had frequent opportunities of witnessing instances of extreme miserliness in beggars & others who died intestate & their property fell to the crown — one who lived in miserable lodgings, but ate nothing but turkey — but it must be turkey from the Kings poulterer — His bread must be from the Kings Baker — If it rained qu'est ce que fait un animal?[1] He put on a kind of hood of brown paper & went himself a great distance to the Bakers for his bread. Died in a grange — discovered his death by the smell of the corpse — found the remains of the last turkey he had eaten. He was a usurer, lent money on pledge — discovered money in marmites[2] — covered with ordure — found morsels of paper written in a kind of short hand — observations on weather — mem[en]t[o] of money-pledges &c but could find nothing of pledges he bought found

[1] What does a person do?
[2] Pots.

a key — which suited a house in another street, where they found pledges treasured up far exceeding the money lent —

[174] Story by Mad^m d. Quandt of the Leipsick Miser — a gent. had lodgings in his house & lost a dog — offered to buy & board another — got the money The gent did not see the dog — but heard him howl at night at length told his servt he must find the dog. They threw open the door where the dog was howling & there was the Miser.

Had purchased houses & chateaus — let them fall to ruin rather than repair them — ready money was every thing to him — Lay 100 crowns on the table & offer it for rent of a dwelling & he was sure to take it before you went — the the [*sic*] house was worth 500.

His children ill with scarlet fever — one died — He kept the corpse till putrid — an other [*sic*] might die & one funeral & coffin do for all — He put corpse in an empty Tun and tried to smuggle it by the parishes &c whom he would have had to pay dues, but was detected & had to pay all & a fine into ye bargain.

N[ugent?] Says the French theatre is cold & deserted — People are tired of the old cold french drama — The romantic taste prevails — I E. they want nature & sentiment. Character of the people changes. Greek & roman tragedies wont [175] suit now.

In Evg — more company comes in. Mrs   Mad Slater [?] & two ladies with her. The Messrs baudry — Mrs DeWitt (Mary Enoch); told me about them — Begged her to remember me to them. Mr sister seems very pleasant woman

From Mad de Qandts go at 10 oclock to Lady
Louisa Harveys — a small Party. Talk with Lady
Adelaide Forbes — Introduced to Mr Ellis — old
gent who has nice daughter & Miss Freemantle there
— pretty girls dressed in red

Return home 1/2 past 11.

[176] Saturday 10. Had vivid dream last night
about the Fosters — Letter from Mrs F. &c &c —
Went out this morning about 1 oclock — to Riding
school — ride for an hour — called upon Bradish & sat
some time with him — Lowell called there — Dined
at home with Peter — In the Evg to Mr Storrows —
read latter part of Macbeth — Stopped in at Galignanis on my way home — read trial of Thurtell [1] &
Hunt

Sunday 11. Had again very vivid dreams last
night This morng read German Play Partzer Wuth
— After breakfast paid Paynes Laundress 19 fr 3 sous.
Went to Galignanis — read records of Thurtells trial
& other news — called on Baldwin & Lowel, neither
at home — called & sat sometime with Sheldon —
talked of the court — &c &c — told me of old french
nobleman from   who appeared always attended
by a Page in Ragged dress. Returned Home Mr Foy
called on me. Accomp[ani]ed him to Mrs Storrows —
afterwards walked on Boulevard with him He introduced me to D^r   an English clergyman here with

---

[1] John Thurtell (1794–1824). His murder of William Weare, and his
famous plea for himself became the subjects of stories and songs. See
Trial of Thurtell and Hunt, ed. E. R. Watson, Edinburgh [1920].

his family — invited me to his house on Monday evg his daughters birthday

[177] Dined at Gen¹ Sir Geo. Aireys. Large family of children. Lady Airey very pleasant, One of the Daughters said their family had been called a republic, & so it seemed to be — all on very familiar terms — Sat with the family till 10 oclock — Very pleasant, domestic scene This day recᵈ letter from Livius dated Berlin —

Monday Jany 12. Read in Mullers Universal Hist[ory]. Wrote to Mrs Speakaling, (Powells friend) — Went to Galignanis read accᵗ of Thurtells execution ridiculous fuss made about it in Papers — romantic reporters of newspapers make Thurtell a hero. Ride in the Manege — call at Mad Bonets & get hkfs for Mrs Foster — Send them in Evg to Airey to take — Dine at home — go in Evg to Theatre Francais. Ecole de[s] Vieillards — Talma & Mmle Mars admirable — afterpiece la Tapisserie — contemptible —

[178] *Tuesday Jany 13.* Studied till past 10. Went to Galignanis — Then to Manege where I rode for 2 hours — called at Mrs Gestiers — found the ladies at home — Lunched & was snowballed by Miss Barton — retᵈ home — Went to Mr Foys where the Storrows were, getting the picture finished — stayd there till 4. Accompd the Storrows home then returned home — dressed & went with Peter to dine with the Gestiers — pleasant dinner & Evg — take leave of the Beasleys who start tomorrow for Havre — return home a little after 10.

Wednesday Jan 14. Very cold weather — Feel

symptoms of having caught cold — great hoarseness — stiffness of the muscles of throat — After breakfast send copy of Salmagundi to Galignani — go there return him Don Juan — read papers — send pomme de terre juices with verses to Miss Barton — go to riding school — exercise an hour & half — return home Bradish calls on us — receive reply from Miss B. with verses. Dine at Mr Forsters — Chaplain to Embassy — At dinner Lord Earley.   Dr. Thurlow nephew of the Chancelor — Dr   Miss [179] Polke the two Miss Bridgemans &c besides the 2 Miss Forsters — at dinner more names mentioned Polke grew quite warm in converse — In evg Mr

Mrs Thurlow & Lady Early came in — Music & dancing to Piano — Lord & Lady Earley old acquaintances of Peters who they met when on their Honey Moon on Lake Catherine their names then Mr & Mrs Ogden — invited me to come with him & see them — retᵈ home in cabriolet with Mr Bathed my feet & took a Tisan ¹ —

Thursday 15. Cold somewhat better — took Tisan this morng. Wrote letter to Sullivan Mr. Artiquenave called — paid Landlord for 3 Months rent of apartments for the ensuing quarter, on acᵗ of Mr Payne 375 frs 65 Cent[ime]s — called at Mr Douglas sat some time with Miss Drew. Dined at Grattans. Present Lady Vavasour — Miss Pollard. Mr Horace Smith.² Mr Greathead, Mrs Grattans Brother &

¹ Tisane, herb-tea.
² Horatio Smith (1779–1849), co-author with his brother, James Smith, of *Rejected Addresses*, with its parodies of Byron and Scott.

sister — Peter & myself. Horace S. pleasant, but a
[180] cold witty man — Great head a literary com-
[mon]place man — Strong made with firm inflexible
features — After dinner some compy came in &
Peter & myself escape as G^t Head & Smith came off.
Went to Mr Storrows & passed the evg — Mr Jamieson there — Stopped at Galignanis on my way home
& read papers —

Friday 16 — went to Manege at 11 oclock exercised from 1/2 past 11 till 2. Ret^d home — left card
at Genl Aireys — at the Harveys called at Lady
Granard — found Lady L Harvey & Miss Harvey
there — Sat for some time talking with Lady Granard Lady Adelaide & Lady Caroline Forbes — who
were amusing themselves with the whimsicalities of
their little black pug Gipsy daughter of Imp de-
ceased — ret^d home — dined tete a tete with Peter
— napped after dinner till 9 oclock — read in letters
on Lond & Paris & went to bed a little after 10.

[181] *Saturday 17.* read early in morng — Paris &
London Sensible but prosy — After breakfast read
Gressets Ver[t]-vert or history of a Parrot [1] — excellent — full of wit & waggery & delightfully versi-
fied — Went to Galignanis — Then to the Storrows
— accompd them to Mr Foys — who finished their
portraits — Returned home in coach with Storrows
who waited till I went upstairs — found Cockburn

Horatio Smith's recollections of Irving are printed in detail in *The Literary Life,* ed. W. S. Walsh (New York, 1884), III, 13.

[1] Jean Baptiste Louis Gresset (1709–1777), author of *Vert-Vert.*
English editions were published in 1759 and 1793.

had been to see me & left the 7 Nap[s] he had borrowed
— dined with the Storrows — Mr S from home —
after dinner the girls recited from Racine — played
music — told stories — read italian — part of Metasta-
sios [1] Themistocles — Mr Jamieson came in — called
at Galignanis on my way home — Ret[d] home at 10
oclock

Sunday 18. This morning the boys came out of
school for the day. Read the morning service to them
& pointed out the beauty and solemnity of the prayers
&c. Went with them & Peter to the Louvre where we
passed between 2 & 3 hours retd home — and at 5
oclock went to Mr Storrows to dinner — In the evening came in Mr & Mrs and Miss Wiggins — Mr &
Mrs Appleton — Mr Hillyard Mr   of Germany —
talked much with the latter about German literature
— Stopped at Galignanis on my way home & read
papers.

[182] Monday 19. Read in Gresset — commence
Schillers Don Carlos [2] — at 12 go to Biblioteque du
Roi — Then to Manege — rode for $2\frac{1}{2}$ hours — return home dress & go with Peter to Mr Guestiers to
dinner — at Dinner meet Mr & Miss Birmingham —
Col   Lady & her sister — Mr   a Swiss protestant parson a little man with Spectacles — calls all
the french who were at Waterloo Brigands — Mr
Birm[in]g[ham] says tho royalist — yet when in
Eng[d] I heard of the fate of the battle of Waterloo it
made me feel sad — Little parson said (with zeal) he

---

[1] Pietro Bonaventura Metastasio (1698–1782), poet and librettist.
[2] An edition in English was published in 1822.

felt no such thing they were Brigands & he did not care if all had been massacred — ah me says Mr B. you are not really french — The Col. said he heard the coups [1] of cannon — at the Battle of Waterloo & each went to his heart he was with the King &c. The Duke de Berri [Berry] was with difficulty restrained from going with his squadrons to the fight — It would not do the King said, to fight ags^t frenchmen —

After dinner Mad^m Thickler & her sister came in — a pretty little German woman of Berlin — is only 23 years of age & has been married 6 years & has children one 5 years of age — We had music & danced Quadrilles.

Returned home at 12 oclock

[183] Tuesday 20. Read in Don Carlos — but felt quite unfit for any mental application — went out a little after 12 — to Galignanis to read papers called at Mr Foys — but he was not at home — walked across Thuilleries gardens called at the Harveys — found Eliza Harvey confined to the house with an inflammation in one of her eyes — sat there till seven — Met at their house with Col Dr Burke a french Englishman with his arm in a sling — Dined at home with Peter — Went in Evg to Mr Storrows — Mr Brimner came in — Accomp^d them all to Mr Lows — passed the Evg there & then returned & sat a little while at Mr Storrows — Rec^d & accepted invitation from L[ord?] Genl Sir Robt [2] Airey to dinner on Thursday

---

[1] Shots.   [2] Perhaps an error for Sir George Airey.

Wednesday 21. Read part of the Morng. Still troubled with a cold, & out of order. A Mr Wilkinson & Mr Richards (a cadet from West Point) called on me Mr Wilkinson had been desired by Vice President Tompkins [1] to remember him to me. He had seen Mr T not long since — went out at 1/4 past 2. Went to Manege and exercised on horseback for an hour & quarter. Fine weather. [184] Dined at home with Peter. In Evg — went to Lady Susan Douglas, a small party — Introduced to Dr McLauchlan, who is of Quebec & a friend of Colin Robertson. Says his Brother is with Robertson — that Robertson makes about 2500 a year—Is at Lake Winnipeg. Introduced to Dr Lasan a very pleasant man — To Miss Caldwell commonly called Puss Caldwell sister to Lady Baltimore [?] — oddly dressed — in red & green feathers & Scotch plaid gown Speaks of her cousin in America — Caldwell who has built a town on Lake George. Told me history of their having been robbed on arriving in Eng^d when at London they were perpetually at Bond S^t. They are now in a state militant with their Landlady who is an inveterate french fine lady.

Lasan tells me that the old nobility grew more & more presuming & intolerant — They are looking forward to indemnification from Gov^t.

Old card playing lady — with still buckled wig — rouge — looked as if herself and head dress had all

---

[1] Irving had served under Daniel D. Tompkins (Governor of the State of New York from 1807–1817) in the War of 1812. See *Public Papers of Daniel D. Tompkins* (New York, 1898), pp. 514–516.

been cast in a mould — Such a card playing dowager as you may see in cathedral towns & watering places in Eng^d.

[185] *Thursday Jany 22.* Heavy & clogged in my faculties from cold. read in Don Carlos — call at Galignanis read papers & return home & lie on sofa all day reading Don Carlos. Send Books to the Kings Library & get out Hist of Normandy [1] — Dine at Genl Aireys — present Mrs Robertson — widow of Genl Robertson who served in America — a fine lookg old Lady who had evidently been a beauty & was still careful of her appearance — fine person — carefully dressed — fine flaxen wig, well created & very becoming. Col & Mrs   Col Thornton a very agreeable gentlemanlike man both in appearance, manners & conversation — The dinner was extremely pleasant. Lady Airey gave anecdotes of their visit to Janina to the court of Ali Pascha. His Harem — Women not fat — his favorite a pretty girl of 16 — asked her if she was happy — Happy — to be sure, why not — lately I was a poor albanian girl now I am a queen, *perhaps the greatest queen* in the world. The more favorite members of the Harem were young girls.

The seraglio is the Palace where the men &c inhabit — the Palace generally — The Harem is the part which the women inhabit.

[1] See letter of Irving to Van Traet [Paris], January 22 [1824], in the Bibliothèque Nationale, Paris. From a recently discovered manuscript we know that this book was a volume of Louis Le Vavaseur de Masseville's *Histoire sommaire de Normandie*, Rouen, 1698.

[186] Lady Airey found on dining she could not get water nothing but wine — She told them she thot they could not drink wine — "Oh no — they ought not even to see it — but the order was that the dinner should be served as much as possible in the English style —" — It seems they thot the English drank nothing but wine.

The women of the Harem used to envy the English Ladies their liberty to ride about &c.

Miss Airey told me of several old families quartered in apartments of the chateau of Versailles — fine quarters but poor living — poverty of some of the old families — some 500 francs a year — one servant woman — 2 Rooms — but extremely proud — looked down on the parvenus — would not visit them — In Versailles great jealousy of precedence among the English — one Honorable Lady who leads the ton [1] & has claim — the rest all in dispute. Great backbiting — &c &c Gardens not frequented — as nobody goes — nobody will go —

Old frenchmen in Allée de Reine [?] — Pigtails & violets.[2]

[187] Genl Aireys Story of Irishman — who asked another why he did not go to some public amusement — 'why my wifes been dead but a month —' Well — what of that — shell never be deader.'

Gent "Broke down in Post Chaise after driving a

[1] Fashion; prevailing mode. A favourite word of Irving's. *Cf. Salmagundi, passim.*

[2] A note for the essay, "My French Neighbor." *Cf.* p. 89, footnote 2.

(111)

mile or two — who the devil would have thought of
the carriage breaking down in this way"

"I your honour said Pat — for you see Ive brought
a bit of cord in my pocket —

Col Thornton mentioned a peculiarity of a lady in
Eng^d whose hobby was to dress her head like a pot of
flowers & sit at the window, & was highly delighted
if it was mistaken for such by the passers by — (She
might have been cured of this whim-wham, by some
unlucky boys throwing a stone to crash the flower
pot)

Old Mrs Robertson said when she went to Eng^d
several years since with her hat ornamented with
flowers after the then french fashion the people in the
streets cried here comes a walking garden.

[188] *Friday Jany 23.*   Morning, read in Bib.
Roman[1] — quite out of writing mood — rainy day —
went in Cabriolet to the Gestiers & sat some time
with Mrs G & miss B.   Found there Col.   The
same I met at dinner a few days since. He was in the
service of the Emperor — when Nap. quitted Paris in
1814 he ordered him to blow up a powder mag^n — by
which half Paris would have been destroyed — he
promised to do so — but did not do it. Alexander was
so delighted with his conduct that on entering Paris he
took an order from about his neck & put it round the
Colonels.   He was rec^d in the Kings service — when
Nap ret^d from Elba he declared the Col should be shot
— the Latter made the best of his way to Eng^d he

---

[1] *Cf.* p. 39, footnote 7.

was with the King at Ghent the time of the battle of Waterloo he says every sound of a can[n]on went his heart — The Duke de Berri wanted to go to the Battle — The Col has rec^d no advancement from the Bourbons.

[189] a french gent. came in while I was there — Mr

promised the Gestiers to bring the Boys & dine with them — on Sunday — Ridiculous note of Rougemont the Bankers about the Jew Rothschilds Ball

Dined at home with Peter. In Evg went to Mr Storrows. Mr   the German came there in the course of the Evg.

Saturday, Jany 24. Wrote half a page at Author[1] — went 1/4 past 12 to Galignanis — Then to Mad^m De Quandts—not at home. Mr Villamils meet there with Mr   who brings me a little letter from Mrs Storey. Talk of the old Emigrés Looking out to full indemnification — one old fellow from S' Domingo says he would not give up a single little negro — (*Nigretto* — Mr & Mrs Grattan came in.

Call at Countess Granards. Meet there Mrs Ellis

Dine at Mr Storrows — receive letter from Mrs Van Wart — Evg go to Italian opera with the Storrows — Don Giovanni — Zuchelli [?] plays the Don.

[190] Sunday. 25 Jany. At breakfast a letter is handed me coming by Post. dated Perth, Jany, from Miss Mary Robertson Nason, niece to Colin Robertson — a strange Raphsodical [*sic*] letter — the girl

---

[1] "The Poor-Devil Author," (*op. cit*).

evidently deranged — requesting a lock of my hair &c &c.

The Boys came out of School & Breakfasted with us — went afterwards to the Louvre — while they were looking at statues &c I called on Foy & sat with him a little while — then ret^d to the Louvre — on returning home rec^d a very acceptable letter from Mrs. Foster — all well at Brickhill — Dined with Peter & the boys at Mr Gestiers — a Mr Felix   there — very young — & hearty — In the evg played Charades — Tableaux — &c — Epoux [1] — Tableau — 1 Table — 2^d eau. 3 Tableau — Reveil D'Abril [2] — Blue Beard — a little dancing & then retd home.

[191] Monday 26. Write to Mrs Van Wart — read the Wanderer [3] a poem by Capt Medwin — has many beautiful passages. Called on Capt M promised to dine with him tomorrow & go with him to night to Mrs Popkins. [4] He is cousin to Mr Shelley. [5] Character of Julian in the Wanderer is Shelleys. ret^d home — Mr Foy called at 2. Sat for my likeness — Letter from Payne — Mr   calls. Quite a Bore — Dine at home with Peter — after dinner sleep till 1/2 past 8. Much better for this nap having suffered all day from a restless night. At 9 oclock Capt Medwin calls for me — go to Lady Susan Douglas — The Villamils &

[1] Husband and wife.

[2] *Réveil d'Avril*, Return of April.

[3] *Ahasuerus the Wanderer.* Cf. p. 99, footnote 2.

[4] Irving used the name Popkins in the *Tales of a Traveller* ("The Adventure of the Popkins Family," pp. 356–363), and thus incurred the ill-will of this family.

[5] Medwin was first cousin to Shelley's mother, Elizabeth Pilfold.

Grattans there & Lord Miltown & several Spanish. Lady Milman & Miss Caldwell come there. Music — Escape with Capt M & go to Mrs Popkins — fine Hotel —— crowded rooms — good music burlesque &c. Introduced to Dr Mrs & Miss Gibbons & several others—found Lady Airey & daughters there. Pretty woman there — a Mrs Crofts and her sister Miss

came away at 1 oclock just as a little girl began recitations

[192] *Tuesday 27.* Jany. read miscellaneously wrote letter to Sullivan. rec^d Letter from John Irving, N York. Went to Mr Storrows — examined Box of Books & took out such as were valuable — Dined with Capt Medwin — present Mr Jenkinson & Mr S' Aubin [1] — conversation about India Sports &c &c &c. ret^d home & went to bed — instead of going to ye Ambassadors

Wednesday 28 Wrote Letters to Payne. Mrs Storey — Mr Murray. Called at Admiral Harveys to see him before departure. Lady Louisa brot me home in carriage — Mr Kenney called & sat some time — Mr Foy gave a sitting for my likeness. Dined at home with Peter. Evg to the Theatre Port S' Martin — 1 piece L Amour & Lappetit 2^d Cuisinier de Buffon 3 Gascon with 3 visages 4 Petit Danaïdes [2] ret^d home by 1/4 past 11.

[193] Thursday 29. read in Curiosities of Litera-

---

[1] Edward St. Aubyn, son of Sir John St. Aubyn, of Cornwall.

[2] *L'Amour et l'appétit; Le Cuisinier de Buffon; Le Gascon à trois visages; Les petites Danaïdes.*

ture[1] — write letters to E. Irving, J K Paulding,[2] Mr
Livius, Mrs Foster — Mr Foy came at three &
painted on my portrait. Capt Medwin called but
was not admitted — Dined at home with peter.
Passed Evg at Mr Storrows — readg Petrarch —
Addison [3] &c

Friday 30, read — finish letter to Mrs Foster — &
send it off for post together with letters to Mrs
Storey Payne — Sullivan — Bills brot of Mr Paynes
— but Decline answering them — Visit from Mr
Goodrich of Connecticut [4] — brot letters from John
T Irving — Exercised at riding school — rec^d letter
from Payne enclosing 50£ to pay certain bills — he
has concluded bargain with managers 200 g^s. Dined
at Mr Storrows — present Mr Mrs & Capt Low. Mr
Mrs & Mr Sheldon — In Evg played at Backgammon
&c.

Saturday 31. Wrote to Payne — & Livius — Pay
Bill of Mr Paynes in favor of   for 250 fr. call at Mr
Storrows. Leave card at Gestiers — call on Sheldon
— Mrs Welles — (leave card) Stop at Galignanis.
Dine at home with P. Evg at a Ball given by Mr
Mays. Among the compy — was Mad^m Gavaudan

[1] Isaac D'Israeli's *Curiosities of Literature* (1791) was a favourite book
of Irving's. See also P. M. Irving (*op. cit.*), I, 373, 454.

[2] James K. Paulding (1778–1860), collaborator with Irving in various
literary enterprises. Paulding's sister, Julia, married Irving's brother,
William.

[3] Despite the alleged influence upon Irving of Addison, this is one of
the very few references to him in Irving's letters or journals.

[4] Samuel G. Goodrich (1793–1860), "Peter Parley." *Cf.* Introduction
of this volume, xi.

formerly of the Opera Comique [1] — with her Grand
mother & grand Daughter — The old lady half
asleep

[194] [2] *Sunday feby* 1. Beautiful Sunny day — read
in Curiosities of Literature — called a little after 12
on Capt Medwin. Sat with him till 1/2 past one — He
read me a poetical letter of Shelleys giving a description of a ride near Venice with L[ord] Byron & return
to Dresden by water — with fine description of Luna-
tic, a mad house on an island &c &c — Went to Gestiers
—found Mrs G & Miss B at home & Mr G. came in —
had much chat about Bordeaux — See both Ferriers [3]
&c &c — Miss G 25 years old — ret^d to Capt Medwin,
drove with him in his cabriolet to Bois de Boulogne —
all Paris in motion — Long talk ab^t Ld Byron — He
writes at fits — has intervals when he cannot write
sometimes 2 & 3 weeks — Does not revise nor correct
much — writes sometimes in Bed — rises at 12 some-

---

[1] Madame Gavaudan (1781–1850), had retired from the stage in
December, 1822.

[2] On this page, written upside down, is one of the most interesting
passages in this Journal. It is placed in a footnote because it bears no
relation to the chronology of the Journal. It reads: "She died in the
flower of her youth & of mine but she has lived for me ever since in all
woman kind. I see her in their eyes — and it is the remembrance of her
that has given a tender interest in my eyes to every thing that bears the
name of woman." This is one of the very rare passages in Irving's writing
describing Matilda Hoffman, his fiancée, who died in 1809. It is significant
that this passage occurs in a Journal of 1823–1824, the very period during
which he is said to have been a rejected suitor for the hand of Emily
Foster. For a full discussion of this problem in Irving's life see, *Notes
While Preparing Sketch Book &c. (op. cit.)*, Introduction.

[3] Irving lived with this family in Bordeaux in 1804.

times 2 — eats a crust in a cup of tea with Egg — rides
out at 4. When in writing mood writes at any time —
if persons are present he often writes & talks — does
not seclude & deny himself. [195] Never speaks ill of
Lady B. When her father died he wrote a most affectionate & moving letter — wished a reconcilliation[*sic*]
— rec^d no reply but a cold message thro his sister —
When he dines by himself is very abstemious as to
wine — when he has company he drinks freely —
gives away large sums — reads miscellaneously all
the modern works — reads much — does not study —
never touches the classics Is not a good Grecian —
understands italian well — reads history &c relative
to the subject he is writing on — Has an excellent
memory, tho not for dates — a poetical memory.
Does not like to meet strangers who are desirous to
see him — says they expect great things, & he is but a
common man in conversation —

Dined at home with peter. At 7 oclock Major
Wheatly & his son call about some concerns of Mr
Payne — Go to Mr Storrows — Susan rather unwell
— Mr [196] Jamieson there — Mr   the German
— Charades — home —

at 10 oclock go to Dr Gibbings — a very pleasant
party — Madam Pasta there Mr Harte played ad-
mirably on the Piano Pasta sang charmingly — Miss
Gibbings sang also very well — Introduced to Miss
Allenton — Mr Sharpe — talked with several other
Gent — Count   came up & spoke to me — I met
him at Dresden at Mr Moriers & Mrs Fosters

[197] Monday Feb 2^d Correct part of Salmagundi

— for the Printers. Get S' Ronans Well [1] of Galignani — call at Mr Storrows. Susan unwell — passed
a bad night — Mrs Storrow sprained her ancle this
morng—return home—read S' Ronan. Mr Foy calls
but too late to paint at likeness. Note from Kenney
— has paid one of Paynes Bills. Mr Bradish calls &
sits some time — Dine at home. In evg call at Mr
Storrows — Susan better — Mrs S. lame — Stop at
Galignanis on my way home —

Tuesday 3. Last night & this morng readg S'
Ronans Well. 1/2 past 12. Call at Mr Storrows —
Mrs S. & Susan better — Call at Dr Gibbings find
Prince there. Very fond of society, dances &c & un-
happy if not invited. Mr Wilmot came in & Dr Mc-
Lauchlin Miss Gibbings acc[t] of MacClure whom they
met in Italy — travelling with old carriage — old
Horses & old Servts at snails pace — stopping con-
tinually to examine stones — very old & Superannu-
ated. Irreligious — Yet fears the Devil — Mistook a
Methodist parson for the Devil & addressed him as
such — [198] Called on Mr Sharpe — found him &
Mrs Sharpe & Sir   Sat some time with Mr Sharpe
& Sir

They spoke of Presidents speech which seems to
have given general satisfaction to the English—called
at Genl Aireys & found him & Lady A—Walked with
them to rue Richelieu — ret[d] home. Dined with
Peter. Evg to Opera Tancredi — Sat in Dr. Gibbings

[1] Published in 1823. Irving read Scott's novels as soon as they appeared. Note his criticism of this novel on p. 120.

(119)

Box. Mr Dallas & Mr Mills [1] came in — Pasta vexed in course of Evg by a Song being called for which had been omitted — Pasta being indisposed — Miss G. says Pasta is very pleasant — not well informed, but of good natural talent. Feels strongly what she plays & is often overpowered by her characters — particularly the few first representations — Does not seem to be happy — Her husband gambles — when Pasta sits by her at music the tears will stream down her cheeks. Is a little high tempered & capricious but amiable. Her mother is a fury — and apt to treat people rudely who visit Pasta too often. Pasta has a fine little girl about 7 — who sings — likes to be praised and [199] is jealous of any preferences of her own age —

Bordoni [2] asks 22 francs a lesson. Vain of person &c — has taste but no great voice — is admired by Cinti. Anecdote of Miss Gibbings — her Eng servant being sent for a coiffeur went for a confessor —

Col Thornton — wounded at New Orleans very clever — agreeable — fond of Dancing —

Friday[3] *4.* Last night finish S' Ronans Well, in bed, one of Scotts worst novels & unworthy of the author of Old Mortality. Correct Salmagundi — Pay Paynes Bill favor of Langrome 271 fr. and 8 fr 10 S[ous] costs for Hussier & protest Call at Galignanis & leave copy of Salmagundi. At 3, go to the Storrows — See Susan & Mrs S. who are sitting in Mr S. Bedroom much better

---

[1] Frank Mills, an English friend, who later dabbled in writing plays.
[2] Possibly Giulio Marco Bordogni (1789–1856), a teacher in the Conservatory of Music in Paris.
[3] Irving's error. Wednesday.

— Dine at home with Peter — Evg go to a party at Lady Susan Douglas' — introduced to Miss Fitzgerald. old Maid — Blue — loud talker — boasts of her independence — One of those women who may roam the world over "sans peur & sans reproche —" secure in their ugliness — (armed with ugliness. Dont dare to look any one in face at [200] this season of the year lest I should be asked to a Ball. Miss Caldwell — goes about asking people to other peoples balls &c — cannot give a party at her own home so entertains her friend[s] miscellaneously at other peoples expense — Grattan & Miss Caldwell talkg slapdash. G one of those fellows that opens his mouth at a venture & trusts god will send him a meaning — came away early with Genl Airey, who sat me down at my lodgings [1] —

[201] *Thursday 5. Feby.* Read in Curiosities of Literature [2] — Rabelais &c. Corrected Salmagundi — Went to Galignanis & read papers — called at Storrows and sat some time with the family — all better — Peter comes in — Called on Dr Maclaughlin — found him with old Dropsical countess whose husband was Chief of the Louvre — She has had dropsy for 50 yrs — is now 82 years old. An Eng gent came into Maclauchlins while I was there — remarkably well informed about America — clear, distinct & precise in his information — Talked of the possibility of falls

[1] This page bears also miscellaneous figures in Irving's handwriting.

[2] Irving's intimacy with Isaac D'Israeli (1766–1848) began in 1817. An interesting description of the elder D'Israeli occurs in a letter to Peter Irving, London, August 19, 1817, quoted by P. M. Irving (*op. cit.*), I, 373, 374.

of Niagara receding & draining Lake Erie — Dined at Capt Medwin — present — Mr Latinn Mr Douglas — Mr S' Albyn, Mr Grattan Mr Kenney, Mr Jenkinson — Latinn very pleasant — Irish servant whose master was undergoing treatment for certain malady was asked how his Master was. "Oh your honour hes very bad — theyre now driving a Post chaise into him —— Oh indeed? — Oh yes your honour & whats more there [they're] going to put a cathedral (catheter) into him tomorrow

From Medwins went with Kenney to Vaudeville — Saw an indifferent piece *les mauvaises têtes* — Kenney slept at my lodgings.

[202] *Friday 6. Feby.* Kenney breakfasted with us — Anecdotes of theatres — difficulty of getting piece played on acc^t of feeling of actors. Poverty of the Drama as to great actors — Paid Kenney 375 francs for Paynes Bill to LeMoine. Write note to Henry to come to breakfast with me on Sunday. Took cabriolet & called at Gestiers — Mrs G indisposed — On Mr Gates, in room looking on Garden — shabby room in fine Hotel — room furnished with cast off finery of the better apartments — Old faded scenes on Silk bed curtains &c Left card at Mr Chenevix. Called at Mr Moriers — Met Genl Knazervitch & Count   just coming out Genl gave me an embrasser — Mr & Mrs Morier at home — chatted for some time about his brothers book &c.

called on Mr Goodrich, rue Odeon—Mr Storrows — family better — Met there Mrs Welles, Miss Wiggins,   Mr & Mrs Sheldon &c dined at home with peter — Evg — went to Lady Louisa Harveys — talked with Lady Adelaide Forbes — Mr Ellis.

From there went to Mrs Alcocks — very pretty party fine apartments — dancing on the carpet [203] presented to Col & Mrs Alcock — Mrs Waller — Maj & Mrs Oden — Mr Dallas. Met there Mr Morier — Mr Chenevix. Lady Thomond — D^r & Miss Gibbings — Anecdote of old Lady favorite of french King — not long since on coming out of the royal presence she carried something very heavy — bag burst and gold pieces tumbled all about — Soldiers employed on the stairs in picking them up — report of Lady Cunningham being out of favour at Brighton.

Old French nobleman 85 — he was last week the youngest of a party of 6 — he is an emigré was a minister of Louis 16

Old russian nobleman with many stars — Mr Morier set me down on my return.

Saturday 7. Read miscellaneously & look over Mss: but cannot write — go to Galignanis & read papers. Ride at the Manege — on the way meet Cockburn who has moved to 24 Rue Chausee Dantin [Chausée-d'Antin] receive from Mr Moriers a vol of travels [1] of his Brother — Dine at Mr Gestiers — present Miss Barton — Mr & Mrs Meyer & Peter. Mrs G did not appear at table, not being well — pass the evg there & return home at 10 oclock.

[204] Sunday 8th Feby. Last night disturbed con-

---

[1] One of David Morier's brothers was James Justinian Morier (1780?–1849). The book was probably *Journey through Persia, Armenia, and Asia Minor*, London, 1812.

tinually by carriages going to & from Masquerade at the opera. Read Moriers Journey to Persia in the night — Henry & Irving breakfasted with us — after breakfast go to oratoire to attend prayers, but find the church vacant. Go to Mr Foys — Meet a Mr   there converse about sympathy between the arts. Rules applicable alike to painting Writing — Sculpture, Music & architecture — all the imaginative arts — Present state of the arts & of Literature in England — an Era — great rivalship — greater glory in excelling — Some will excel — as in forest some trees will shoot above the others, tho when in the forest we cannot see their superiority we perceive it when at a distance — so posterity will do justice to those who rise above their contemporaries — no school of painting at present in Italy — Eng^d & France the only two schools.

After leaving Mr Foys walk by the Tuilleries & across the garden — went to the Manege & saw the scholars riding — returned home — boys went to Mr Storrows found letter from Capt Holdridge who has executed Williams [1] tombstone Went to Galignanis & read papers —

[205] Dined at Mr Storrows — present Mr Foy Mr Brooke of Manchester — The boys — Peter & myself — in Evg Mr Sheldon came in —

Monday 9th Last night slept indifferently.

This morning finished correcting Salmagundi — Write to Capt Holdridge — Mr Dodge consul at Marseilles — & to Leslie — Mr Grattan calls on me — at 4 oclock set off in Gondole for Versailles to dine

---

[1] *Cf.* p. 40, footnote 1.

with Kenney — dull dreary day — overcast — Arrive at Versailles at 6. Lose my way — do not get to Kenneys till 1/2 past 6. Find company waiting — Mr & Mrs Greathead — Mr & Mrs Horace Smith — & Mr Spurrier — son of a Merch[t] of Perth who left him 200,000£ — forced out of house of Com[mons] — for having gained his Election by bribing — a great player of Ecarté — Felt very heavy at & after dinner — In the Evg — other compy came in. Lady Vavasour & Miss Pollard — could not rouse myself to conversation — Slept at Kenneys but did not get to him till 1 oclock

[206] *Tuesday 10*. After tolerable night rise at 8. Breakfasted between 9 & 10 — Walked with Kenney to Club room where English men meet to read papers & play ecarté — returned to town in Gondole — got home at 2. Give corrected copy of Salmagundi to Mr Galignani — Mr Foy called on me at 1/2 past 3. Dined at home — passed Evg at Mr Storrows — Mr Artiquenave there — Feel quite torpid — cannot rouse myself to literary exertion —

[207] Wednesday 11. Very tired & disheartened — read for some time — Gave Marianne letters to put in post office for Leslie — Mr Dodge & Capt Holdridge — Walked out — to Galignanis — To Foys — (not at home) — Lounged in the Louvre — Called & left card at Major Macans — At Eng Ambassadors Called on Cockburn who I found in a pensionnat [1] Rue Chausee Dantin — Left card for Brimner — Mrs Welles — Mr Dorr — hunted for Mr Amblers

[1] Pension?

lodgings, but he had changed them (9 Rue St James) ret^d home — & Mr Foy called on me & sat for some time — Dined at Mr Lattins — a very pleasant party — Count D'Armond & his sister the countess D'Abeyne a very charming pretty woman & spirituelle — Mademoiselle a woman of uncommon talents — Lord   Miss Fitzgerald — Capt Medwin Mr Grattan Mr Hussat — extremely agreeable — In Evg came in a Mr Brent Mons   who has a Chateau near Pont L'Eveque, part built in time of Louis 7 his mother has translated Annette de Linden Mad. wanted me to write about St Johns eve [1] Mr Lattins daughter Mrs Mansfield — a very pretty & charming woman — had five children She took me to Genl Aireys.

[208] Evg at a Ball at Genl Aireys — came home at 12 oclock

Mem. Mr Lattin has an excellent bust of Washington [2] by Houdin [Houdon] in Terra Cotta which he got in America. He knew Washington in Philadelphia & once made him laugh heartily — whereupon those who were present said you have done that which no one else has done.

[209] Thursday 12. Send letters to E. Irving — J K Paulding & Mr Cargill — write preface to Salmagundi —

Feel intolerably triste — cannot bring myself to

---

[1] A theme which, through the influence of Scott, was frequently in Irving's mind. *Cf. Notes While Preparing Sketch Book &c. (op. cit.)*, p. 50, footnote 3.

[2] Irving planned a biography of Washington as early as 1825. He completed this work in the year of his death (1859).

write on my work — tho near 6 weeks have elapsed without writing — go to Mrs Storrows read till lessons are over — go with the Ladies to the Louvre — See Medwin & Jenkinson there — Miss Barton — Miss Collins — Mr Foy — very chilly at Louvre — return with Ladies at 4. Dine with Peter at Mr Mays — present Mrs   & her husband & Miss   In Evg go to Lady Louisa Harveys — a few people there besides the family — return home at 11.

Friday 13. Read — wrote a little on the early hist[ory] of Wm the Conqueror[1] — Called on Mr Lattin & sat with him some time. Little Cabinet with books — Dined at home with Peter — In Evg at Mr Storrows — met there Capt Allen of the Cadmus & Mr Jamieson. Capt A. gave us anecdotes of Hunting the Civilized Indian — Mr Jamieson gave anecdotes of second sight Mr & Mrs Appleton —

Read papers at Galignanis — gave G. Preface to Salmagundi[2] —

[210] Saturday 14. Feby. Very much out of spirits — but finished a translation of anecdote of Wm the Conqueror walked out to Galignanis — then to Port S' Martin to look after a play — called & left pamphlet at Mr Appletons to be taken by him to Eng^d for Payne — called & left card for Villamil — called on Mrs Walker — shewn in to saloon where was an old paralytic woman. Thot myself mistaken, but found it really was Mrs Walker. Mother in law to the Mrs

---

[1] This manuscript, recently discovered, is published at the conclusion of the Journal. See pp. 247–257.

[2] This edition was published by Galignani and Baudry in 1824.

Walker who invited me — another paralytic woman passed into the door — was glad to make my congé & be off — Met Medwyn & walked with him — told me how insolently he was treated by Murray who never answered his letters &c & finally when he requested an answer in London, having offered the Mss of his poem to be published at his own expense — recd the Mss back without a word in reply.[1] Met Grattan who walked a little with us. Dined at home. In Evg went to Storrows & read Medwins poem to the ladies

[211] *Sunday 15.* Wrote to Mrs Van Wart & sent the letter to Mr Appleton to take to Eng^d Mr Walker called on me to engage me to write for the European review at 16 £ st[erlin]g a Sheet—Declined.[2] Went to Capt Medwins who read me journal of a painter while prisoner of the robbers near Rome [3] — Accomp^d Medwin to Jenkinsons — fine family of daughters & spaniels — Jenkinson has been painting at Landscapes about 4 years & has made great proficiency — Dined at home with Peter — In Evg went to Mr Storrows — Mr Richards & Mr   there — stopped at Galignanis on my way home — returned home at 11.

[1] Irving was to experience Murray's careless and indifferent treatment of authors during the writing of his *Columbus* in Spain, in 1827.

[2] Irving, after his editorship of the *Analectic Magazine* in 1812–1814, steadily refused substantial offers from English periodicals, to be either editor or a regular contributor.

[3] This entry indicates the source of "The Painter's Adventure," in *Tales of a Traveller*, pp. 364–375. The later notes concerning Foy show that the chief source of Part III of this book ("The Italian Banditti") was in these conversations, and not, as has been stated, in Irving's own journey to Italy, in 1805.

Monday 16 — Awoke very early — full of uneasy thoughts — light my lamp & read in order to dispel them — At breakfast talk of Italian story — determine to try it — go to Foy — converse with him on the subject — he relates an anecdote or two which excite me — return home & commence — Medwin calls & sits for some time — recommence at ½ past 1 — write till 4 oclock on introduction — Dine with Peter — In Evg go to Lady Susan Douglas & meet the Villamils. Mr V introduces me to two gentlemen from South America — [212] Grattan talks to me about his intention of going to London to bargain for his projected work — Meet Medwin as I come out who goes home & sits with me till ½ past 12.

Considering the smallness of this globe what a great part of it is uninteresting & almost uninhabitable, consisting of desarts — flat monotonous plains &c &c. The beautiful parts are but few & limited & these in fact have been made by convulsions, which have broken the even surface of the original world — thrown up mountains — made crags — precipices vallies &c &c So also with the moral world — It is the convulsions & revolutions that have made all that is romantic and picturesque in morals & manners — what a dull world this would be for poets & painters had there been no deluges or earthquakes and no war — a milennium would be death to poetry — a dead sea [1] —

[1] Such moralizing is characteristic of Irving's other journals rather than of this matter-of-fact record. *Cf. Notes While Preparing Sketch Book &c. (op. cit.), passim.*

Rec^d a letter this day from Mrs Foster and Emily
[213] *Tuesday 17.* Wake very early — get up at 6
oclock & write till 8 — at introductory part of Italian
tale — after breakfast write to Grattan a humbug
letter about his work, which he is to shew to the Booksellers — He is an arrant literary trades man — one
who bolsters his name & placards it in all ways &
manners — resume my pen and write all day at the
italian story — finish the introduction & commence
the tale — write 28 pages this day — clear & neat
writing — Dine at Lady Louisa Harveys — meet no
body besides the family except Mr Drummond & D^r
Chirnside The latter has been much in service as
military surgeon & stands high in his profession. He &
Drummond gave many particulars of the battle of
Waterloo [1] where they were both present. Drummond says there never was an occasion when so many
gentlemen ran away. The officers & men were quitting the ground continually — many of the Guards
especially — who had been mere sunshine soldiers —
enlisted for mere home service & parade. The D^r says
the whole regiment of Duke of Cumberland went off —
but this was the fault of the Colonel who could not be
brought to bring his men into [214] the reach of fire.
Speaks of the splendid appearance of the french Curi-
assers [*sic*] as they advanced when the sun was out &
glancing on their armour — Speech of a little lad a
drummer who had taken shelter in a square during a

[1] Irving's interest in the events at Waterloo found expression in a
brief but well-written essay, "The Field of Waterloo." See *Wolfert's
Roost*, pp. 235–238.

charge — 'look my boys — there come the Tin
Jackets again." Vivacity of the french charges — It
soon subsided however when it came in stubborn con-
flict with the steadiness of the English [1] — The Artillery did most execution ripping up the masses of
french horsemen who strewed the field — French
officers of horse always advanced in front of their men
— The french require it to inspirit them on tho it is
exceedingly dangerous to the officers — The officer[s]
often rode in advance flourishing their swords with
their white Hkfs about the hilts & riding up to the
columns to tempt them to throw away their fire —
Squares sometimes attacked before & behind & obliged to make fires in two directions. Lancers dangerous in action the hussars with their sabres were not
match for them — They were very wanton & cruel.

[215] In the Evg some other company came in — I
came away about 11.

Wednesday. 18. Feb. Slept ill last night — awake
very early this morning — read in bed. Moriers
Journey to Persia — rise unrefreshed — while breakfast things are removing scrawl the Story of the Bold
Dragoon [2] — After breakfast resume the Italian
Story, rewrite what I wrote yesterday and add Eight
or nine pages — feel haggard from want of rest last
night & dress to go out — receive letter from Livius
from Calais, with pamphlet story of Euryanthe,[3] in

---

[1] Cf. idem, p. 235.

[2] "The Bold Dragoon; or the Adventure of My Grandfather," in
Tales of a Traveller, pp. 47–59.

[3] C. M. von Weber's three-act opera was first acted at Vienna, on

German — also receive a letter from Dr Spiker — King of Prussias Librarian — requestg early copy of my next work [1] — ride for an hour in the Manege — Dine at home with peter — Pass Evg at Mr Storrows — Mr Jamieson there — return home 1/2 past 10.

[216] Thursday 19. Wake very early in Morng & try in vain to sleep again — After breakfast resume the Story of the mysterious picture [2] — Capt Medwin calls but I continue writing — finish the story by 1/2 past 3 — having written 23 pages since 1/2 past 9. Dine at Dr Maclaughlins — present several gentlemen whom I knew by sight but not by name except Col Thornton — Thornton speaks of the handsome manner in which Genl Jackson sent back watches & Epaulettes that had been taken from officers at New Orleans. Speaks of the custom in war not to fire upon individuals — Even if reconnoitering parties advance too near, when no actual engage[t] is going on, they are hailed & desired to keep back.

Story of discovery of foul play at the club packs of false cards found there — Pasta supposed to be at the

October 25, 1823. In Dresden Irving had translated German plays, but he apparently made no use of *Euryanthe*.

[1] During the winter of 1822–1823 Irving had enjoyed in Dresden a reputation as a distinguished American man of letters. *E. g.*, see the Dresden newspaper, *Abendzeitung*, July 23, 1822. S. H. Spiker was an important agent in introducing Irving to the German reading public. He himself translated several works. *E. g.*, *Gottfried Crayon's Skizzenbuch*, Berlin, 1825.

[2] "The Adventure of the Mysterious Picture," in *Tales of a Traveller*, pp. 69–80.

In the evening some other company come in —
I came away about 11.

Wednesday. 18. Feb. Slept ill last night
— awake very early this morning — read in
bed. Morier's Journey to Persia — nice unrefreshed
— while breakfast things are removing scrawl
the story of The Bold Dragoon — After breakfast
resume the Italian story, rewrite what I
wrote yesterday and add eight or nine
pages. Feel haggard from want of rest last
night & dare to go out. Receive letters from
Irving from Calais, with pamphlet story of
Margaret, a German — also receive a letter
from Dr Spiker. King of Prussia's Librarian, requesting
an early copy of my next work. Ride
for an hour in the Maneje. Dine at
home with Peter. ~~Rumble~~ Pass left at Mr
Storrow. Mr Jameson there. Eleven home.
To bed 10.

FACSIMILE PAGE OF THE JOURNAL, 1823–1824 [215]

bottom of it — by which means she has lately won 36,000 francs from an Englishman

In Evg — taken by Gen[1] Airey to a Ball at the Miss Fieldings — Introduced there to the Miss Constables — Mrs Bernard a friend of Lady Charlemont [?] Lady Gage

From thence go to Ball Masque — at the club rooms — very dull — came away at 1/2 past 10

[217] *Friday* 20. Sleep ill last night — after breakfast this morng resume & rewrite the stories of the Aunt [1] & the Bold Dragoon 23 pages at 4 oclock go to Galignanis. Galg[i] proposes my editing an edition of British Classics — promise to think of it — He is about publishing Knickerbocker.[2] Dined at Medwins with Mr Jenkinson & Mr Mills. I was oppressed by torpor & heaviness — After dinner at 10 oclock went with Mr Mills in his cabriolet to a Ball at Mr Moriers — very pretty — Staid until 12 & came away with Gen[1] Airey — who set me down home.

Saturday 21. An indifferent night — After breakfast call at Mr Foys — not at home — beautiful morng — walk on Pont des Arts. Stop at Galignanis — talk a little about their projected edition of English Classics [3] return home — rewrite early part of the hunting dinner.[4] Mr Gates calls on me & brings a little letter from Mrs Storey — continue writing till

---

[1] "The Adventure of My Aunt," in *Tales of a Traveller*, pp. 40–46.

[2] This edition of *A History of New York* was published by Galignani in 1824.

[3] This project was never finished.

[4] "The Hunting-Dinner," in *Tales of a Traveller*, pp. 15–21.

three — dress & then try to nap on Sopha — at 6 go
to Mr Lattins to dine. Meet there Mrs   Miss Fitzgerald — Mr Underwood, whom I formerly met at
Jeffreys — & Mr

Underwood mentions having left a diary of the
courts of Paris during the siege at Birmingham which
I may have a sight of.

Story of the Red man — slipped at foot of the
staircase — Tell him — the Redman is here [218]
Napoleon bowed & told them to admit him High
words passed between them the attendant heard high
altercation & anxious lest something might occur —
opened the door, when he saw the red man had just
bolted up the chimney his tail working in the ashes.

Old french Chateaux — have magnificent apartments — only partly inhabited

Chateau   once defended against the soldiers of
Henry 4. fine tower & chapel left & mills in the
cellars with which they ground corn. Suits of armour
— scull cap &c

Fontain[e]bleau — recollection of Francis 1 —
Henry 4 Napoleon —

Accompany Mr Lattin to Countess D'Abeyne —
at her fathers —Duke D'Armond—shewn into handsome apartments — ottoman—Old madm D'Armond
is fine old lady — remains of Beauty — flaxen hair
— now light grey.

Countess D'Armond — fine eyes — bad teeth Mad.
D'Abeyne splendidly dressed for a ball — Bird of
Paradise feather &c Talk of french Domestic life —
French marry with eye to family — not mean selfish

— families live more together — Family — coterie — society — gd humour Thinks the french made best of parents [219] choosing — saves young ladies the trouble French women all fond of husbands —

Nugent who came in says love is not to be considered.

Do you think so said Countess —

Condemn English habit of wandering & the coldness & indifference with which they detach themselves from their native place or neighborhood.

Returned home in Mr Lattins carriage — at 11

Sunday 22. Rewrite the Story of "My uncle & the Marquis." [1] 14 pages The Boys come from school. At 2 visit Mr Foy, who tells me anecdotes of Ital robbers. Leave card at Mr Ellis — Hotel Castille [?] — Dine at Mr Storrows — feel much out of sorts & come home early — bathe feet & go to bed. Receive this day letter from Consulat at Marseilles —

Monday 23. This morning write introduction to Robber tales — 12 pages — interrupted by various circumstances. Galignani & Didot [2] call to engage me as editor of their Edition of British Classics. Refer them to Peter — at 3 visit the Gibbings Mrs G at home — a russian gent there — Miss Gibbings and Miss Fairfax come in — the latter very [220] talented — writes italian poetry — call & leave card at Mr Hackets — return home — Mr Lattin calls in carriage for me with Mrs Mansfield — Miss   & Mr Nugent

[1] See p. 165, footnote 2.
[2] Probably Firmin Didot (1764–1836). The Didots published, with Galignani, several editions of Irving's writings.

Dine at Countess De Beynes — present Marchioness
D'Armond — Mrs Mansfield — Miss   Mons
D'Orloff [1] — Mr

after Dinner Count & Countess D'Armond came
in.

Countess De Beyne says in Louis 14 the nobility of
France rec[d] its blow. Richelieu destroyed it   They
have had title — pretension acknowledged of ruling
but no power. Not a nobleman who could bring 10
men into the field — however in Engd tho it is not
shewn Nobility have great power & a great name can
command thousands. In France nobility went with
the King & were lost. In Eng[d] with the people. In
Eng[d] the Royal Dukes are very great. The Prince is
always in opposition. In France the Prince was at
the head of rebellion — but ruined.

Countess DeBeyne noted for the excellence and
exactness of her table. Every thing that is convenient
— Miss   told her that a gentleman the day before
had requested her to look out for any thing worthy of
mention as uncommon & to report it to her — Miss
found before her a cut glass decanter of wine
𝔇 without bottom [2] in an Ice cooler — It was so
made—said the countess that it might enter easily
among the lumps of ice. Salad Knife & fork of Plat-
inum—Cups are red—green &c. [221] Lattin says the
french have no feeling for the antiquities of their own
history or country — of the middle ages. Do not

[1] See p. 163
[2] Irving at this point in the manuscript drew a sketch of the decanter.

feel the beauties of the gothic style &c. Have not the deep feeling of the English for what is solemn — melancholy &c — affect it because it is the fashion — but it is shallow & mere pretence — Speaks of chateau of   mentioned a few days since — nothing of the old castle — but one of the Defendible chateaux of the French Barons — old moat — dry & partly filled up — Old popes house — Chamber haunted by Duke de Guise — (Garden wall painted cut in cyphers is common in old Buildings)

Went in Evg to Mad. De   pretty apartments — Family assembled in a neat Saloon   The Duke of Talleyrand [1] comes in — fashionable man — considered the french model of Politeness — several other gentlemen & ladies come in we left it & came home at nearly 11

Duke of Talleyrand, older brother middle sized man upwards of 60 — pleasing countenance, with continual smile. Hair creped [2] & powdered and tied behind —

[222] *Tuesday Feby 24.* Wakeful in the night — write 5 pages — Story of Popkins [3] — all the worse for writing — went out before breakfast — visited Foy — breakfasted with him at caffe to talk of Italy &c returned home but could not write much. Went with Peter to Galignanis — talked of the Editing of British authors they off[d] 20,000 fr — stated my terms, Walked on Boulevard with Peter — visit Pauscinias

---

[1] Joseph Charles Maurice Talleyrand (1754–1838).
[2] Frizzled.
[3] "The Adventure of the Popkins Family" (*op. cit.*).

[?] of Rome & Naples. retd home dined and slept heartily till 1/2 past 8. Took warm bath & went to bed.

Wednesday 25. Awake early, felt greatly relieved by the fine [?] sleep of last night. Wrote in bed on the robber story — [on ?] the adventure of Popkins &c 10 pages before breakfast — after breakfast wrote the concluding adventure of the attack of the Escort[1] 10 p. Wrote a little at the Lucien Story.[2] Called at Galignanis. Called on the Harveys. Alcocks. Thomond — Welles. left card[s] at all. Walked on Boulevard with Peter. Dined at home — in Evg went to Boarding school concert at Mad^m Clements with the Storrows — Afterwards to a party at Lady Susan Douglas. Genl Airey sets me down home.

[223] *Thursday 26.* At 6 oclock, write at the Lucien Story. continue at it all day & translate 26 pages. receive proof of introduction to Salmagundi. Opera ticket seat from the Gibbings — Dine at home. In the Evg go to Opera & sit in Dr. Gibbings Box — L'Inganno Fortunato and Nina [o] la pazza per amore — fine music & good singing on the part of Pasta.

Friday 27. At 4 oclock in morng — write at The Lucien Story till 6 — napped — rose 1/2 past 7. Wrote note to Lady Louisa & Mrs W —

[1] "The Belated Travellers," *idem*, pp. 333–355; or "The Adventure of the Englishman," *idem*, pp. 410–418.

[2] The "Lucien Story" was probably "The Painter's Adventure," *idem*, pp. 364–375. In America it was said that Irving obtained this story from a manuscript narrative of a servant in the employ of Lucien Bonaparte. See the *United States Literary Gazette*, 1824.

Wrote till 2 oclock at Lucien story. Near 20 pages today — rec[d] letters from Capt Holdridge, at Heyers — & an old one of 13 Nov. from Newton, which had been delayed in Post office Visited the Guestiers — Mrs G at home — sat some time with her. Mrs Thickler & another lady came in — Met Mr Lattin & Miss Called on Sheldon — Dined at home — passed Evg at Mr. Storrows.

[224] *Saturday 28 Feb[y]*. At 4 oclock morng — finished translation of Lucien Story — After breakfast write 2 additional pages — went to riding school — call on Capt Medwin. Called at Mr Lattin — Saw him & Mrs Mansfield — her lovely appearance on entering the room — Lattins story of Duke Fitz James & another person — The other charged Fitz J. with having insulted him — ended by strikg Fitz J across face with his whip — Went immediately to Bois de Bolonge [*sic*] without going home — He and Fitz J send second for Pistols — Fitz James had the first fire shot his adversary thru the breast who fell Second said hes dead — & advised Fitz J to fly — he was just going when the wounded man rose on his knees — Stop said second — you must return & receive his fire Fitz ret[d] but the other fell dead — Fitz J had scarcely ever fired a pistol — The other was a practised & sure shot—

In time of Louis 16 — shortly after his marriage at a masqued Ball a person appeared as a wind mill — Said many strange, import[ant] & true things to the Queen. Monsieur &c They did not dare to molest the mask but ordered him to be watched as they were incensed

—[240][1] he got near the door & escaped unseen leaving the shell of the windmill standg — man appeared as corner of a house — stickg up satirical affiches [2] as any one notorious appeared —The present King when Monsieur [3] was famous as being a great mark — full of wit & repartee

Dine at Mr Chenevix — fine Hotel — compy — Lord Granard — Sir   Shea — Capt —   Miss Knight — Mrs Young Mr & Mrs Ellis &c &c. retd home in Sheas carriage — Miss Knight authoress of Dinarbis [Dinarbas][4] &c — governess of princess Charlotte.

[225] *Sunday. 29.* Broken nights sleep — noise of carriages all night in consequence of Masquerade. Call, after Breakfast, on Capt Medwin. Not up yet. Go to Mr Foys, have long talk about Italy &c — bring home picture of the girls — Write out a sketch of the hints he gave—Dine at home— letter from Mr Lake — In Evg. go to Mr Storrows — Mr Richards — Mr & Mrs Low there

Monday. 1 — wrote this morng to Mr Lake returng his book — called at Galignanis & read papers. Galg. apologized for not havg called to talk about lit^y plan— Mr Didot being absent. Ret^d home & wrote account of Robbers with anecdotes — 12 pages. Called & left

---

[1] The conclusion of this anecdote and a few other notes were written in, upside down, on p. [240] of the manuscript. They are, therefore, inserted here in sequence.

[2] Bills, or posters.

[3] *i. e.*, his title during the reign of his brother, Louis XVI.

[4] Ellis Cornelia Knight (1757–1837). *Dinarbas; A Tale*, London, 1790.

cards on Count Lavindowsky [?] & Mr Price Mr
Gates called. Dined at home. After dinner the boys
came from school. Took them to the theatre Gymnase Coiffeur & Perruquier Rodolphe — Petites Sat-
urnales — L'Heritiere — returned home & supped —
rec^d letter from Lake with his book again

[226] *Tuesday 2 mardi Gras* — Distracted last night
by continual passing of carriages — felt exhausted
this morng. Henry & Irving breakfasted with us —
called on Medwin — Mr Mills called there — much
conversation about Italy & the Abruzzi [1] — returned
home went to Galignanis — To the Storrows dined
there games of various kind[s] in the Evg — Mr
Jamieson there — ret^d home at 12 Irving unwell.

Wednesday 3^d Irving quite unwell this morning —
give him epsom salts — He remains at my lodgings
all day. Henry returned to school — rewrite part of
Painters narrative remain in the house all day —
Irving continues ill — give him an emetic — Mr
Storrow calls in the Evg — Irving sleeps in my room
— I sleep on sopha in saloon —

Thursday 4. passed last night on the sopha in the
saloon. In the morng Irving continues ill — Send for
French Physician, Dr Dumenier [?] who prescribes
warm drinks. Write all day at Bold Dragoon. Mr
Texier calls; mentions that his daughter is about to
be married. Go out at 3 oclock. Leave card at Count
Orloffs. Mr Mays — call & pass some time at Lady
Louisa Harveys — Jealousy between [227] Spaniel,

---

[1] See *Tales of a Traveller*, p. 322.

Folly (alias Benjamin) & a red squirrel — Dine at Medwins — present Mr Lattin, Mr Mills — Mr Henniker — Mr Jenkinson — Mr.   & Mr.   talk of Duels — of gallantry &c. Story of Sir Hennikers of Major   at the battle of Waterloo who had been wounded eleven times & swore he would not quit his gun & was killed on the cannon — A french officer who had three times taken a cannon — swore he would not leave it — bestrode it & was killed on it.

Friday 5. Passed last night on Sopha — Irving very feverish — In morng — correct Knickerbocker — receive letters from Leslie & Sullivan — visit Storrows — not home — Mr Mills with whom I sit a long while conversing about Pelasgian cities [1] — return home — Mr Foy calls — Dine at Mr Villamils — present — Mr Grattan, S'Aubyn Gates. Capt Medwyn Mr Light — & Spanish gent — Other company comes in in the Evg — talk of Spanish literature —

Mrs Mansfield calls for me & takes me to Hotel D'Armond. Introduced to the countess — [228] to the Princess —   Splendid apartments — magnificent hotel — finest in Paris. Company of the first fashion — finely dressed — several very fine women — Gent & ladies keep apart — a great deal of talking & laughing — Count D'Armond married one of the richest heiresses in france — she has fine eyes, but is short & deformed in person — They are not happy together.

Saturday 6. Passed last night on sopha. Irving

---

[1] See *Tales of a Traveller*, pp. 322, 323.

better this morng. Physician pronounces his malady the measles. Write at various parts of the Sportsmans tales [1] — Visit from Mr Lee of N York who brings books & letter from Miller — a hearty, hard, business looking young man — Get Books out of Royal Library. *Micalis Italia avanti il Dominio dei Romani* [2] — Mr Storrow calls — Walk out at 1/2 past 3. Fine day. Meet Sir Fredk Henniker and Mr Wyburn near Thuilleries — converse some time with them. Walk through Gardens — along champs Elysee — where I meet Price [3] on Horseback — looks uncommonly well. Has been at Vienna & in Bohemia intends to return to Dresden. Went to Jenkinsons meet there with Mr Oldnixon — has been 5 years in [229] America. Jenkinson & Medwyn come in with the girls & a legion of dogs. Walk back thro Champs Elysee &c — with Jenkinson — &c &c &c Oldnixon tells anecdote of losing himself in the woods in America on a Hunting party.

Dine at home with Peter. In the Evg — go to a small party at Lady Thomonds — meet there the Granards — Alcocks — Count Chalanni — Sir Geo Shea &c &c Music from a Russian Prince who plays & sings well — one of the Miss Sheas [4] sings well —

Talkg of Lady S. D. — She goes about haunting

---

[1] "The Hunting-Dinner" (*op. cit.*).

[2] *L'Italia avanti il dominio dei Romani* (Florence, 1810), by Giuseppe Micali (1780–1844).

[3] Stephen Price, the American theatrical manager, who succeeded Elliston in 1826 as director of Drury Lane Theatre. Irving knew Price through their common friendship with Payne.

[4] Irving knew this family well in Madrid, in 1827.

her own house in quest of the tea cup that any one of the company has set down. Misses silver &c Looks like the ghost of a Housekeeper that had forgot to lock up the spoons before she died.

Talkg with Col Alcock. Until Nations are *generous* they never will be wise — true policy is generous policy — all littleness — selfishness &c may gain small ends but lose great ones — it may appear chivalrous but it is true — Expedients may answer for the moment — they gain a point but they do not establish a principle — there is a return of the poisoned chalice —

[230] Old Marchioness D'Armond — very white — with very light gray hair — Looks like the white woman of Wesel or rather like the widow of the Italian in Don Giovanni.[1]

Party at Lady Thomonds — Elegant apartments in one of the fine french Hotels — solid but elegant architecture — Saloons richly furnished — blue silk hangings — fine carpets — &c &c — company in groups — some person with maimed fingers who plays well on Piano & sings duet with Miss Shea —

Group at Piano, with harp beside it. group at round table in center looking at caricatures & choosing from among collections of costumes, dresses for the Ambassadresses fancy ball — groups of ecarté players in another corner Gent in blue ribband

Group by Fire place on Sophas & arm Chairs — conversing — group in another corner round a table

---

[1] Presumably Mozart's two-act opera, first performed on October 29, 1787, at Prague.

where Russian Prince is reading fortunes in pack of cards to a beautiful English Countess (Lady Adelaide Forbes) her sister Lady Caroline leaning over her shoulder — Others round the table & one pretty pale female in black with black velvet hat & feather (Lady Julia [231] leaning across the table listening — (Scene & subject for a Travellers tale [1] — *The fortune told*) Gent tells mysteriously things that affect violently a fair lady who retires suddenly.

Story of masqued ball told me by Princess   A few Evgs since at a masked ball one gent — told another go & whisper to yonder lady these words which I shall mention to you — The words seemed to be of no particular import — The Gent whispered them to her — She was violently agitated; uttered violent ejaculations & hurried out of the Ball — The Gent declared he would never repeat those words again — Each person is curious to know what these words were —

Sunday 7th Passed last night in Irvings Room; on Sopha — his night restless — Physician this morng pronounces his complaint the chicken Pox — rewrite part of Italian Story this morng. Mr Mills calls — Drive out in his cabriolet — rain — Dine at Mr Welles.   Present Mr & Mrs Wiggins Mr   Mr Greene Peter — Miss Wiggins — return home early. find Irving very restless with delirium —

[232] Monday 8. Passed last night in Irvings room who was very restless. This day write at the Italian Story

---

[1] This material was not used in *Tales of a Traveller*, or elsewhere.

Write at Italian Story — Dine at home — Evg Dr Calls — Doubts whether I-gs complaint is not the Small pox — pass the night in Igs Room —

Tuesday 9. Irving very much broken out — has no delirium to day — Dr calls at noon — pronounces comp^t the small pox confluent — opens pustules with hands — I write this morng at Italian Story. Mr Storrow calls — tells me of Henrys having same comp^t at the Pension. Drive there with him. Find Henry in the Infirmary. His comp^t very light — Does not think it necessary to remove him. Dine at home — Irving better towards Evg — Pass the night in his room — finish Italian Story. Was to have dined to day with Lady Gran^d but find excuse

[233] Wednesday 10 — Irving seems better this morng — very little fever — no delirium — This day I rearrange plan of author — call at Henrys school — Henry doing very well — complaint quite light — Dine at home in evg Irving has more fever & a little delirium but soon falls asleep & awakes more composed — pass the night in his room he sleeps very well

Thursday 11. Write from 5 oclock this morng at Author — Irving quite comfortable. Mr Galignani calls this morng about my editing suite of English Authors — we cannot agree about the first condition Viz — an advance of 100£. He goes off to consult Didot — Doctor calls — finds Irving in excellent train — Says that had he not been previously vaccinated he would have had a severe fever today — the vaccination had mitigated the comp^t — receive from Mr

Miller 3 vol of Pilot [1] — go out & walk in Tuilleries
— call & leave card for Sir Fred^k Henniker [2] — Mr
L'Assan   Dine at home & pass evg in sleepg.

[234] *Friday. 12 March.* Irving quite free from
fever and in good spirits — Get him into the next
room, where he lies on sopha — Write all day rear-
ranging author story — receive letter from Barham
Livius, dated London 7th — Go out & visit the Storrows — Dine there & stay till 7 oclock — Susan [3]
gives me poem.

Saturday 13. Irving convalescent.   Try to write
prelude to Wolfert Webber but cannot.   Write letters
to Mrs & Miss Foster & send them also send letter to
Mrs Van Wart — Mr Bradish calls — Walk out with
him   Call & leave cards for Sir Fred^k Henniker — call
on the Harveys & sit some time with the young ladies
— call on the Gibbings — & Genl Airey & leave
cards — call & sat some time with Lattin who has had
attack of the gout.

Lattin says young fellows full of animal Spirit —
life — fire &c apt to exhaust themselves — become
pallid — nervous, full of ailments — Like fox hunters
who begin by riding at every thing dashing over
bridge & ditch in 3 or 4 years are cautious — tired —
exhausted — Wear themselves out.

[235] Dine at home with Peter — Gallignani called
today & acceeded [*sic*] to my terms — after dinner lie

[1] James Fenimore Cooper's *The Pilot*, published in 1823.

[2] (1793–1825), traveller, and author of *Notes During a Visit to Egypt,
Nubia, the Oasis, Mount Sinai, and Jerusalem*, London, 1823.

[3] Susan Storrow, daughter of Thomas W. Storrow.

down to nap & wake at 9 oclock — read papers at Galignani & return home — to bed

Sunday 14. write Prospectus & terms for Collection of British Literature—Galignani calls—& agrees to my terms—250 francs a vol. 2500 fr in advance — Write part of introduction to Wolfert Webber — not in good mood — Sir Frederick Henniker & Mr Wyburn call — receive letters from America — Visit the Storrows — Dine with Sir Fredk Henniker — Present Capt Beaumont — Mr. Wyburn Mr Bradish — I was in a Stupor — Came home at 11

Doctor visited Irving today

[236] Monday 15. Write introduction to Wolfert Webber — Recd an elegant present of books from Galignani and Baudray — for my corrections of Salmagundi and Knickerbocker — consisting of 33 vols octavo elegantly bound — of choice french authors — Racine, La Fontaine — Moliere &c — Called at Galignanis — called at Lady Aireys — called & sat for some time with Lady Granard — she talked of Paris in old times splendid hotels in Faub[our]g S^t. Germain — house parties rich houses & retinues — Superb equipages—people in those times dressed richly — gay colours — swords

Fine piles of buildings — steeples — towers—fine churches — rich abbeys —

Nobility only went down to their estates occasionally to squeeze tenants or to pass a little time in fete — carried Paris with them — no rural pleasures — formal walk after driving in formal alleys &c

At home met Mr Morton — who sat some time

with us — perplexed what to undertake as a business —

Evg passed at Mr Storrows — Mr Jamieson there who took leave as he goes to England —

[237] *Tuesday 16.* Rewrite story of Antiquary and Robbers [1] — called & left cards at Mr Chenevix — Mr Moriers — walked through garden of Tuilleries — delightful morning — rode at Manege — returned home Kenney called & sat for some time — dined at home — passed Evg at Mr Storrows —

Dr. called this morng.

Wednesday 17. Wrote a little this morng — at Buckthornes story — merely arranging it — Mr Galignani called & brot prospectus which I altered. Grattan & Kenney called — Called at Mr Gestiers — but Mrs G had drove out — rode at Manege — Mr Foy called & sat a little while — Dined at home — Evg at Mr Storrows — Mr Lowell was there.

Thursday 18. Wrote at some parts of Marquis Story [2] &c — Merely copying corrections &c Wrote to E Irving & to Sullivan. Mr Mills called — rode in the Manege — Left card at Medwins — Henry came out of school & dined at my lodgings. Dined with Lord Granard — present Col Hamilton — Mr Dale Mr Seabright &c Lady Rancliffe told me of a [238] history of France in Engravings in the King's Library — also a Hist of Bavaria — of a town in Auvergne little known or visited — where the houses are all gothic of the style succeeding to the early gothic —

---

[1] "The Adventure of the Little Antiquary," in *Tales of a Traveller,* pp. 321–332.   [2] See p. 165, footnote 2.

French have begun to imbibe a taste for the middle ages since intercourse with the English. Their illustrations of Normandy — Brit[t]any — praise of it.

Mem: to give discription of a French road and French days Journey.[1]

Lady Carolines little dog Gipsey — that nourished a perpetual Heartburn —

Lady Granard told me to *mark her words* it would one day be known Scott only contributed the poetry & touched up the novels — written by another hand: His causes for father[in]g them were generous & would redound to his credit.

Evg to Lady Louisa Harveys — The Ellis family took flight — fearing to catch contagion from me — Talked some time with Miss Knight authoress of Dinarbis & Governess to the Princess charlotte —

Friday 19. — Corrected slightly the Mss: of Author &c — writing fit gone — 1/2 past 12 went to Lady Louisa Harveys — accomp[d] a party consisting of the Harveys — Mr Drummond Mr and Mrs   of Amsterdam & the Marquis   to S[t] Denis — a cold raw day — Church dismally cold — visited the tombs of the Kings &c

[239] Dined at home — Evg at Mr. Storrows.

Saturday 20. Touched up story of Wolfert Webber a little in the announcement — Wrote to Payne & Livius & sent letters — Mr Storrow called — went with him & left cards for Shaw — & Lowell — found Mr Morton at home — calld & sit some time at Mrs Stor-

---

[1] This sketch was never written.

rows—got 30 naps of Mr S. Stopped a little while at Galignanis — Dine with Frank Mills — present Sir Henry Mildmay — Mr Guester — Capt Medwin — He says that Moore had talents but not genius. Thinks he shines in smaller pieces but not in great attempts —

Went to opera — saw the latter part of Tancredi — sat in Churches box after Church had gone out C. much altered — thinner than when I saw him in U S.

[240]¹ *Sunday 21*. Read miscellaneously — rub out pencil writing in Mss. Henry comes from school —Medwin calls —read Italian story to him—Dine at Mr Storrows — In Evg go to Mrs Jenkinson Sir Geo Shea & daughters just leaving — Col.   Capt Medwin — Mr Mills there — come home in Mills Cabriolet

[241] *Monday 22*. Write this morng at Goldsmiths life ² Mr Shaw & Mr Wilson called on me. At 2 oclock went to the oratoire to attend the wedding of Florentine Texier with Mons Therion — much pleased with looks & manner of Bridegroom — return home & find letter from Murray — full of kindness &

¹ At the bottom of this page, upside down, are notes which form a continuation of the anecdote of the windmill on p. [224] of the manuscript. *Cf*. p.140, footnote 1.

² This essay was written for the first volume of the series of English Classics, and, as it happened, was the only one published. Irving never finished this task. He later used this essay as a basis for his biography of Goldsmith, published in 1849. Volumes of the original essay are rare. One of these is in the library of Doctor Roderick Terry.

friendly professions Offers 1200 guineas for my new
work in 2 vols without seeing it till in print. Letter
from Miller — offering from Mr Carey [1] to buy the
Am copy right — Walk with Medwin — who tells of
his havg with Mills written a satirical work on the
English in Paris. Livius calls on me — Distressed
about his sister — wishes me to carry message to
Dana — Dine at Mad^n Debourcals — wait a long
time for dinner — large french party Have dinner —
return home — find Livius there who talks about the
affair of Dana — also of Theatrical matters

receive letters to day from N York introducing Mr
Kissam [2] & Mr Law and sendg me writers on Washington [3]

[242] *Tuesday 23. March.* Livius called this morng
declined carryg message to Dana — Dressed in court
dress & 1/2 past 11 went with Sheldon our charge
d Affaires to the opening of the chambers of deputies
— Went first to Tuilleries to Salle des Ambassadeurs
— Introduced to Mons   Secy of the King and Mons
       also to Mon.   secy of the Russian Ambassador
— who had been in America — a young man fine
complex^n In the Salle is Mon   one of the oldest &
richest families of Russia — refuse[s] to take any
title. He is a lively witty man — a large man with

<hr/>

[1] Of Carey and Lea (Carey, Lea, and Blanchard), publishers, who, in
1835 and later, published some of Irving's writings.

[2] Of the New York family of this name, intimate with the Irvings.
See *Historical Magazine*, April, 1860.

[3] Perhaps for the biography which Irving contemplated.

gray hair brushed close all over his head. Popes
nuncio — red fleshy long Italian face long
aquiline nose blk eyes — hair standing in
a stiff penthouse cue another priest —
with him — yellowish face[1] — large nose —
little cunning mouse eyes — under a hanging lid &
deep eye brows.

Drive to Hall of opening — a magnificent saloon
with crimson silk hangings — high gallery round it
crowded with ladies — throne at upper end — I was
with diplomatic corp in entrance at lower end —
Many fine women finely dressed — King[2] read his
speech in a faltering broken, blundering voice —
prompted [243] by his premier gentleman — M.
Blacas When the names of deputies were calling to
take their oaths the King fell asleep repeatedly —
Monsieur frequently spoke to him to awaken him.
Premier gentleman acted as flapper & coughed &c.
Kings legs muffled up — He was wheeled in. Great
shouts of Vive le roi — a feeble little voice heard
after all the rest — probably some expectant of a
chateau —

The prince magnificently dressed in Ermine & em-
broidered velvet — The members in uniform, blue &
silver & white & underclothes — Before entering the
chamber we had assembled in a salon of the Louvre.
Here I was presented to the Russian ambassador
— saw Deseyes[3] who pleaded the cause of Louis 16
— he is bent with age —

[1] Here Irving drew a sketch of the nuncio.   [2] Louis XVIII.
[3] Raymond, Count de Sèze (1750–1828).

After returning home & chang[in]g dress I called on the Harveys & sat a little while then on Mills — Met Livius — walked with him Met Cornell — who walked with us. left card for Kissam & Law. Dined at home — In Evg saw Marriage of Figaro badly sung & badly acted to a poor house —

[244] Wednesday 24 March. In bed corrected Goldsmiths life — after breakfast went to have my hair cut — called on Mills — Talk with him about the New Forest — promised to pay a visit to his sisters with him — Medwin came in — ret^d home — lunched — went out with Peter to call on Mr Kissam & Law — found no one home but a Mr Tredwell — who appeared in a little Went to Galignanis — At home Jones called on us — arrived in town yesterday — Met Livius just before dinner — who showed a copy of a letter he had rec^d & written &c Dined at home with Peter & Irving — Evg called on Mills & went with him to splendid fancy ball at the Ambassadors — Mills as a Neapolitan Fisherman — Lord Worcester a Knight Templar. Ballet of the 12 seasons —

[245] Thursday 25. Went to bed between 4 and 5 at 6 got awake & took warm bath till 7 — slept till ten — breakfasted & went with Peter to Livius — took 2d Breakfast — Met there Baron de Walsh — musical amateur & Viscount   Afterward went home — wrote to Murray — requiring *1,500* gs — sent it with letter from Irving to Mrs V.[1] to post Called on Mr Low — Jones — Mr Lattin — sat with him & with

[1] Mrs. Van Wart, Irving's sister.

the Lovely Mrs Mansfeld. Mr & Mrs Marsh came in
— Lattin mentioning Lucians account of the Gouts
deriding all the other maladies as being insignificant
in comparison to him —

Called on Mills — not at home — ret[d] home —
rec[d] letter from E. I. by the Marmion — Dined at
home — In Evg went to Mr Storrows — The Boys
there — Henry came out of school to pass 3 or 4 days
with me — not being well

[246] *Friday 26.* Wrote early this morng at Goldsmiths life. Jones called & sat some time with me. Dr
Maclaughlin & Mr Greville called — promised the
latter to dine with him on Tuesday next — nearly
finished Goldsmith — received the tale of Eureka
[?] from Lady Rancliff. Troubled to day with pain in
my side — body bloated — called on Mills — walked
with him & Medwin — Mills showed me his poem.
Well written but cruelly severe — Left card at Ambassadors. Dined at Sir Geo Sheas — present —
Mr Middleton — Young — Seabright — conversation
lively — but too much taken up with talking about
persons of whom I know nothing — A party in the
evg — & music — oppressed with drowsiness & the
pain in my side — & came away — Threatening
symptoms in my legs today.

Saturday 27. Pain in side — took pill last night —
finished revision of Goldsmiths life this morng — rec[d]
letters from Payne, Mrs Foster & Mrs Van Wart —
wrote to Payne rec[d] letter from Mr Dewey N York —
rode in Manege visited Lady Granard & Lady Rancliff — Latter told me of french Lady who followed

her husb^d to sea as Midshipman. When he died she had passage when she retired from society & said she saw & conversed with her husband

[247] Dined with Mills — Medwin there and Mr Hook [1] Latter told excellent story about Dr.Parr — some discussion on Dr Ps character who was pronounced a great Humbug — Mills doubted him as a grecian — He certainly has produced nothing in print to warrant his reputation. He repeated some excellent characteristic touches that he had met with in a Methodist journal —

Evg went to Miss Fitzgeralds — a dance to the Piano — Danced a quadrille with Mrs Mansfield & another with Caroline Drew. came away at 2 oclock —

Sunday March 28. Henry & Irving with us still — A snowy wintry morng — After breakfast called on Foy — sat some time with him & took notes of Italian scenes & incidents — Went to the Storrows & sat for some time — at 2 oclock went to Galignanis — till near 4. ret^d home — Livius called — Dined at Welles — present — Mr Waller — (Stockbroker) Morton — Jones — Sheldons 2. ret^d home at 10

[248] *Monday March 29.* Irving & Henry ret^d to school — Tried to write at Wolfert Webber but could not do any thing of consequence — rode in Manege Dined at home with Peter. Evg — went to concert at Mr Forsters — an Italian Improvisatore there, a great

[1] Theodore Hook (1788–1841), the wit and novelist. Samuel Parr, at this time seventy-seven years old, had interested Irving in 1817. He describes the old scholar in a letter to Brevoort, Birmingham, January 29, 1817, quoted by P. M. Irving (*op. cit.*), I, 360.

bore — left there at 11. Went to a Ball at D^r De Coucey [Coucy] L'Assan — Talked with Villamil Grattan — Medwin — The Aireys — &c &c introduced to Lady   Henry & Lady Se[a]bright — got home near two oclock —

Tuesday — 30th This morng write description of Wolf^t Webber[s] Daughter — Mr   a miniature painter called a little before one to take my likeness — Medwin called in during the Seance — & sat with me some time afterward — Promised me a sight of his Journal in India and also his Italian Journal — Rode in Manege — Mills called, went with him to his lodgings — read me lines in Milman [1] — Took me to dine at Mr Grevilles. Present Sir Geo Dallas [2] — Mr Light — Lady Lake — Mr Mills — Mrs Greville [249] Mr Light mentioned anecdote of French humanity at the storming of S' Sebastians the English were at first repulsed with heavy loss — left many of their wounded in ditch & the tide coming in so they were drowning — a young french officer was seen on the top of ramparts waving a Hkf — They thot it was a bravado & fired at him repeatedly — He contin^d his signal — descended the breach — at length it was discov^d that he was entreating them to take away the wounded who were drowng — To his humanity many owed their lives & among the number a f[rien]d of Lights who had lost a leg & who told him the story —

[1] Perhaps from Henry Hart Milman's (1791–1868) *The Martyr of Antioch*, or *Belshazzar*, both of which appeared in 1822.

[2] (1758–1833), the writer on politics.

The name & fate of the officer I believe are alike unknown —

Went afterwards to opera saw last scene of Romeo & Juliet — Pasta sublime in the address to all'ombra avvenuta [1] — Pastas last appearance — called for by the audience & appeared, face streamg with tears — after opera introduced to Lady Mildmay —

[250] *Wednesday March 31.* After breakfast, feeling good for nothing went to Galignanis & read papers — cold variable dismal weather, with falls of snow — ret^d home & sat for my miniature — afterwards called on Medwin & sat for some time with him reading his Journals — called & left card for Sheldon ret^d home — Dined at Lord Granards — present Miss Knight — Lady Rancliff Ladies Adelaide & Caroline Forbes — Lord Henry Mr beasley — Mr Mills.

Miss Knight says France has nothing of the picturesque excepting where it borders on other countries — towards Spain — towards Switzerland — French borné — hemmed in by rules & method into mediocrity — Every thing made artificial — Their very trees not allowed to grow naturally. French esprit Miss K says tends to shew itself in little pamphlets — (Yes does it not at present find vent in the small periodical papers — The vaudevilles &c of the small theatres are also vehicles for public petulance) French rather deficient in picturesque costumes In fact they have not the picturesque & do not wish for it.

[1] *Cf. Romeo and Juliet,* III. ii.

North of Eng^d much colder & more bracing than
the foggy west.

ret^d home in Mills cabriolet —

[251] Thursday. April 1. Fine sunny morng — tho
still rather cool — read remarks on Moliere, called &
sat with Jones. Called on Sheldon — went with him
to call on Mr Brown — Am — Minister just arrived
— found him at Grand Hotel de Wagram — He is a
very tall but good looking and Gentlemanlike man —
called afterwards on Mr Lattin — not out of Bed —
Met Mrs Mansfield & sat some time with her.

Called on Medwin & walked with him — Ordered
new waistcoat — Called at Mr Storrows only Minny [1]
at home — Stopped in at Galignanis Dined at Mr
Chenevix. Present Lady Hawarden Lady Milman &
Miss Caldwell Lady Brabason [Brabazon] & Daughter — Mr Nugent — Mr Seabright &c &c sat next
Miss Brabason & talked a good deal — In evg introduced to Lady Hawarden.

Called afterwards with Mr Nugent at the Countess
De Beynes — She was out — ret^d home at 10.

[252] Friday April 2. A wretched rainy morng —
cold & cheerless — read Molieres life — went to
Manege & rode for a couple of hours — called on Mills
ret^d home — called on the Storrows & at Galignanis
— Gallignani just recovering from severe illness Mr
Dorr called & sat with me today —

Dined with Medwin — Mr Jenkinson & Mr Mills
— Talked of smugglers — used to throw down Jen-

---

[1] Ann Louisa, daughter of Thomas W. Storrow.

kinsons fence, but left barrels of brandy as recom-
pense — Used to cut across the country across bogs
where nothing else could go — Exciseman who followed was stuck fast with his horse till morng. —

Mills 2 Kegs of white Brandy intercepted one
moonlight night —

Went in Evg to a small party at Lady Louisa Harveys ret^d home at 1/2 past 11.

[253] Saturday April 3. My birth day — wrote
part of a letter to Mrs Foster — dozed — Mr Storrow called & went with Peter to Mr Browns — Called
on Mills & left names—called on Sir Wm Brabason—
Went to Manege & exer[cised] for an hour & half —
ret^d home — Dine a[t] Miss Fitzgerald. Present Mrs
Mansfield Mrs & Miss Reynold[s] — Mr Dinon —
Capt Medwin, Mr Grattan — Mr Fitzgerald Poet
from Caen —&   at dinner Dinon denied that
Mad^m Talleyrand had mistaken him for Robinson
Cruesoe —

In Evg — Mrs M. comp[laine]d of the bad taste of
confession in catholic religion — The awkwardness of
havg to meet priests at dinner face to face — to whom
you had confessed every thing Old gent the Baron
Weber came in in the evg — He was foster brother to
Marie Antoinette — a stout old gent — with white
head —

The Poet from Caen went about complimenting
every one — fell into his hands after much evasion —
The french carry on a trade of compliments. They
seek it of one another — They interchange [254]
praise. I think it requires a degree of hardihood to ad-

vance up to an author or a lady & praise his book or her face without any ceremony. It is stopping a man on the Kings highway & praising him.

Sunday April 4. Henry & Irving breakfast with us — After breakfast call with them on Jones — find Dorr there. Then call on Livius Rue de Provence — Send boys to Mr Gestiers and call on Mills. Sit with him some time. Saying of Frenchman — that the Politesse between gent was like the cotton that china was packed in to keep it from injuring one another —

Mills suggests two stories. The Enthusiast & the Sceptic. Thinks Dinon [1] a Humbug — says he was once thrown from houses with the old man when he had a medal mania.

The old man had written about medals & coins & knew nothing about them — Wanted Mills to come & tell him what he had. Ret^d home —found letter from Mrs Foster — ret^d to Mills — called with him on Grevilles — found Lady Lake & Mrs Greville at home — went afterwards & drove with Mills in his [255] cabriolet in Bois de Boulogne — a fine day but grew cloudy & cool — Met Cornell &c ret^d & dined at Mr Storrows Mr Lowell there — In Evg the Lows & Sheldons — came home at 10

Monday — 5. read Story of Freyschütz — part of Don Juan. Wrote to Mrs. Foster — Mrs Van Wart Mr Miller — copied 3 pages in Robber tales — sat for miniature — called on Mills found him busy on MS of K[night]s templars — Medwin came — we

---

[1] This collector of coins reappears in the "Adventure of the Little Antiquary," in *Tales of a Traveller*. See pp. 321, 322.

walked out — called & left cards for the Gibbings —
Fairfaxes — called at Mr Lattins — Mrs Mansfield
there — Miss & Mr Fitzgerald — ret[d] home — Dined
at Mills — present Sir Henry Mildmay — Mr Greville — Mr Edgill Mr Mills Capt Medwin — Sir H
Mildmays story of April fool made on Mrs Coldfield [?] She was to have a party to dinner. Fox wrote
a letter in character of Count   saying that he had
just arrived, enquiring to have the pleasure of introducing his hungarian friend the Prince of Seidlitz
Powders who only stayed two — three days in Paris
— Rec[d] a note from Mrs Coldfield invited him & his
friend to dinner — Various speculations [256] at
dinner. The Prince did not appear — what kind of
man would he be — fair dark &c &c curious name —
said Mrs C — like an English Physic — Hungarians
did not recollect such a name suspected him to be an
impostor — at length at 9 oclock a letter with bl[ac]k
margin arrived from prince regretting he could not
attend as he had just heard of the death of his cousin
the Bishop of Epsom Salts who died at Cheltenham
— signed Poisson d-Avril.[1] P.S. A card had been
p[ri]v[a]t[ely] engraved Prince of Seidlitz Powder —
at —   Hotel — The Miss Coldfields send after
him at Mrs Marchs[?], the Duchess of   &c so have
to bring the Prince of Seidlitz Powders there

ret[d] home at eleven having stopped in at Galignanis —

[257] Tuesday 6. Fair weather Read Pilot till 1/2
past 12 — called at Mr Storrows & sat till 2. Went to

[1] April-fool joke.

Manege & rode till 1/2 past 4. Dined at Count Orloffs [1] (son of Orloff who strangled Paul) Present Jones
Admiral Tchieff [?] — and three ladies who appeared
to be of the household — Countess so infirm as to be
wheeled about in her chair — Count has private
theatre — fine apartments — presented me with his
Tour in France — (P S (I am told he is prone to pull
the long bow) Countess fond of short stories Had read
of *Magic blanc* —

In Evg went to Duchess of Duras [2]—Lady Rancliff
introduced me — met there Cuvier — Baron de Humboldt — Countess De Beyne &c Pictures of Europa [?]
hanging up — Duchess a fine interesting looking
woman a little turned of 40.

Humboldt said there were 10,000 mad people in
France.

[258] Wednesday 7. April — tolerable weather —
a little rain in the middle of the day — After
breakfast went to Manege & rode — called on Mills
— Medwin comes in — took 2ᵈ breakfast towards
twelve — retᵈ home & sat for miniature — read in
Don Juan — Mills called — read Robber stories — I

---

[1] Count Gregory Vladimirovich Orlov (1777–1826), author of *Voyage
dans une partie de la France, ou lettres descriptives et historiques à la Com-
tesse Sophie de Strogonoff*, Paris, 1824. Count Orlov's father, Alexis
Orlov (1737–1808) is said to have murdered Peter III, at Ropsha.

[2] Various letters of Irving in the possession of Yale University describe
his friendship with this lady. See also letter of Irving to Mrs. Catherine
Paris, Paris, September 20, 1824, P. M. Irving (*op. cit.*), II, 213–217.
"The Duchess of Duras is one of the finest women of France, idolized in
the world of taste and literature . . ." She wished Irving to write a book
concerning her chateau, in the manner of *Bracebridge Hall*.

feel quite out of conceit of them to day — & feel down in spirits — Count Orloff called — told some circumstances concerning the Robbers — Their outrage upon Mr Lackington consul at Naples & his two daughters near to Naples [1] —

Dined at Mr Gestiers — present Mr & Mrs Meyers — Miss   Mr Gestier mentions the distress of french at sinking of funds and diminishing the Interest.

Mills today mentioned the hubbub in a city of Sicily from a kind of whispering echo in one of the churches by which one might hear all that was said at Confession — The scandalous anecdotes discovered of wives — daughters &c &c

ret^d home about 10 oclock

[259] Thursday Apl. 8. Out of Spirits — distrustful of my work — particularly robber stories — Dress & go out after breakfast — to Foys who was not home — called in at Galignanis — promised to dine there on Saturday — ret^d home for a time called on Medwin, not at home — called and sat some time with Livius — called at Mr Lattins — who was somewhat better — He quoted saying of a Germ[an] writer — He loved to breathe the country air — the fresh free air that had never been contaminated by flattery — that had never been voiced into a lie as in the city.

An Irish lady & her nice fresh daughter came in & sat some little time — One that a man would feel no compunction in begetting children upon —

[1] *Cf.* "The Inn at Terracina," in *Tales of a Traveller*, pp. 303–320.

Mrs. Mansfield came in also.

— Called on Mills — Sir Geo Shea — neither at home — called & sat for some time with Lady Airey.

Mr Foy called on me

Dined at Sir Robert Wilmot — Present [260] Lady Belmore & Miss Caldwell — Lady Hackett — Dr Young & several young gent — rather a dullish dinner —

In Evg — stopped in at Ital[ian] Opera & saw part of Tancredi sat in Dr Gibbings Box — Miss Gibbings introduced me to Mr Henniker — brother of Sir George

Friday 9.th After breakfast went to riding school & exercised for an hour — called at Mills — borrowed Albertis Italy.[1] Mills read scraps from memorandum & — ret[d] home & sat for miniature — rec[d] book & note from Sir Henry Mildmay — went to Louvre & saw Foy who ret[d] Mss of Robber tales. Ret[d] home and found Mills at my room readg Robber tales — called & took leave of Mrs Gestier — saw a perfect miniature of her by Guerin. ret[d] home — Mills still there — Advises me to touch up the Frenchman tale [2] — Dined at Storrows — present Mr Mays Mr Sheldon — Mr Dorr Mr Reed — Mr Brimner

afterward went to Dr Gibbings — pleasant music from Miss Gibbings — Sir Geo Shea invited me to his seat in Hereford Shire — Introduced to Mrs & Miss Fairfax

[1] Irving refers probably to Leandro Alberti's *Descrizione di tutta l'Italia*, Bologna, 1550.

[2] Probably "The Adventure of My Uncle," in *Tales of a Traveller*, pp. 22–39.

ret^d home at 1 oclock

[261] Saturday. 10. A rainy day — felt good for nothing — had gone to bed at 2 oclock last night — passed the day lounging on sopha readg life & Eloge [1] of La Fontaine &c — Dined at Galignanis — present a Mr Cooper one of the Editors of the paper — two french ladies & 2 french Gent. Galignani said the Variety — Gaiete & one other theatre on Boulevard were the only theatres that made money —

Abonnements [2] in theatre not transferrable 4 Editors to paper — & to mag[azine]. Mr Stretch — Grattan — Greathead ret^d home 1/2 past 10.

Sunday 11. awoke at 4 oclock & could not get asleep again—read Moriers travels—After breakfast called at Jones', & found that he had left Paris yesterday — called on Livius who played several airs & told several adventures — called & sat with Medwin — till Seabright came in — Ret^d Home Livius called on me & we went together to the conservatory of Music Concert by Mad   heard   on violin Zuchelli sang

[262] My seat was cold & I came away after first act — ret^d home & napped till time to dress for Dinner — Dined at Jenkinsons en famille — only Medwin there. House over run by Dogs — In Evg — some company came in — The Villamils — Singing & pictures — ret^d home ½ past 12.

Monday. 12 April. Woke early Went out before breakfast and rode in Manege. Breakfasted with

[1] Appreciation, or criticism.

[2] Subscription-tickets.

Mills — clear serene, but in the course of the morng — some rain &c. Called on Col Aspinwall [1] & left cards. ret^d home — rec^d letter from Payne — sent 100 francs in his name to Col Wheatley — write to Galignani, requiring explanation about literary enterprize. —

Dine at Sir Henry Mildmays — present Marquis of Worcester. Mr. Fox Mr   Mr Mills — Mr.

In Evg — Mrs Mansfield calls & takes me to Countess de Beynes — meet considerable society. Meet there Count Orloff and Count Casimir [?] return home about ½ past 12 —

[263]   *Tuesday 13.* Read miscellaneously this morng — at ½ past 12 Miniature painter called and had a sitting. Mr. Foy called to take leave as he sets off tomorrow for Italy. At 2 oclock called at the Storrows and sat with them till 4 Returned home and dined.   In the evening went to vaudeville & saw Leonide [2] in which Pauline Geoffrey played charmingly & a pleasant fairy burlesque called *Le pied de Nez* [3] Philip & Jenney Colon played well

Wednesday 14. Read Moriers travels. Looked over Buckthorne Mss: Idea struck me of work called

---

[1] Colonel Thomas Aspinwall, for many years Irving's literary agent in London. Aspinwall said: "Such of the works of Washington Irving as were written out of England after 1824 were confided to my disposal, and published under contracts made by me as his agent." See *Proceedings of the Massachusetts Historical Society*, VIII, 32–38, November, 1891. This article includes a memoir and a portrait of Colonel Aspinwall.

[2] *Léonide, ou la vieille de Suresne.*

[3] *Le pied de nez, ou Felime et Taugut.*

Buckthorne & his times [1] — Sat to Miniature painter.
Mr Morton called — Mesr Galignani & Didot called
to arrange about terms — agreed to every thing &
paid me 2500 francs down — called on Mr. Storrow —
get 30 Napoleons — sat with the ladies till 5 o clock
— ret[d] home dressed & dined at Grevilles. pres[en]t
— Mr & Mrs G & Lady Lake, Mr Hinchcliff — Mr.
Fox, Mr Mills Mr Drummond

ret[d] home at 10.

[264] Thursday Apl 15. at 12 Mr Greville calls on
me, we call for Mr Hinchcliff and go to Major Lights
— where we pass some time looking over his collection
of drawings — Panoramas of Malta, Messina, Alexan-
dria, Cairo — Views of places in Italy — Tyrol —
Switzerland — Wales &c call on Major Aspinwall [2]
Walk with Peter in the Champs Elysees — Long-
champ — Henry & Irving come out from school —
write to Mr Lemoine about Miss Hankworths affair
— Dine at Welles — Present Mr & Mrs Brown —
Col & Mrs Aspinwall — Mr & Mrs Low — Mr & Mrs
Sheldon — Sheldon Secy of Legation — Mr Dorr —
Mr Brimner — Mrs Sheldon — Mr Codman — return
home at 10 oclock

Friday 16. Henry & Irving with us — wrote introductory remarks to Goldsmiths life. Rec[d] Letter
from Payne, inclosing 40£ on acct of Theatrical
writings — called at Galignanis & gave part of Goldsmiths Biography — Rec[d] invitation to dinner from

[1] The final title was "Buckthorne and His Friends," in *Tales of a
Traveller*, pp. 135–299.

[2] Colonel Aspinwall.

Russian Ambassador which I declined — called on
Mills — left card Sir Robt Wilmots — called & sat
for some time with Mr. Brown — left card at Sir H
Mildmays — sat some time with Mr Lattin — Dine
at home — Evg at Mr Storrows.

[265] Lattin was without pain — head & stomach
in good order — case of the man that might be called
a happy man if he did but know it. Spoke of Long-
champ — prefers it to S' James Park — because you
have all classes — likes to see the women — Fiacres
cabriolets cabs & all so happy — None of that exclu-
sive cold superciliousness & ennui — Happiest people
— Rousseau says go into a country —the place where
discontent & ennui is is the Palace & the person the
most ennuied is the King — when in Lond: in compy
asked a lady if she had been in the park — what —
Park on Sunday — faugh — never — how absurd
you are said Lattin — You are the very people that
should go on that day to shew yourselves — to en-
courage the people keep up the hearts of lonely &c

Saturday 17. Fine morng—feel literary fit coming
on. Write all the morning at the French Story in
Strange tales,[1] adding historical anecdotes. Mr Galignani calls about corrections &c. Miniature painter
calls & gives me a sitting. Medwin calls & takes
leave as he goes to Geneva — write a little more then
called & left card for Morton — called on Mills, not
at home — called & sit some time [266] at the Harveys. Admiral ret[d]. Dined at home. Sir H[enr]y

[1] The first of the four divisions of *Tales of a Traveller*.

Mildmay called & left card — called in the Evg and passed Evg at the Harveys — a foreign lady with them who speaks english well —

Sunday April 18. Wrote all this morng on various parts of Strange Stories. Went out at 2 oclock & called on Mills. Left card for Russian Minister. Fairfaxes — Gibbings. Dined at Mr Storrows — present Mr Morton & his two sons. Peter. Henry & Irving — dancing in Evg — read papers at Galignanis on my way home — ret^d home at 11.

Monday. 19. Touched various parts of Strange Stories — Mr Galignani called &c. talked about prospectus &c Mills called — read part of Mss: of Strange Stories — walked with him to see Medwin who is ill in bed with touch of the Liver — Then walked in the Tuilleries — fine day — a great deal of company — Dined with Young at the Circle — Col Young Col from India Dined there — with Mr — Mrs Young — another Mr Young related to Jeffrey — Mr Mills — Sir W Brabazon — Mr Wilder &c In Evg went to Lady Constables — Magnificent Hotel — gilded rooms &c — Miss Fairfaxes — Miss Knight — Lady Adelaide Forbes — Lady Thomond & the Ladies OBrien. Saw the album in which Moore and myself wrote —

[267] Tuesday 20. Wrote a little retouching the opening of Wolfert Webber — fit left me & I had to desist — walked out to Mills — ret^d home walked out with Peter — called on Bradish who has been ill for some time & is still confined to his bed — tho getting better — called by on Medwin, who had gone

(170)

out. Ordered Boots & shoes at Gays. Called & left
cards at Count Orloffs. Walked with Peter in yᵉ
Tuilleries — a beautiful day. Called at Staubs &
ordered clothes — Dined at Didots — Went thro his
printing establish[men]t — 38 presses — 250 hands
— casts his own type — a complete labyrinth — at
Dinner Dr   son & daughter in law who is very
pretty — two other gentlemen & ladies — no demand in France at present for fine Copies — of valuable works. Didot printed 152 copies of Phaedra
[Phèdre] — Loss — has them yet on hand — folio —
splendid — one copy in Vellum — 50£ — retᵈ home
11 — found note from the Duchess of Duras with
present for Ticknor [1]

[268] *Wednesday. 21. April.* Wrote this morng —
on Wolfert Webber — sent home Moriers book with
letter — Sat to miniature painter for the last time.
Called at Storrows & went out with them to Auteuil
— country beginning to look beautiful — day uncommonly fine — Dined at Mills — with Greville —
Edgill — Medwin Peter & Mills. Greville noisy &
talkative — spoiled the dinner party [2] — Came home
at ½ past 10 —

---

[1] Irving acted at various times as representative in Europe for George
Ticknor (1791–1871). For a full account of their relations when Irving
was in Spain, see *George Ticknor, Letters to Pascual de Gayangos*, ed. C. L.
Penney (New York, 1927), *passim.*

[2] If this was, as is probable, Charles Cavendish Fulke Greville (1794–
1865), it may be said that he had no better an opinion of Irving than Irving of him. See under the year 1829, in *The Greville Memoirs, A Journal of
the Reigns of King George IV and King William IV* (London, 1875). Greville found Irving deficient in cultivation.

*Thursday 22*ᵈ Sent book & note to Capt Cadogan
wrote alterations on Wolfert Webber — but did not
feel much in the vein — Livius came in — walked
with him in Tuilleries from 3 till past 5. Mills & Medwin joined us — fine day — Trees putting out their
leaves — women lookg pretty — old genˡ 70 years old
— whom Medwin has met in all parts of the world —
stoppd in at Rue de la paix & bought breastpins —
Dined at Storrows — present the Aspinwall family
and Mr. Consul. Went afterwards to opera. Mr Gibbings box. Saw Montelli for the first time in Cener-
entola — fine voice — well recᵈ — came home in Mr
Gibbings carriage.

[269] Friday 23. Wrote at Wolfert Webber makg
alterations — no excitement — miniature painter
called & brot home my likeness — called at the Storrows & sat some time with them — called on Mills —
not at home — walked in Tuilleries — left card at
Miss Fitzgerald — called & sat with Mr Lattin —
who is recovered — Dined with Mr Morier — present Sir Patrick   & daughters — Mr Ogilvie — Mr.

Evg — at a small party at Lady Thomonds —
talked with Lord Thomond — Mr Chabanais Ladies
Adelaide & Lady Caroline Forbes — came home at 12
— found letter from Van Warts.

The seasons seem to have an average of cold & sunshine — though apt to be irregular — fine weather is
like ones income — a certain amount for every year
— sometimes we have an unusually fine season but it
is but enjoying two passions in one or spending next
years allowance in advance — We are sure to suffer

(172)

for it. We had an unusually fine season two years
since & we have not yet recovered [270] from that extravagant summer — so prodigal of sunshine —

Saturday 24. Wrote a little at Wolfert — but was
not in good mood. Wrote note to Henry inclosing
letters — called at the Storrows — at Mills — Dined
at home — afterwards called at Mills — went home
— slept 2 hours — Went to the Fairfaxes — where I
found Mills & Miss Knight — talkg of French — former prejudiced — Miss K more candid & moderate —
promised Mrs F to pay her a visit at Gilling castle if
I came to York shire — not far from York — went
afterwards to Frascati — annual Ball — Trumpery
& Strumpeting — introduced to Lord Howick son of
Earl Gray — came home at 2

Tuesday 25 — Took warm bath at 6 — at seven
fell asleep & slept till 9 — Tried to write this morng
— but could not get on — Mr Cornell called & Mr
Geo Jay — Went to Mills — drove to British Ambassadors & left card — calld at Jenkinsons — drive
in Bois de Bologne — all the world there — talked
with young Fairfaxes — Miss Gibbings — ret[d] home
— dressed for Duchess de Duras — did not get there
till compy was seated at table — Morier there —
Duchess daughter a fine woman — Duchess spoke of
her chateau in Touraine Old Norman buildings —
went afterwards to Storrows — then to Jenkinsons —
& ret[d] home.[1]

[271] Chateau built about time of first Crusade

[1] At the bottom of page [270] are these words, upside down: **Morier
Orloff Douglas.**

mementos of Cath[erine] of Medicis — Her library with her cypher.[1]

Monday 26. Write on W. Webber — till near three — call at Storrows — dine at home — go to the Variete — See La Neige — Sol[l]iciteur — Porteur d eau. Les Blouses — theatre hot — feel sleepy & uncomfortable —

Tuesday 27. After breakfast go with Peter to Place Royal in the Marais — thence to the Library of Monsieur — Then along the Quais — beautiful weather — Visit the Storrows who are on the point of leaving town. Adieux of Victoire & the other servants &c &c. Stop at Galignanis get prospectus — Call & leave cards at Mr Alcocks — Mr Browns — Call at Sheldons & get new passport — Leave card at Medwins Dine with Livius. Go to comic opera See the Mechant Ange — pleasing — Then the opera in 3 acts of Joseph by Mehul [2] — very much pleased with it. Weber thinks it the best french Opera extant — a Debutant Mr Lefraillade — handsome good voice — acted well home by 11

[272] Wednesday 28 — After breakfast write half a page at Wolfert Webber — Go to Galignanis — then to Biblioteque Royale with Peter. Then to police about Passport — Then to Mr Storrows — go with him to look at houses — then call at Ad[ml] Harveys & sit some time with Ladies — Meet Mills & walk with him — Dine at home with Peter Evg to Gymnase — See Les Femmes Romantiques. L Heritiere Mansarde

---

[1] *I. e.*, monogram.   [2] Étienne Henri Méhul (1763–1817).

de[s] Artistes Partie et Revanche — retd home well satisfied

Thursday 29. After breakfast went to Police for Passport. Office hours just commencing — dirty desks, with days provender in cupboard — Old court yard of the Police Hotel — Bought Books on my way home — Van Trump &c — went out to Auteuil & passed the morng in the garden with the Storrows — a delicious day — Trees in blossom & young leaf — on returning home find letters from Paulding & Pierre Irving [1] — with copy of the play — Call at Lord Granard — Dine at Welles — present Col & Mrs Aspinwall — Mr & Mrs & Miss Wiggins Mr & Miss Hinkley — Mr Morton — Pringle — March [273] ret^d home at 1/2 past 10 —

Friday 30. rec^d 500 fr from Mr Storrow — called at Foreign Ministers & left Passport to be signed. Called & left card for Dr Gibbings — Mr Villamil — walked with Young — called on Mr Lattin — saw Mr Griffiths there — Dined at Mr Lattins — a Mr Dillon there

Story of Archbishop Dillon — 8 Dillons killed in French Service at Battle of Fontenay King asked if there were any more of the family — Yes — one left — Then We take care of him said King — He was accordingly put in the church — tho nature intended him for a soldier — fine magnificent grenadier looking man — and face that looked as if he drank tho he was temperate — Lived well. In country dined with a

[1] Irving's biographer, Pierre M. Irving, or another nephew, P.P. Irving.

curate who had detestable oil — why mons — he cried, what oil is this — monseigneur it is the same that burns before the image of our holy saviour —

In Evg Grattan came in —

[274] May 1. Saturday. A rainy day — Arranged & burnt papers, letters &c — Went to Foreign Minister for my passport — but having mislaid the receipt could not get it — vexatious regulations — Called on Mills & walked with him — Wrote this day to Payne — rec^d letter for Henry from Mrs Van W — Dined at Miss Fitzgerald — present Mrs Rennik & daughter. Mrs Mansfield — Capt Medwin Mr Fitzgerald — Mrs Rennik told me the story of a married lady in love with her own Brother in law who after death appeared to her & left the mark of his burning hand on her arm — She wore a black ribband on it ever afterwards — Mrs Rennik said the Ladies son was her own Brother in Law & told her of his mothers wearing the ribband — Took leave this evg of Medwin — who starts in the morng for Geneva

[275] May 2^d After breakfast went out to Auteuil — rainy day — found Henry & Irving there — the latter indisposed Dined there & returned home in Evg —

May 3. Fine weather. Bot Trunk — 90 fr — Hair brushes 6 fr. Ret^d home Col Aspinwall called & told me stories about Kidd [1] — called on Mills then on the Jenkinsons, Mills played off a hoax upon the

---

[1] From Aspinwall Irving derived material for "Kidd the Pirate," in *Tales of a Traveller*, pp. 426–434.

Jenkinsons with a pretended note from Mr Payne —
Purch[d] Necklaces.

Dined at home — Henry & Irving with us — went
in Evg to Gymnase Lusitains & Cuisinier — Leyster
of Fauxbg — Mansarde des artistes — Demoiselle et
la Dame —

May 4th About 11 oclock drive in Cabriolet to Bar-
riere de Passy — Walk thru Passy to Bois de Bologne — Beautiful day — hear cuckow [cuckoo] for
first time this year — go to Mrs Storrow — give the
girls necklaces — walk in Bois de Bologne with Mrs
Storrow & the girls — return to house at 4 1/2 —
[276] [1] Call at Dr Gibbings — Dine at home — after
dinner call at Mad[m] de Courvilles Evg at the Ambassadors — a great deal of company presented to Lord
—— Lady   Lady —— ——   ret[d] home at 1/2
past 1

Wednesday May 5. Wrote conclusion to Goldsmith
life — call on Mills — On Lady Granard — Mr Lattin
— Mr Bradish, where I met with Mr Barton a very
genteel young American — Leave card for Mrs Welles
— Dine at Mr Browns — present — Mr Sheldon —
Col & Mrs Aspinwall — Mr Bradish, Mr Barton
Mr McCrea of Virginia — Mr Barnet —

Evg to a Ball at Mrs Crofts — introduced to Gen[1]
Upton — Lady Harvey introduced me to her daughters came home at 1/2 past 12

[277] *Thursday 6.* This morning wrote story of the

---

[1] The first ten lines on page [276] of the manuscript have been almost
entirely rubbed out.

Devil & Tom Walker.[1] Peter went to Versailles A Mr
Goodwin called on me — So did Mills who talked of
furnishing an article on Secret Societies. Gave him
Buckthorne to take home with him. At 5 oclock went
out to Passy to dine with Livius — No 4 Basse rue.
Found him nearly done dinner having forgot his having invited me. Living out there with a girl with him,
"La solitude est une belle chose &c" said he. While a
chicken was roasting for my dinner we went up to a
Belvedere on top of the house commandg a fine view.
The Landlord an italian who has wrote several things
& speaks several languages told me as a reccommen-
dation [sic] to his home that one could do every thing
there "chiens ou enfants" — Came on to rain — got
carriage & returned home — at 1/2 past 9. Dressed
& went to Miss Fitzgerald — a crowded party — A
cursed bore of an italian improvisatore — a dance
afterward — I was introduced to Lady   the lord
knows who & her daughters — talked a great deal
with Young & Morier & Mrs Mansfield — Mr Lattin
was there & said the improvisatore [278] had spoken
of the resurrection of Greece — he might now speak
of the resurrection of Lattin — (it was his first appearance since his illness) came away at 1 — Mr Mills
set me down

Friday 7. May. Wrote all the morning at Tom
Walker — Henry & Irving called about Spanish mas-
ter. Called at Mr Douglas. sat with Lady Susan &
Georgina Drew. Cashed a 40£ bill at Lafittes Paid

[1] *Tales of a Traveller*, pp. 435–454.

Fredericks bill for shirts. Called on the Harveys —
on Mills who was out — Met & walked with Sir
Henry Mildmay — Dined at home. After dinner
went to Passy but could not find lodgings to suit me.
— Peter accomp^d me — We went on to Auteuil &
passed the evg at Mrs Storrows — Col & Mrs Aspinwall & children came there — ret^d home about 11.
Oclock

[279] May 8 Saturday. Wrote this Morng at story
of Tom Walker — Called on Mr Coles who was writing an adaptation of Burgomaster of Saardam [1] for
Payne — Lives Rue Caumartin No 9 — says they are
trying to get the Adelphi Theatre for Payne — Ret^d
home & arranged Trunk for departure — Mills called
on me — approves highly of Buckthorne — Dined
early — After dinner drove out to Auteuil — took
lodgings at Bains Public[s] a charming Room looking
into a garden

Room board &c. 300 fr per month — pass evg at
Mrs Storrows — walk in the Solitaire [2] with Susan &
Ann Louisa & listen to the nightingale — Return to
Hotel have to wait in saloon till room is ready pretty
girl & plain without a room playing Ecarte. General
comes in with blue cloth cap worked with silver —
girls father — retire at 11 O clock

May 9 — Sunday. Awake at a little after 4. Beautiful dawn. Birds singing in the garden under my

---

[1] C. F. Reynolds's *The Burgomaster of Saardam; or, The Two Peters*
was acted at the Haymarket in September, 1824 as *'Twould Puzzle a Conqueror*.

[2] Retreat, or retired spot. Perhaps connected with the hermit mentioned on p. 181.

window. Beautiful sun rise — get up 1/2 past 7.
Servt brings petit dejeuné [déjeuner] at 8 — a huge
milk pot & little coffee pot that looked like a little
fellow paying his addresses to a tall woman. Write
for several hours at the adventure of my Uncle, in-
serting particulars of Duchess of Longueville.[1]
Breakfast a la fourchette at [280] eleven. The Genl —
the Baron & his daughters — prodigal Son, & Hard
times at table [2] — afterward go to Mrs Storrows —
find Peter there — Walk in garden — After they have
Lunched we walk in Bois de Bologne — lovely day
— hear the Cuckow Mr Bushy — Mr Storrows clerk
comes out — plays on flageolet — dines at Mr Storrows — pass some hours in the garden — tell the
story of Lilly of the Valley.[3] Sit by moon light in the
saloon till ten & then return to my lodgings —

Monday May 10. Awake early — Birds Singing —
beautiful morng & delicious weather. Breakfasted in
my room between 7 & 8. Wrote a little at the Story of
Tom Walker, introducing dialogue between him &
D[evil]. on subject of the bargain — rewrote the story
of the Young robber [4] — breakfasted at 11 — a la

---

[1] See "The Adventure of My Uncle" (*op. cit.*), pp. 32–36.

[2] Anecdotes or incidents for Irving's writing.

[3] Irving's faculty of story-telling is well illustrated by his tales for
children. "My dear little lady," he wrote Susan Storrow "... It puts
me in mind of a story which I'll tell you. Once there were two little rose-
buds that grew in the corner of a garden, in a quiet sheltered corner. One
of the buds ..." Irving to Susan Storrow, Birmingham, June 25, 1824,
in the Harvard University Library. He was to recall these happy evenings
with the Storrow family two years later during his loneliness in Madrid.

[4] "The Story of the Young Robber," in *Tales of a Traveller*, pp. 393–
403.

fourchette — previously I took a stroll in our garden
which is extensive. Met the Baron & the Gen[1] —
before sitting down to breakfast the Baron addressed
me by name & said he already knew me by my works
— pleasant breakfast — returned to my chamber &
wrote till 1/2 past 2 — dressed and went to Mrs Storrows. Read Italian with [281] Susan in the garden —
ret[d] home to dinner — Pleasant dinner — The Baron
remarkably agreeable — has a pleasing mode of
treating his pretty daughter & has son a handsome
lad of about 18 — Spoke of the old solitaire [1] in the
Bois de Bologne — some said he was a hermit —
others a protestant priest — After some badinage the
Baron observed to his son he has one title of great
dignity — what is that Papa — that of Vieillard.[2]

Baron spoke of the Impertinences of France, among
the young men particularly — a thing which one
never met with in Germany —

After dinner went to Mrs Storrows — walked in
the Garden till near nine oclock — came home 1/2
past 9 — & went to bed.

Tuesday 11. Slept ill last night — often awake
heard 1, 2, 3 4, 5 & 6 strike — rose at 7. Breakfasted
wrote at Robber tale. Recd letter from Peter. Dejeuner a la fourchette at 11. at 12 resumed my pen &
wrote at robber tale till 1/2 past 2 — Peter arrived.
Walked with him to Mrs Storrows & in Hotel garden
till dinner — there had been rain in the morng —
afternoon very pleasant — Peter dined at Hotel. At

[1] Anchorite.　　　　[2] Old man.

dinner much talk of the Gen[1] & Baron about war.
Cavalry officers always charge at the head of their
[282] troops — often the first to be Killed. Napoleon
—used a small glass scarcely larger than opera glass in
the field—Knew the situation of his troops—put the
glass to his eye & took it away almost immediately.
The Infantry is what is most effective in battle —
They can sustain a battle alone — but neither cavalry
nor artillery can—The most destructive fire is that of
musketry — when men get close together in wood —
deploy & shoot each other down like rabbits — Artillery kill comparatively fewer men. At the battle of
    the french threw 47000 balls — had each killed
its man what slaughter there would have been —
some killed several — but the greater part flew harm-
less — Great time and patience requisite for a retreat
en echellon [1] French bad at a retreat —

Marmont [2] — brave, but improvident showy —
fanfaron [3] — liked parade — talked finely — a shewy
man at table — much orgueil.[4] [283] passed evg at
Mrs Storrows — walked in garden — music — came
home at 10 —

Wednesday 12. Rise at 6 — rainy morng — wrote a
little at robber story — resumed my pen after breakfast and wrote during the day till 1/2 past 3. Constant rain. Dined at home — conversations about
Bonaparte

----

[1] Echelon. In ranks.
[2] Auguste Frederic Louis Viesse de Marmont (1774–1852), Marshal of
France.
[3] Boaster.   [4] Pride.

Baron de la Salle a Livonian young man set out from home & travelled to paris for the purpose of killing Bonaparte — In mounting the stairs of the Tuilleries he let his pistol fall — seized it with marks of apprehension — was seized & taken before Emperor. Said he wished to rid the world of a plague — Nap — ordered him to be confined but to have every thing he liked. He had eau de vie & used to get drunk in prison. He continued in prison until the time of Naps first downfal[l] when he was liberated — When Nap was replaced on the throne he returned again & was taken in the same place on Tuilleries staircase — He had large quantities of fulminating powder about him He fell in the [284] By a singular coincidence he fell in the [1] very same place of the Staircase — The fulminating powder exploded, he was terribly burnt — & taken home almost lifeless — The Baron visited him when in this situation — he died of his scorching.

Passed Evg at the Storrows — Music.

At table today much conversation about the descent upon Eng[d] The Genl [said?] that if they could have landed they would have had London immediately — The Baron did not believe the invasion was ever really intended — if it had taken place he thinks it would have been instead of Moscow the rock on which the emperor would have been wrecked —

Gen[l] says the English are good troops — They fight well. They learnt it by fighting the French in the Peninsula.

Little Doctor said the English were the only en-

[1] Irving's repetition.

emies of the french that acted with consistency & character. They were always opposed and always the same the rest changed about, one time truckled to the Emperor another time rose perfidiously against him

[285] *Thursday. May 13.* Still experience a want of Sound sleep at nights. Wake early & rise unrefreshed — get up at 6 this morng — Write this morng on alterations of tale of my uncle — Feeling rather worn & exhausted I set off for town between 10 & 11. On arriving at Paris went to Mills — Left my ms: of robbers with him — went home — Mr Beasley is quartered for a day or two at our Lodgings — called at Galignanis — they are very anxious to get Agent for America — Get a few books of them — ret^d to Mills found Edgill there — Mills pleased with the alterations I had made in the Robbers story — return to Auteuil — pass rest of the day & evg with the Storrows — return home at 10.

Friday. 14. Commence writing before 8. Rewrite Poor devil author — Morng held up — at 2 oclock go to Mrs Storrows & walk in garden — read Heaven & Earth [1] — dine at home. Evg at Mrs S. Charles & Sam home

[286] *Saturday 15 May.* Slept well last night Showery day — rewrite Hist. of Manager & introduction to Literary dinner [2] — rec^d letter from Mills — at 3 oclock called at Storrows. Mrs S in town. Staid

---

[1] *Heaven and Earth, A Mystery,* by Lord Byron, London, 1824.

[2] "Literary Life," "A Literary Dinner," and "The Strolling Manager," in *Tales of a Traveller,* pp. 135–143; 278–299.

there to dinner — read Italian — Evg told story of
Number [of?] ms — ret[d] home 1/2 past 9.

16 Sunday. slept well last night — Wrote a little
at various parts of Buckthorne &c — Beasley &
Peter came out at 10 — latter brot me letter from
Mills. Inclosing note concerng Pelasgian Cities.
Walked with them to Mrs Storrows. After bidding
them farewell ret[d] home & rewrote part of Buckthorne &c and arranged 1st vol of the work.

Dined at Mrs Storrows & passed Evg there —
wrote letter to Mrs Van Wart. Ret[d] home at 10.
Cold rainy weather. Had to keep a fire at Mrs
Storrows.

[287] *May. 17. Monday.* Wrote alterations to
Buckthorne & send off Mss: of first volume by Marianne to Peter to have it copied. Walked in garden at
Mrs Storrows — Susans birthday 17. Day Sunshiny
but cool — nightingale singing in day time — While
at Mrs S. Mills called and left a line mentioning the
death of Lord Byron at Missolonghi April 19. Dined
at home. Return in evg to Mrs S. Birth day f[ê]t[e] —
Mons. Cansano comes in & talks nothings the whole
evening — return home at 10 oclock — cool enough
for fire at Mrs S.

Tuesday May 18. cold enough for a fire in my room.
rec[d] letter from Payne — transfers to me the furniture of the apartment — make various corrections in
Mss: of robber tales &c call at the Storrows — Go
into town — Stop at Mills — he mentions a subject
for a narrative death of Murat — Sir Henry Mildmay
comes in — vexd at the talk of a satirical person

(185)

called Lounge in Tuilleries. — On my way to lodgings Meet Mr & Miss Gibbings. At home get Mss: with corrections from Peter — call at Galignanis — ret[urn] home — visit from Dr Kissam and Mr Agree with young man to copy Mss at 5 sous a page — small page dine with Peter — Return to Mrs Storrows read Italian — then part of Moores fire worshippers [1] — return home 10

[288] Wednesday May 19. Wrote at Kidds anecdotes in Wolfert Webber — corrected various parts of work until near 4. Went to Mrs Storrows — walked in garden — dined there — read italian and part of Moores Fire worshippers.

Thursday 20. Slept well. Rewrote various parts of Wolfert Webber — notes to it &c — rec[d] letter from Mills. Went into town — Saw Mills and agreed to start with him on Monday — dined with Peter — ret[d] in the country Walke[d] out — arrived at Auteuil 7. walked in Mrs Storrows garden — read italian — Miss & Mr Walker — Music — returned home at 10 1/4

[292] [2] Friday 21. — Slept well. This morng — rewrote parts of Tom Walker & latter part of Wolfert Webber — till 1/2 past 11 Walked in the Bois de Bolougne — with the Storrows. Italian lesson — dined with them — passed Evg — there and ret[d] home at 10.

Saturday 22. Rainy day. packed up trunk — went out at 1/2 past 12 — to Storrows — sat there till 4 —

---

[1] The third section of *Lalla Rookh*, London, 1817.

[2] Pages [289], [290], and [291] are blank.

(186)

read fire worshippers — Italian &c — ret^d paid Bill at Hotel & took leave — ret^d to Mrs S. dined there — sent for trunks in Evg & slept at Mrs Storrows — farewell

Sunday 23. Rainy morng — Took leave of the family & ret^d to town. Call^d on Mills — Left card at Mrs Mansfield — Called on Coles — Galignani — corrected Mss: dined at home with Peter & passed Evg at home

[293] *Monday May 24* — Galignani called on me — We signed agreement about the Collection of British Literature[1] — At 10£ a volume for collating & correcting Biographies and notes &c. Write letter for him to Ebn^r Irving to appoint agent — wrote a private letter to E I. to same purpose — Livius called on me — Freyschutz to be played early next season — Called at Douglas, found Grattan there, who goes to England in a few days — Mr Douglas just ret^d from Italy — where he had nearly been taken by the Brigands — Mr Cornel called on us — Dined at home with Peter —

JOURNEY TO ENGLAND

Left Paris at 1/2 past 6 oclock with Mr Mills in his carriage — rainy cold Evg — Drove through Nanterre &c &c arrived at St Germain & put up at

[1] "Mr. Irving is to select the authors and the parts of their works to be published. He is to collate and correct the Biographies and notes . . . but it is expressly understood that he does not obligate himself to contribute any original matter. That is to be left entirely to his own discretion." From the manuscript of this contract, in the possession of Dr. Roderick Terry.

Hotel D Angleterre — shewn into a handsome carpeted salon — Had tea in English style A good fire & [294] sat & chatted till 1/2 past 10 — It was like a winter evening —

Tuesday May 25. Anniversary of my departure from America [1] — Rise a little before 6 — breakfasted between 6 & 7 Left S' Germain about 8. Day cool & cloudy but clears up gradually and after part is fine — travelled all day without stopping — passed Rosny — fine avenue along the grounds bordering on the road — Great bend of the Seine — high hill just after leaving Rosny which commands a fine view — Mantes in distance — from which we had made a great detour in coming by Rosny — Pont de la arche a pretty place — a mere village —

Early in day after leaving S' Germain pass by Poissy — beautiful trees on the Seine — [295] — noble view of Rouen at a distance from Hill of S' Catherine — like Tupps hill on Mohawk [2] —

Arrive at Rouen 8 oclock — put up at Hotel de France — order a dinner & a roaring fire.

Wednesday 26 Rise at 7 — Diligence preparing to start in court yard — Looks like 3 coaches fastened together — Noahs ark — people entering — the birds (3 ladies) in front — the animals in center & the creeping things behind. English servant cleang his masters shoes in court yard. My ladys maid displaying herself at window.

[1] May 25, 1815.

[2] Irving's associations with the Mohawk River, in New York State, began in 1802. To these he often alluded in later writings.

Exorbitant bill at the Inn. Mills quarrels with Landlord & Landlady — we start at 10 oclock — beautiful weather — cool but clear [296] Race on the road between postechaise and driver of mallpost [1] — Indignation of Postechaise against the latter whom they call a Sacré Savoyard — arrive at Dieppe at 3 oclock — rusty little old town — battered motheaten walls and gateways — little old castle like a wart on a hill — Still there is a picturesqueness about it — put up at Hotel d'Angleterre kept by Taylor — quite an English house — Sorry for it — should rather have had french hang to the last to enable one to enjoy the contrast of England. Walk on Pier — Tame looking English — Little old Englishman with tawdry cap & slatternly wife — Tall Englishman with white hat white pant[loons] & big belly. — one whom I'll warrant they call *a gentlemanly man*. Old Englishmans daughter walking with french subaltern officer & evidently pleased with her beau. At dinner Mills wishes me to write on the subject of the story of Girls of the town & to draw pictures of their wrongs.

Took tea. Evening fine star light — Lights gleaming on harbour —

[297] Thursday May 27 Left Dieppe at 10 oclock on the Rapid Steam boat — beautiful day on board were Sir   Paul Mr La Touche Mr Farr Mills — Had fine smooth passage landed at Brighton on the flying Pier at 8 oclock Put up at Old Ship Tavern — Take tea with Mills & traveller

[1] Malle-poste, mail-coach.

Friday 28 — Great vexation at the Customs house — Ridiculously strict — Take petty articles from Travellers — Leave paynes dressing Box to be retaken to France Left at 11 oclock in Coach for London Mr Farr — Mr La touche & Mills were fellow passengers. Warm sunny day country beautiful — passed thru Cuckfield & Croyden Arrive at White horse cellars at $\frac{1}{2}$ past 6 — leave trunks there & go to Covent Garden theatre — see 2^d representation of Charles 2^d [1] — took trunk &c to lodgings provided me by Mills in [298] 22 Henrietta S Cavendish Sqr — where I am stowed away in a room that a cat could not turn in.

Saturday 29 — Breakfast at Leslies with him & his sister — go with him to Mr Bridges [2] where we dine on cold tea ales &c. Call at Newton — visit the Exhibition with Newton Superb painting of Leslies Sancho in Chamber of Duchess — excellent painting of Newtons Mr Pourceau[g]nac [3] Call on Mills who I find suffering under Ennui — Call with him on Moore — find Moore in high spirits The success of Capt Rock [4] has quite elated him — letter from his wife — says My dear Captain Rock I found 3 pounds in your drawer [299] & went to stores [?] to buy you a present

[1] The play in which Irving and Payne had collaborated. *Cf.* p. 62.

[2] Probably Sir Samuel Egerton Brydges (1762–1837), the bibliographer and genealogist, whom Irving knew well.

[3] Newton's *M. de Pourceaugnac, or the Patient in Spite of Himself* and Leslie's *Sancho Panza in the Apartment of the Duchess* were first exhibited in 1824.

[4] *Memoirs of Captain Rock, the Celebrated Irish Chieftain*, London, 1824.

— My ticket on Lottery has drawn a blank — Tom brags to every body that its all her own — Called with Moore on Lady Landsdown — charming handsome woman — Called at Lady Donegals who was too unwell to see me — Saw the Miss Godfreys & Miss Barbour — called on Mr   Moores old friend — who invited me to accompany them to Bath — Met Moores friend Mr Nevins [?] & promised to dine with him on Monday — called on Murray. Cordial reception Murray told me at once that he would give me 1500 Guineas for my next work without [300] seeing it — Met Mr   Later Mr Cohen there — Dined with Newton — Mr Foster came in & sat part of the Evg — called with Newton at the Storys but they were at the Opera — returned home at 11.

Sunday May 30. Slept very ill — Breakfasted with Rogers in company with Newton Leslie and Procter [1] the poet. Rogers said that when Lord Byron & Lady Caroline Lamb quarrelled — Lord Byron told him When man & woman fall out the one that keeps the ground longest wins. Lady Caroline gave in ten minutes before me

Lady Caroline took all Lord Bs letters — made a funeral pyre of them put his miniature on top — had a number of young girls to dance round singing a kind of incantation [301] & burnt them — but mark you they were only copies — & what made this ridiculousness complete was that there was no one present to be taken in by it but herself *& she was in the secret.*

[1] Bryan Waller Procter (1787–1874).

He said when Lord & Lady Byron separated Byron told all his friends & Rogers among the number that he alone was to blame

Rogers thinks Murray the great loser by the burning of the Mss: as he bought a post obit work not to be available until the death of a man younger than himself — of course he ran a great risk — unexpectedly the death of that person makes the Mss: available in the course of a year — but he is deprived of his bargain Rogers says Moore does not recollect the Mss: & he says he does not believe Moore read it — As while in paris he [302] was so continually engaged — he had not time to read even his Billets doux —

Rogers suspected he himself was handled harshly in the Memoir as Moore did not show it to him —

Jones called for me & took me in his gig to Dinner to Mr Williams — Met Newton & Col Aspinwall there ret home at 10 1/2 —

[303] Monday May 31 Breakfasted with Leslie — Powell [1] came in after Breakfast—Went to Paynes whom I found surrounded with newspapers conta-[in]g critiques on his new comedy a Mr   and young Holcroft there

returning home called on Mills — walked with him — called on Wm Spencer [2] — who invited me to take up my quarters at his lodgings — to which I gladly

---

[1] Peter Powell, an intimate and whimsical friend of Irving's during the latter's association with Leslie and Newton in London, in 1820.

[2] William Robert Spencer (1769–1834), man of wit and poet. His lodgings were at 4 Mount Street, Grosvenor Square.

consented — called on Lord & Lady James Stewart
— then on Mr Mrs Holloway where I met Mr John
Neal author of Logan [1] &c —

Returned home — touching at Newtons — found
Payne at my lodgings — revised his play — At 7
called on Mills & accomp^d him to Mr Moores to
dinner — where I met with Mr & Mrs   of Wiltshire. Mr Lattin — Mr Becker — husband of Miss
ONeil — Dinner very pleasant much conversation
but I was nervous & uncomfortable — Sat at [304]
table till 11. More company came in in the Evg —
but I came away & returned home

Tuesday June 1. Breakfasted at Newtons — called
at Mills; who introduced me to his brother Charles —
a neat genteel man, with the quiet, sensible english
manner — Strolled with Mills to Newtons who accompanied us to the gallery. Then went with Mills to
his Elder Brothers — a Bachelor, who keeps estab-
lisht in town & country — great Sportsman — a perfect Gentleman. Tea table standing — took tea between 1 & 2 — Fine old chased silver Tea Kettle —
on stand with tea & sugar set to match. The Elder
Mills talked of the Forest men about new Forest &
the river — Knew scarcely any thing — had no law
— believed the river belonged to them & they had a
right to all it produced — faithful to one another,
honest witness sometimes — but tho 500£ a [305]
reward had been offered they never betrayed each
other

[1] *Logan, A Family History*, Philadelphia, 1822. The author was John
Neal (1793–1876), the American novelist and critic.

(193)

Called at Lady Donegals found Moore there who sang several of his new songs for me & then accompanied me home.

Dined with Newton at the Storeys and accompanied them to Drury Lane theatre — Miss Stephens [1] benefit — a vast deal of bad acting & bad music. Comedy of Errors concert & no sing no supper — Moore joined us at theatre — Walked home together afterwards — witnessed row with two young men, who were taken in charge by the watch.

Wrote to Mrs Van Wart & Mrs Foster.

[306] *Wednesday June 2*^d Breakfasted at home — marked omissions in play of Ch^s 2^d [2] left card at Hoffmans — called at Paynes and left Mss: Went to Mr Williams got 85£. Called on Col Aspinwall who gave me particulars of Kidd.[3] Called on Miller — who accomp^d me to Price, who is ill of gout — Sent letter to Peter. Called on Mr Philips M.P. and on Murray.

Dined with Jones — present Mr & Mrs Welles — Mr Burt — Mr Brook — Mr Newton Col Aspinwall — Mrs Welles gave me a Seal — returned home at 12.

[307] *Thursday 3*^d — Breakfasted with Mr & Mrs

---

[1] Catherine Stephens (1794–1882) acted with Elliston at Drury Lane, from 1823 to 1827.

[2] After witnessing his play Irving wrote: "It succeeds very well, though the critics attack the *language*. The fact is, the first act is extremely heavy, in consequence of being extremely ill played . . . I shall assist Payne in pruning the piece to-day, and I have no doubt it will have a good run." Irving to Peter Irving, London, May 31, 1824, quoted by P. M. Irving (*op. cit.*), II, 193–195.

[3] *Cf.* p. 176.

Welles. After breakfast accompanied them, with Jones Chas Williams to Epsom Races a cloudy cold uncomfortable day — Returned home 8 in the Evg — went & took a solitary dinner at Hatchetts (White Horse cellar) & returned home

Friday 4th Breakfasted at home — write preface for Payne — went to Newtons — returng homeward met Moore accompanied him to Lady Donegalls whom we found in her drawg room. Walked with Moore all the morng — he was making various visits, errands &c &c called at Murrays.

Dined with Mr Charles Mills, met there Mr Frank & John Mills, Mr Drummond & two other gentlemen — much talk about racing. In Evg went to Miss Whites met there with Moore, Lady Morgan [308] Mr & Mrs Croly [?] Lord & Lady James Stewart. Moore sang for us — Went afterwards with Moore & Newton to Mrs Inmans [?] — Heard Pasta & Rossini — introduced to Duke of Sussex [1] & — his eldest Daughter Miss Vuppel [?]. Met with brother of Sir Geo Shea — ret^d home at 1.

rec^d letter today from Mrs Foster

Saturday 5th called at Paynes with Ms: to be copied. Left card at Mr Rush's called at Sothebys [2] — promised Mr Sotheby to come to him at Epping Forest on my return from the country. Called at Mr Rogers. Rogers anecdote of dinner invitations — was going in country Invited by Lady Jersey to come on

[1] Probably Augustus Frederick, Duke of Sussex (1773–1843).

[2] Probably Samuel Sotheby (1771–1842), the antiquary and book-seller, although Irving may allude to William Sotheby, the author.

certain day & dine — when he returned to town —
She would take no denial — happy to get him at any
rate—he promised if he returned he would[309]come.
Was asked by Lady Barbara Ponsonby — he had
so often — disappointed her — must come &c &c —
The Duchess of Somerset told him he must come —
She was always at home & would be always glad to
see him &c &c He returned to town at the day —
called on Lady Jersey — Well you are coming to
dine — thats so good of you — This is so friendly —
Well — make no stranger of me — I could dine elsewhere — Lady Barbara Ponsonby has asked me &c

Why really — to treat you as a friend — we are
expectg a great many our table is full & if you could
dine with Lady Barbara — You see I make no ceremony &c —

He went to Lady B. Ah — you are come to say
yes — thats so good of you — I shall never forget it
&c &c.

Why I have come to accept — but yet dont put
yourself to inconvenience — I can dine else where —
why really we have [310] issued invitations as many
as our table will hold — but Mr Luttrell has not replied — If you could see him & know whether he
comes or not. If he does not come & you would take
his place we would be so obliged — He had now his
dernier resort — the Duchess of Somerset who was
always glad to see him & would always take it as a
favor to dine sans ceremonie So he called on her —
but she never said a word about his coming to dinner
— In fine the man of many friends eat his dinner

alone at a coffee house & spent a miserable triste evening at a theater.

Called at Lady Spencers [1] — found her in saloon looking on the park — she was writing billets — a hearty woman, talks heartily — laughs heartily at her own speeches when [311] there is no joke — says the devil occasionally — hates the french — Says Englishmen are taken up with hunting — racing & shooting — Lord [2] & Lady Derby came in — his lordship a little bald roundheaded amiable man — Lady Derby tall & thin, and evidently has been elegant — once Mrs Farren [3] — Complimented me about my works — Invited me to visit them at Knowsley — Lady Morpeth came in (whom I had once seen at Holland house — afterwards Lord Spencer — called & left letter & card at Mr Moriers Dined at Lady Donegalls en famille — the two Miss Geof[f]reys & Barbara — very pleasant dinner — staid tea & then went & saw part of Matthews American olio [4] — very stupid & tedious — went behind the scenes & saw Matthews afterwards — & then returned home —

[312] Sunday 6. June—Called on Newton—Mills — Payne — early — returned to Newtons and

---

[1] Wife of John Charles Spencer, Earl Spencer (1782–1845). An interesting letter from Lady Spencer to Irving is in the possession of Dr. Roderick Terry.

[2] Edward Stanley, twelfth Earl of Derby.

[3] Elizabeth Farren (1759?–1829), an actress praised by Hazlitt for her "fine-lady airs and graces."

[4] This was presumably Charles Mathews's *Trip to America* (1824), with its caricatures of various American types, black and white.

walked out to Lord Lestourls[?] — called on Sir John
& Lady Maria Stanley — promised if I came in their
neighborhood in Lancashire to call on them. Called
on Rogers & accomp^d him to his Brothers at Padding-
ton. Rogers stopping to speak with various persons
on the way the Duke this Sir Harry that — stopped
to hear music — observed that he liked to hear music
in warm weather — Pass the White Conduit house —
speculates upon the character and concerns of people
whom we meet — tells anecdotes of Lord Byron when
he saw him at Pisa in Italy — His sister at dinner &
several nephews —

In evg thick fog came up — ret^d by coach — pretty
woman in it — Rogers facetious —

[313] *Monday* 7th Rise at 6 — Write to Mrs. V. W.
Sent 5£ to Payne by twopenny post. At 8 start in the
Telegraph [1] Southampton coach, with Mr. Mills on a
visit to his brother in law Mr Compton at the Manor
house. Stoney cross near Southampton in the new
forest. Fine weather for travelling, pleasant & sunshiny — Whitsuntide — pass several mutual relief
societies dressed with cockades — On the hill in sight
of Southampton we find Mr Comptons chariot waiting for us — neat equipage — his own postillion in
bl[ac]k jacket & white breeches & white toppd boots
— footman on Dickey — delightful drive through the
New forest — wild & rough Enter the park: looks
like wild land — weeds, fern — undergrowth of
brambles, &c — Suddenly come in sight of the house

---

[1] "A fancy name for some kind of carriage." *New English Dictionary.*

— with ornamented grounds about it contrasting the wildness of the forest — beautiful distant prospects [314] Spire of Southampton Church & — Fine apartments in the house — Mrs Compton a frank pleasing intelligent woman with a prepossessing countenance Mr. Compton tall, manly & handsome about 36. find him at some chemical experiment. At Dinner we have General   Fane & Sir Vivian who both distinguished themselves on the Continent [1] — dined at seven.

retired to bed at 11 — north room

[315] Tuesday. June 8. Lovely morning — fine view of the forest from my window — small church at a distance on hill — cuckow heard. Write in my room till breakfast time — Breakfast near 10. Coffee — tea — marmalade — eggs — cold meats on side table — After breakfast Mr Compton & Mills have a fishing net on the grass to examine — Go to the Library — eastern exposure — pillars east end — portraits — sophas — arm chairs — tables &c of all kinds. Go to my room & work at Mss: At ½ past 1 — walk out with Mr C and Mills — pass by small church — Visit stone where William Rufus was killed — Shallow valley with clumps of trees. As we descended into the valley we met a funeral going up hill towards the church. Found two gentlemen on horseback at the stone one hammering at it with a stone to chip off a memento — stone quite defaced — called

[1] Sir Henry Fane (1778–1840) fought at Victoria in 1813 and Orthes in 1814. Sir Richard Hussey Vivian (1775–1842) served in Flanders, Holland, Spain, and France.

at Mr Comptons nieces — in small cottage suffering under a paralytic stroke.

[316] Return home — Loll on grass with the children — at ¼ past 4 mount the horses & ride with Mr Mills & Mr Compton to visit   remarkably pretty woman called at the Kings house & saw the iron stirrup of Wm Tyrrel[1] and it has remained his private property ever since.

Dined at home — ret[d] to bed at 11

Wednesday June 9.   Early in morng ex[amine][d] Mss: of Wolfert &c — beautiful morng — at 12 we set out on fishing party Mr Compton Mr Mills on horseback one of the Boys on pony & I drove Mrs Compton, two of the children & the tutor in a low car drawn by black horse — called Dusky Sludge ride thro beautiful forest scenery — glades, heather, groves of birch — &c saw herds of deer — groups of light horse, as to morrow is review day — Huge trumpeter — groups of horsemen riding at distance thro forest toward stoney cross—helmets gleaming — repast under tree by brook.

[317] the gents drag a forest brook for trout catch very few.   Horses get away from peasant & gallop about the heath — we are attended by one of the forest Keepers.   Return home thro woods by a track across turf — beautiful forest with green carpet of grass under it — get home at 6.   Dress for dinner — Sir Geo Ross a great Bavard.[2]   Col Russell — Mr & Lady   & Mr

---

[1] Irving probably alludes to Walter Tirel or Tyrrel (*fl.* 1100), who is said to have killed William Rufus.   [2] Talker; gossip.

Thursday 10th Rainy day — Col. Russell at the house, having come over to review the yeomanry. At 1 Oclock he and Mr Compton rode over to the review, in the rain — the Col in uniform — Wrote letter to Peter & sent parcel contg Mss: of Ital[ian]. Bandit[ti] to E. I. via Mr. Williams. Loitered about the house all day.

At dinner Mr & Lady   Wemyss — Lady Errol sister of Ld Somerville Col Frank Russell, Capt Somerville brother of Lord Somerville [318] Lady Wemyss beautiful — Lady Erroll agreeable — Mr. Wemyss rather conceited — They spoke at dinner of an old curmudgeon of the name of Tunk who lived at Ringwood[1] — passed for rich had several stacks of Barley always standing near the road — had a bank at which the country people deposited their money When he died he was found not to have been worth a farthing & his barley stacks were full of rats — much talk of Box[in]g — racing — parsons &c Retired to my room ½ past 11.

Friday 11. June. Fair weather though cool — receive parcel from Payne contg the residue Mss: of my work. After breakfast Mr Compton, Mills & myself set off for Bitterne on shoot[in]g & fishing excursion. Mr C & myself in gig — Mills on horseback — pleasant drive thro forest by Stoney Cross a lonely public house on bare hill above Rufus stone — pass public house where women go to lay in being ex-

---

[1] The name of this village probably suggested the title of one of Irving's sketches, written many years later. See "The Early Experiences of Ralph Ringwood," *Wolfert's Roost* (1855), p. 279.

parishioner[s] [319] came down upon beautiful broad
fertile valley of the Avon to Ringwood a neat little
market town — pass farm of old Tunks. —

House of Earley the smuggler who cheated his fellow smugglers who trusted a large sum to him to pur-
chase cattle & liquor — got the cattle & liquor on
trust & cheated creditors likewise — died some years
after — His son squandered all away & died of drink
at 32 People about here think that money ill got does
not stay — Rode along thro soft fresh scenery — the
Avon running thro broad meadow land — came to
Bitterne — an old fashioned manor house — pointed
wings — built on old part — vaulted cellars in arch of
Henry VII house built on plan of Inigo Jones — Old
Poll, near the gate comes toddling out of cottage to
open the gate — drive into yard — stables &c all
vacant — find lad to take care of horse & go into the
house. Stone corridors — old fashioned rooms — one
looking out on a quiet bowling green with sun dial —
salt meat room —

[320] Stroll about wet meadows — Mr Compton
gen[1] Fane & a Mr. Fitzgerald of the navy shooting ducks — kill 16 couple & an owl — old Wotton
dragging net — catch one salmon & two or three
Jacks & several roach. Old Wotton fisherman to
Mills Brother — descended from a family of fisher-
men who have lived about there for ages — Wotton
said — so called for 700 years — Always poor as rats
— Wottons son Moses.

We punt about the river — clear out & roused wild-
ducks in sedge — go to land pass thro straggling

hamlet of Avon — Blacksmiths shop used to stand on the site of one where Tyrrel changed his horses shoes when he escaped. A brick Shop in center of road where a cross road comes into main road — hard by the Old Queen Inn — Near it is Tyrrels Ford — so called to this day — Light horseman of the yeomanry sauntering about the hamlet in his uniform. Return to Bitterne — take a lunch of cheese & ale — Servant who had been to Newfoundland and [321] among the Esquimaux. Return home at 5 with Mr Compton — fine ride part of the way thro the forest by   the seat of old Lady Londonderry — see deer in the woods — ride across green sward &c — arrive home at 7 — & dress for dinner — receive letter from Payne

Saturday 12. Receive parcel from Payne — play) Walk about the farm yard and garden with Mr Compton — visit cow house — great number of cows, Norman breed & Norman & Devonshires — Keeps them always in stable — they give more milk & richer — are less trouble — give more manure — it is cheaper & more profitable — they are less troubled with flies — Pigs — two of a wild kind almost wild boars — garden — pigs — pines &c &c — beautiful shrubbery — ride out with Mr Compton & Harry the latter on white pony — dogs — Dash and Truly — day overcast — ride by rufus stone — Through forest — turf — mosses — bogs coverd with bright green verdure — come to Keepers lodge — in a wild [322] part of the forest. Brick house — great number of Dogs — about it who set up terrible barking — pointers —

newfoundland Dogs — fox hounds — Hawks & crows nailed ags^t house — Keeper Mr Hunt, a stout made man — talked of Deer straggling about — difficulty to keep them to the walk — been out these two nights after them — Mr Compton tells of Gypsy encampment near Sir Hussey Vivians — that had been 3 days there Time to send them off — they ought not to be allowed to pass more than one night — Get too well acquainted with the neighborhood Hunt tells of partridges that he had seen — we ride on — through deep forest scenes to the house of Mr Harbin — jolly old fellow who laughs like a crane — White hat — light hair — large sandy face — stout made — coat of dark green with forest buttons — leather leggings — He gets his pony & rides with us — laughs a great deal — tells storys of smugglers — He has lived here between 30 & 40 years — in a bleak high [323] part of forest — came there once on a hunting party took a liking to the place bought it & has lived there ever since. Was once to London — met with a girl of the town — liked her — brought her to the country with him — she lived with him 30 years till her death. His house keeper was burnt to death about 2 months since — had lived with him 30 or 40 years — very old — He lives alone — shoots a great deal — rides about — will not go out to formal dinners — sees any body at his own house — no road to it — but tracks along the green sward.

told of superstitious notion of people that smugglers money never thrives — all money got in that way or ill gotten in any way never stays by the gainer.

Talked of fishing — of Dogs — Deer &c. Had the stud book — a volume of shakespeare &c — on a shelf. We rode over heaths and thro wild parts of the forest — Deer bounding about — Told of the former smugglers — most of them near coast had a smart horse and cart that could turn briskly to any thing

Horse stealers — gypsies great rogues in this way. Horses passed from hand to hand [324] one rides horse off 40 miles gives her to another who rides another 40 miles & so on — gets horse in return —

We come to Bramble hill lodge — beautifully situated on slope of hill with superb prospect over the forest — decent Woman-Keepers wife who talks to us. Keepers boy calls the deer with a kind of chaunt — to browse — throws potatoes to them — then branches of ash trees of which they are extremely fond — pleasant of summer evg^s about 6 to hear the keepers from the different lodges calling the deer to browse. — continue our ride thro forest — beautiful beech trees — Hawthorn in bloom — fragrant — Mr C tries to get Mr Harbin to go home & dine with us but in vain Old gentleman takes leave of us in the lattice near rufus stone and gallops homewards. We return home —

Dine at home enfamille — pass the Evg in the Library —

[325] Sunday. June 13. Cold & rainy — fires in breakfast room & library — breakfast at 10. Write letters to Mrs Foster & Payne — pass the day in the library — reading Congreves Love for Love —

Glanville on Witches — Rabelais — Gilpins New Forest [1] &c.

Library a noble room — with great bow-window. Volumes of yellow composition at each end. Portraits above the book cases — one of an old lady in antique dress who defended the right of the family to the manor against the pretensions of the crown — At the other end of the library — portrait of Knight in armour — Book cases with gilt wire — tables & writing desks of various kinds — sophas — deep arm chairs of all fashions well cushioned — Japan[e]d India screen. Materials for writing in all directions

Box for letters for post office stands in the Hall.

First breakfast bell 8 Oclock — breakfast hour ½ past 9. Cold meats & wines stand on side table until 3 oclock — first dinner bell ½ past 6. 2^d — 7. Dine at seven precisely — afterwards coffee & tea — at 10 oclock wine — lemons & hot & cold water & case of liquors brought in go to bed generally at 11.

[326] Monday June 14. Rise before 5. Shiny morning. Breakfast with Mills — at ½ past 5. Mr Compton rises to take leave of us. A little after 6 we start in difft Post Chaises — He for Mr Edgills near Staines — I for Bath — ride for some time thro the new forest — then thro open pleasant country. Weather held up towards 8 — at ½ past 8 arrive at Salsbury [Salisbury] — or New Sarum — pleasantly situated in verdant valley with little stream slipping

[1] Probably William Gilpin's *Remarks on Forest Scenery*, London, 1791.

through it — Weather fair — visit Cathedral — in remarkably good preservation — of hard grey stone uninjured by time cathedral has a very neat precise style — a wedding going on in it — a Miss Ayre to a gentleman with a name resembling that of Pringle — I stoppd at the Regent Inn.

Numerous old picturesque houses in Salisbury — particularly near the cathedral some with grass plots flower gardens &c before them — Old gate ways — walls moats.

[327] At ½ past 11 — set off for Bath on outside of a coach — fine day — pleasant route through gentle valleys with stream of water on the left — Thro Warminster.

Arrive at Bath about 5. Stop at York Hotel, but go to White Lion having engaged to meet Mr Moore there. Moore not arrived. Difficulty to get a room, the town so full — get a small room no 22.

Dine in Coffee room. Just before arriving at Bath the weather thickened up & began to rain. A cold rainy Evg — Did not know what to do with myself — too cold to walk about—read news papers three times over — dozed & drank tea to pass away time — returned to my room between 9 & 10 & will now go to bed.

[328] Tuesday June 15. Weather cool, but does not rain — go to church to Oratorio. Before the performance meet Sapio who tells me with an air of great mystery, whispering in my ear, that he has an engagement in Drury Lane for 2000£ a year. Meet

Philips [1] the singer, looking like an old half pay officer — Music good. Loder [2] the leader is a good musician & understands his business

After the service the day is fine — I am joined by Philips at the door of the Inn who proposes to introduce me to Catalani.[3] I accompany him to his room where he introduces me to a Mrs & Miss Harvey Speaks in great terms of the latter who is his scholar & of whom he expects to make great things — call on Catalani — suffering with a cold — she is an extremely natural creature speaks broken English and so does her husband — old faddy [4] clergyman comes in Mr. Bowen — Mr. Loder also — On taking leave Catalani shakes hands in English style. Philips with his easy confidence proposes me to walk [329] with him & the ladies — cant refuse — paraded round bath — Introduced in passing to a Mr   a gentleman who writes in the Quarterly Musical review.

On returning to Inn find that Moore has arrived — but gone out — shortly after meet him & Mrs Moore with a Mrs   with them.

Dine with Moore tete a tete in coffee room. Go with him & the Ladies to the theatre — bad concert — vast number of ugly old women there. Bath is quite a perch for these old birds — This morng at

---

[1] Henry Phillips (1801–1876), who established his reputation as a singer in this year.

[2] Probably John David Loder (1788–1846), the violinist.

[3] Angelica Catalani (1780–1849), one of the greatest of concert and operatic sopranos.

[4] Crotchety. Irving uses the word repeatedly in his writings.

Church had seen one dressed in green like old paro-
quet. Return home sup & go to bed about 12.

[330] Wednesday June 16. Breakfast with the
Moores. Mr Elwyn calls on us at breakfast invites
me to dine with him — with Moore &c Go to Abbey
have good seats in the gallery Music — Mount of
Olives by Beethoven — Ach[1] by Brooks & Manners
— Selection from Handel — Insufferably long —
talked with M about the clergy. Stout doric columns
— pillars of the church.

Walked about after the music — dined at Elwyns
— present Mr — Mrs & Miss   the latter beautiful
— Dr Crawford & lady — Mr Mumbleton, a gossipping old beau — Evg — went to the concert at the
room with the   talked much with Miss   a very
beautiful girl — Her father invited me to Farley
[Farleigh] — to shew me the castle — Catalani sang
came home at ½ past 11

[331] Moore says — I have often thought, when I
have had a little too much of Rogers & been where I
could not get rid of him — "who shall deliver me
from this Death."

Jekyll,[2] in crossing one of the courts of Law with
Moore saw the lawyers going across generally two &
two — & one very large man alone — Jekyll immediately observed — the Mourners two & two — *The
Body* —

Sheridan once met his son Tom after the latter had
been guilty of great irregularities — They came upon

---

[1] *Ach! Gott vom Himmel*, Luther's hymn, a paraphrase of Psalm XI.
[2] Joseph Jekyll (d. 1837), politician and wit.

one another suddenly at the turning of a corner. Sheridan addressed him with warmth — Sir I have done with you — &c I have cut you off with a shilling — Tom looked at him wistfully You do not happen to have the shilling about you Sire?' The reply was irresistible.[1]

[332] Thursday June 17. Breakfasted with Moore — rambled together about Bath — He introduced me to a little Bookseller near the Abbey Church — called at Catalanis, who was not up.

Left Bath at 11 in post chaise with Moore for his cottage [2] — drove thro very pleasant country. Moore told me an entertaining story of his becoming acquainted with a lady who had just buried her husband.

Arrived at the cottage between twelve & one — very pleasantly situated, and a delightfully arranged little retreat. We rambled about the fields & to Bowood the seat of Lord Lansdowne — a princely mansion of stone — with columns in front — fine park around — found Lord Lansdowne at home who received us very kindly walked over the grounds with us — pretty water fall — wished us to stay to dinner — accompd us part of the way back — begged me to call on him when I came to town — returned to the cottage to dinner — pleasant dinner — In the evg a

[1] Irving probably obtained this story from Moore, whose life of Sheridan appeared in the next year (1825).

[2] Sloperton Cottage, two miles from Bowood. Moore lived here intermittently for thirty-five years, and is buried in the nearby churchyard of Bromham.

delightful walk — pleasant landscape of village — viewed the village of   with its fine old [333] church — passed the Evg at the rectory — The rector ill abed — large family of sons & daughters — very pleasant ret^d home about ½ past 9 — & went to my room at 10 but remaind readg Lord Byrons Ms: Memoirs till ½ past 12.[1]

Friday 18. Rose at 7. Read more of Lord Byron while dressing. Pleasant breakfast — After breakfast adjourned to Moores study where I prepared a dispatch for Murray of part of the Ms: of Strange Stories.[2] Moore read the whole suite of Strange Stories and expressed a most favorable opinion of them [3] — Dined a little after 2 that I might get to   in time for the coach. After dinner set off with Moore — Mrs M & Mrs Brannagan accompg us part of the way. Had a very [334] pleasant walk with Moore thru Lord Landsdownes grounds to Mr   where we found the coach had just passed. Stoppd there & took tea while they sent for a chaise — Bowles [4] church & parsonage in sight —

Had a pleasant gossipping cup of tea & then took an affectionate leave of that charming fellow Moore. A brilliant in head and heart —

[1] This manuscript made a profound impression upon Irving. He was constantly mentioned in the gossip of the day as one of the very few who had seen the manuscript before its destruction. Moore's life of Byron appeared in 1830.

[2] "Strange Stories by a Nervous Gentleman," Part I of *Tales of a Traveller*.

[3] Moore seems to have concealed his real opinion. *Cf.* Introduction, xii.   [4] William Lisle Bowles (1762-1850).

A beautiful drive to Bath thro pleasant villages —
Chippenham &c Arrive at bath at 9 oclock — 18
miles (in 2 hours) & put up at the White hart —

[335] Saturday. 19. June. Leave Bath at ½ past 7
oclock for Birmgᵐ Distant about 92 miles — Day
drizzling & in the course of the day heavy rain. Rather
uncomfortable — having an outside seat. Pass
through Gloucester, Tewkesbury Worcester — arrive
at Bᵐ 8 oclock. On the way find Hope Richard[s] in
the Coach on the way to visit at Mrs Van Warts —
on arriving take her home with me — find the family
all well — & the little Gills there on a visit.

Sunday 20. tried to write this morng at Story of
Capt Kidd, but could not get under way — Mr
Wright called — Mr Goddard & Mr Goullet of the
royal navy — passed the day at home excepting a
visit to Mr Wrights — In Evg — told stories to the
children —

Monday 21. Get up at 6. Breakfasted with Mr
Van & Hope Richards The latter set off for Liverpool
— a rainy day. Staid at home & wrote Kidds story in
the money diggers.[1] In Evg — played on flute for the
children to dance

[336] Tuesday 22ᵈ June — rainy morng — re-
touched some part of Kidd — made up parcel of the
Ms: of Wolfert Webber & sent it off for America —
with letter to E I. Walked down to the warehouse —
met Rann Kennedy [2] who talked of his long projected

---

[1] "Kidd the Pirate," in *Tales of a Traveller*, pp. 426–434.

[2] (1772–1851), poet and scholar, and from 1807 to 1836 second master
at King Edward's School, Birmingham. " ... My particular friend, the

(212)

poem & his sons gaining prizes at the university —
Met Mr Merinden returned home & remained at
home the rest of the day Told stories to the children
in the evening.

Wednesday 23. Rainy day — at home most of the
day — Sketched adventure of the German Student [1]
— wrote letter to Newton — rec[d] letter from Marianne from Paris —

Thursday 24. copied & finished story of German
Student & sent it to Murray — at home most of the
day — visited the library in the afternoon — detestable cold rainy weather.

[337] Friday 26. rainy day — At home all day —
copy out Hell gate [2] & Capt Kidd — a Mr Caldwell
dines with us — a clergyman of North Carolina Had
been fellow student of John Randolph [3] at Princeton.
Says Randolph at college did not get on well in his
class preferring to read according to his humour —

Rev. Rann Kennedy . . . is a most eccentric character, and is both my
admiration and amusement." Irving to Henry Brevoort, January 29,
1817, quoted by P. M. Irving (*op. cit.*), I, 360.

[1] "The Adventure of the German Student," in *Tales of a Traveller*,
pp. 60–68. This story Irving had heard at Sloperton Cottage from Moore
who had obtained it from Horace Smith (*Cf.* p. 105). The incident is
typical of Irving's use of sources in writing *Tales of a Traveller*. Part I,
which is concerned with German themes, is in debt somewhat to Irving's
stay in Germany and Austria, but this Journal reveals his dependence
upon secondhand narratives and anecdotes. For an able analysis of the
sources of Irving's German stories see H. A. Pochmann, *The Influence of
the German Tale on the Short Stories of Irving, Hawthorne, and Poe* (a
dissertation in the library of the University of North Carolina, 1927).

[2] "Hell-Gate," in *Tales of a Traveller*, pp. 421–425.

[3] Irving met John Randolph at the trial of Aaron Burr, in Richmond,
in 1807, and knew him well in London, in 1830.

read a great deal — Caldwell pleasant man but uncommonly shabby in appearance —

In the evg Charles Storrow arrived —

Saturday 27. fine weather Wrote to Mrs Storrow & Susan & to E I. Touched Cathedral town — part of D° [1] — call at Mr Carter. See Mrs C & Emily — receive letters from Sullivan. Mrs Foster — Peter — Evg — Mr & Mrs Wright & Mr Salt sup with us —

Sunday 28. Set off at 1/4 before 7 in morng for Kenilworth & Warwick. In Chariot with Mrs Van W. & the girls Mr Van & the boys. Mr Salt accompd us in his gig. day cloud[s] up early & is dripping throughout — breakfast at Knowle — ride thro Warwick. Dine at Kenilworth — Mr Van &c go to see Mrs & Miss Blair — Visit Kenilworth [338] Met a Mrs Boddington, wife of a surgeon who acts as cicerone — Stop at Mrs Hawkesworths school & see the Miss Gills. Return home by 8.

Monday June 29th. Altered & sent Poor Devil author to Murray — Wrote to Peter — Col Aspinwall — Dined at home. Mr Ingleby dined with us. After dinner drove the boys in Mr Wrights gig to Aston church [2] — Evg — supped at Mr Wrights on cornbread — present Mr & Mrs Van Wart — Mr Salt Mr Goddard — ret[d] home at 11.

Tuesday 30. Called on Mrs Merinden —

Wrote to Marianne & Mr Storrow — Had my hair

[1] Ditto. Apparently an allusion to a story or sketch which was never published.

[2] Aston Hall in Birmingham had been Irving's model for the castle described in *Bracebridge Hall* (1822).

cut — Dined at Mr Kennedys. Present Mr & Mrs Greene Mr & Mrs Garbet Mr & Mrs Cooke & Mr terribly heavy dinner. Talk about livings & clergymen & colleges &c &c — get home ½ past 10 tired to death

[339] Wednesday 30th. At ½ past 10 start in the coach for Oxford — fine day — dine at the Red Horse [1] at Stratford — get to Oxford by 7 oclock — great dilemma. The colleges vacation commences today — every coach chaise &c engaged to take students home — take tea in coffee room of Mitre tavern — apply at coach office till 11 — at night — filled with students applyg — pay the men at office double fare to furnish me a place — get off at 12 in top of coach — have a dismal night — two lubberly students & a bull dog leaning on me all night — Arrive at London at 8 —

Thursday July 1. Breakfast with Newton — call on Murray — who promises proof sheets in a day or two — visit Lady Donegall — write to Mrs Foster — Buy shaving case &c. Lunch at Newtons & at 4 oclock set off with Newton and Willis [2] for Sullivans at Weybridge — pleasant ride — arrive there at 7 — Dine & go to bed at ½ past 10 — heartily tired & sleepy

[340] Friday July 2d Damp morng — Breakfast at 9 — walk about grounds — find a singular high road

---

[1] At this inn Irving composed in 1816 the first draft of his essay "Stratford-on-Avon" (*The Sketch Book*, 1819). The Red Horse still has a room containing "Geoffrey Crayon's Sceptre," and other relics of Irving's associations with Stratford.

[2] An Irish landscape painter.

cut thro the turf by ants from one tree to another —
— ride out with Willis — fine view from Hills over a
woody country towards   Rode to the village — return about 2. Neighbor comes in — a round headed
young man — hard & loud — takes Newton off to
look at Hogarth prints — Walk with Willis & Mrs
Sullivan to haunted house — ramble about & dine at
¼ before 6. In Evg walk out again — a Mr   passes
the evg with us — retire to bed at ½ past 11.

Saturday. July 3ᵈ Beautiful morng — Breakfasted
early with Sullivan who drove me in his pony gig to
Hounslow. Passed Horse guard on the road on the
way to Hounslow for review — at Hounslow get on
coach for London. Road thronged with troops — carriages & four — Post Chaises &c all going to the field
day at the Heath.

Arrive in town ¼ past 10. Stop at White Horse
Cellar — go to Murrays not at Home [341] Clerk
throws me all aback by telling me Murray does not
intend publishing my work till November. Call again
at Murrays & wait for 2 hours. Murray out to see
Hobhouse [1] about Lord Byrons remains which have
just arrived. Wrote to E I to stop the publication in
America — Walk out & meet Mills — Walk about
with him — stop in at Bully Andrews who gives me
ticket for opera — call again at Murrays — see him
— he agrees to publish the work immediately [2] —

---

[1] John Cam Hobhouse, Baron Broughton of Broughton Gyfford
(1786–1869), statesman and Byron's executor.

[2] *Tales of a Traveller* was published on August 25, 1824. It was far
more unfavorably reviewed than *The Sketch Book* and *Bracebridge Hall*.

write another letter to E I. Dine at Johnny Gaunts
— go home — nap — dress and go to opera — Romeo
& Juliet. — Romeo — Pasta — Juliet — Renji [?] de
Beyne [?] — the Father by Garcia — finely performed
crowded house. Meet Trotter [1] — introduced me to
his cousin Mrs Linsay a pretty woman. Took me
behind the scenes — come in to Lady   Box her
daughters the Miss Frazers there — Met Mr Chas
Mills Mr Scott &c &c. at opera — returned home ½
past 12 — slept sound [342] P. S. Some question
whether the Dean of Westminster will permit Lord
Byrons remains to be buried in the Abbey — The
Bishops only chance for immortality is to refuse —
They talk of its being a private funeral!

Sunday July 4. Rose after 9 — Breakfasted at 10.
called on Jones sat with him till 12. Went to Camp-
bells [2] — a breakfast to a large party. Genl L'Allemand — Genl Pope — Lord Dillon — Sir Chas. Morgan — Mr Colburn &c.

I was introduced to Genl L'Allemand —

Walked afterwards with Colburn to New Road.
Called at Leslies No. 1 S' Johns Place Lisson grove
north. Found him & his sister at Dinner. Dined
with him staid to tea — his first day in his new house

See the *Literary Gazette*, August 28, 1824; *Literary Chronicle and Weekly
Review*, August 28, 1824; *Blackwood's Edinburgh Magazine*, September,
1824; and *Westminster Review*, October, 1824.

[1] Captain Trotter, an English army officer, whom Irving had known
in Dresden.

[2] Thomas Campbell (1777–1844). Irving edited an American volume
of Campbell's poetry in 1810. Irving and Campbell were intimate from
1816 to 1825 and from 1829 to 1832.

— We afterwards walked in Regents Park — He & his sister went to Mr Dunlops — I called on Payne — not at home — ret^d home at 9 oclock

[343] *Monday 5.* While at breakfast rec^d note from Jones telling me of Van Wart & Wrights arrival & breakfasting with him — rec^d first proof of Tales of a Traveller went round & took second breakfast with Jones. Walked with Jones & Van to Vans Lodgings & to Inns of Court — called at Davidson the printers White Friars to make arrangements about the printing of the work — He told me that Tegg [1] had intended printing a 2^d vol of Salmagundi but had desisted on Davidsons remonstrance. Went to 4 Mount S^t & got a letter left there from Payne & one from Mrs Foster — P.S. Payne called at 12. Says he expects to get the Coburg [2] & wants to get dramatic assistance.

Called at Murrays. He shewed me a great parcel of letters in his Iron chest which he said was from Ld Byron — Thinks the Dean will refuse sepulture to Lord Bs body in Westminster Abbey.

Arranged with him about preparing a corrected edition of Salmagundi.

On my way home was taken up in her carriage by Mrs [344] Story & her pretty daughter — took me home & waited till I dressed — found Payne waiting at my room who talked again about the Coburg — Mrs Story sat me down at the Albany. Dined with

---

[1] Thomas Tegg (1776–1845), a London bookseller famous for his cheap reprints and abridgments. He had published a London edition of *Salmagundi* in 1823.

[2] A theatre.

Jones — Van W & Wright — went afterwards to Haymarket saw 12 oclock precisely [1] — Sweethearts & wives [2] & Fish out of Water [3] — House hot the pieces grotesque but overcharged & fatiguing came home about 12.

Tuesday 6. July. Called an[d] sat some time with Jones. Wrote to J.K.P.[4] requesting essays from Salm^gd — Sent letter to Galignani. Set off for Bedford. At coach office met Payne who came to take leave of me. Set off for Bedford at ½ 2. Passed thro Islington — Barnet — Hatfield pretty place — fine view of the church with trees about it & the old brick mansion of Lord Salisbury to the right. Country very rich & fertile — Arrived at Bedford ½ past [345] 8 — found Mr Fosters servant & gig waiting for me. Took me to Brickhill — where I arrived about 9 — & was welcomed by the family in the kindest manner.[5] A Mrs Rorderer there on a visit

Wednesday 7 July. Rose at 7 cloudy morng — after breakfast wrote to Peter & Sullivan — Walked in the ground[s] & to Bedford with Mrs Foster & Emily. Called at Mrs Fosters sister in law — saw Miss Eleanor Foster — a beautiful girl — ill with rheumatic gout — called at Old Mrs Livius [6] — monastic lookg house — Yew trees in the yard —

---

[1] Milner's play, *Twelve Precisely; or, A Night at Dover.*

[2] Kenney's play.

[3] A play by Joseph Lunn (1784–1863).

[4] James K. Paulding. *Cf.* p. 116, footnote 2.

[5] See Introduction. All traces of the Foster family in Bedford have vanished.

[6] Apparently the mother of Irving's friend, Barham Livius. *Cf.* p. 3.

Walking thro Bedford saw the Bumbailiff in a gig
driving a young lady. He is the dandy of Bedford.
Dined at three. Weather clears up beautifully —
After tea walk with Mrs F. & Emily — set out to
drive Margaret [1] & Flora in Pony cart — The Pony
stumbles — comes down, breaks [346] his traces & the
shaft of the cart — We walk about the ground & then
return — After supper walk by moonlight with Mrs
Foster & Mrs Rhorderer — Mrs Foster talks of the
great number of noble Palaces in the western Part of
Germany along the Rhine & the Nacar [Neckar] —
Bonne [Bonn] — Coblentz [Coblenz] Mantz [Mainz]
Biberich — [Biebrich] — Mannheim — Worms —
Heidelberg — Wurtzburg [Würzburg] Stutgard [Stutt-
gart] &c &c — these princes must have been rich —
palaces some of them now falling to ruin — Ecclesi-
astical buildings also —

Italy also — convents in remote places that did a
great deal of good — people in their vicinity more
civilized —

went to bed about 11

[347] Thursday 8th July. rose at 8. After breakfast
corrected proof sheets of my work & sent them to
Murray. Sent duplicates to E.I. via Miller Lond.
Drove with Mrs Foster in Pony car to Mr Grimshaws
— Livius Brother in law — He was from home —
Mrs Grimshaw at home. Cottage covered with roses
& Honeysuckles — Garden beautifully laid out in
bed of flowers — roses of all kinds — superb white

---

[1] Margaret Foster, the eldest daughter of John Foster, by a previous
marriage.

Poppys — magnificent walnut Behind the house — House very prettily fitted up & furnished — Returned home to dinner — After dinner walked in the Hay fields — Beautiful weather — Warm, sunny, but airy — Haymakers busily employed taking advantage of the weather — perfume of the hay stack when it begins to get warm. Sheep draw to the summits of the hills — a sign of good weather

At tea a Mr Mardin calls — the curate of the parish — formerly an officer in the army & has been wounded — a zealous clergyman we had sacred music — He expounded a chapter of the bible & prayed [1] —

Took a walk by moonlight round the [348] lawn with Mrs Rhorderer before going to bed — Beautiful moonlight night — nearly full moon — perfume of the flowers & the new hay — went to bed between 11 & 12 —

Friday. 9 July. After breakfast talked for some time with the ladies about american bird[s] Went to my room; made alterations in some parts of Buckthorne story — Sketched preface to the work. Rec^d Proof sheets & a letter from Payne — Corrected the former & replied to the latter — Sent the whole by post; with additional Mss to Murray. Showery morng — held off for a little while — walked half an hour with Margaret & Mrs Rorderer — At dinner we

[1] Irving was not at ease in the atmosphere of this religious household. "I felt out of tune there where you were all wound up to so high a key. I was a little jarred too by the well meant but unskillful and unseasonable handling of some of the professional persons I met there." Irving to Emily Foster, Paris, August 23, 1825, in *Yale Review*, January, 1926.

had Mrs Frederick Foster & her sister and Mr Latrobe nephew of Latrobe the American architect. After dinner walked a little — Music in the Evg — Retired about 11.

[349] Hot climates produce smaller quantities but higher qualities of plants [1] — Fruits of finer flavours. Wheat of superior quality — More temperate climates produce the greatest abundance but of moderate quality. The spices are of tropical climates — almost vertical.

Saturday 10. Wrote this morng retouching the Stroll[in]g Manager [2] — Rec⁴ proof from Murray. Visitors — Mr Simeon — fellow of S' Johns Cambridge & professor of theology.[3] Mr Madan & Mr Tatham — Mr Simeon very eloquent — soft spoken — waxes warm and eloquent — says a blow in the stomach causes instant death & produces no rigidity in the members — posed by a sudden question of Mrs Foster. Backed by scriptural quotations by Madan — Makes a kind of volunteer sermon & then proposes prayers from brother Madan — All kneel down and pray.

[350] return to my room and write. After dinner walk with Mrs Foster — Margaret & Mrs Rorderer to a small church at a distance. Tombstones of the

---

[1] In 1805 Irving was an amateur student of botany, a subject, as the notebooks show, in which he never entirely lost interest. See "Washington Irving's First Stay in Paris," ed. S. T. Williams, in *American Literature*, March, 1930.

[2] "The Strolling Manager," in *Tales of a Traveller*, pp. 278–299.

[3] In spite of minor errors in this description, the visitor was probably Charles Simeon (1759–1836).

George Palmers father & son the former had two wives the latter three —

Farm house of the present Geo Palmer a long brick building, with pointed wings. Clusters of chimneys — One window over grown with yew & ivy — Sundial leaden water spouts &c

In Evg — Mrs Foster had been to Mrs Livius & seen Mr Simeon — Mrs Livius was telling a sad story of a clergyman receiving a messsage from a lady in trouble wantg to see him but he must come blindfolded — He complied. Found her in bed — recollected to have often seen her at church — said she was a jewess — wanted to be confirmed in the church but her relatives opposed it & finding her resolute had determined to make way with her — and there said she [351] pointing to a heap of stones in a corner of the room are the stones with which they are going to stone me to death to morrow — ah madam said Mr Simeon had I been there I could have accelerated the corner stone for I swallowed the stories after the ceremony.

Nay said Mrs Livius — Mr Greene told it me with tears in his eyes. Ah — said Simeon — Greene — Is not that the gentleman who was tired with the version of the Whales swallowing Jonas & so put it that Jonas swallowed the whale — Indeed! — said Mrs Hale — Mrs L[ivius's] niece — why I did not know that any one held that belief.

fine day today — sunny — airy — wind &c &c good Haymaking

[352] Sunday 11 July. Fine weather — Rec^d proof

from Murray. In morng went to church to S' Pauls Church. Heard Mr Simeon preach a sermon for the benefit of society for converting the Jews. Took the weak plea of our having derived the doctrine of salvation from the Jews because the saviour & the apostles were Jews — So they were naturally but not originally. In as much as they preached the doctrines of christianity the Jews persecuted & destroyed them

Busy little sexton like nodd[in]g monk — had long wand of office & went tattapping about on tip toe conferring with church wardens about drawing a window curtain &c —

Dined at one in town with the ladies — Returned home — wrote a little at Robbers story — Returned to Bedford took tea & sent my despatch to Murray. Went to church & heard a good sermon from Mr Maddan — Returned home about ½ past 9. On the way I was introduced [353] to the Livius's —

Monday July 12. Wrote to P.I.[1] requesting him not to come to Eg^d. Set off in carriage with Mrs Foster, Emily & Flora — & two boys & Trappaneger in Pony waggon for Ampthill. Beautiful day. Ampthill park. Immense old oaks — short, massive & enormous — were considered in Oliver Cromwells time too old for use — fine views from the Park. Passed by the largest oak. — hollow — on this are lines by Lord Holland — gentlemanlike poetry — on summit of a Hill is an antique stone cross marking the place where the old castle stood — Catherine of Aragon was confined there.

[1] Peter Irving.

Drove to Woburn Abbey. Fine avenue of trees. Large palace built round a quadrangle. Saw the marble gallery — Canovas Graces in a recess at one end — statue of the Dukes daughter a child with a dove on its bosom by Chantry — a son of the duke — a child also — opposite — at the other end of the gallery in a recess Busts of Fox — Ld Holland — Grey — Spencer &c &c

[354] — curiously laid out French garden round the house. Heathery — China Daisy — little gardens of the young Lord & Lady with Grottoes Arbours &c with their names over them. One who had gone to sea had an anchor in box, planted beside his arbour in remembrance of him. Riding house — Went through the main building — fine saloons drawg rooms & galleries richly gilt — & furnished in magnificent yet pure taste — fine paintings — Among the curiosities saw the walking cane of Charles 1. of ivory — and of the Russell who was beheaded —

In a corridor a collection of pretty models of Spanish costumes — A biscuit coloured —

[355] Walked through the Park to Woburn — great herd of deer — Woburn a neat village — dined at Skinners — who invited us in at tables — a showy man — full of bows — Mr Foster came to Woburn in gig & dined with us.

Beautiful drive home in Evg — stopped at Millbrook church. Situated on a ridge of Hill — with deep rich glen on each side with houses of village and a fine look out over the broad flat of Bedfordshire —

arrived home after ten — quite tired — drank tea had pleasant chat and retired —

[356] Tuesday. 13. July.   Beautiful weather — Wrote all day correcting Robber tales — despatched the Mss to Murray — The ladies were at the meeting about Jews — In the Evg walked to Bedford with Mr F. He gave me an acc^t of Moravian establishment — of making roads. Mac Adam only has 14 or 15 inches deep of broken stone — which answers as well & better than the old mode of having a foundation of large stones as used in Germany —

took tea at Mr Fosters Brother—Pretty Eleanor better than when I last saw her. Dr Palley there — made dry grave jokes —

came home about 12 — a beautiful moonlight night

[357] Wednesday 14. July.   Fine morng — about 11 oclock clouds come up — Severe thunderstorm which prevails more or less through the day —

receive proofs — & a letter from Payne & Marian[ne]. Finish correcting Robber stories — write to Payne — Newton & Mrs Van W. Go to Bedford — & bespeak place in coach for tomorrow to town — at the George. At dinner we have company. Mr. Mrs. Miss & Young Mr Higgins. Old lady with surfeit on face — a wig on with wreath of small roses. Veil — yellow shoes &c &c daughter pretty. Father — a man with head clumsily cut out of a block

Mr Payton & daughter in gig from a Hall 17 miles off. Pleasant gentlemanly stuttering man — I saw

him 9 years since at Vanwarts — Daughter a fine girl
— Dinner — much talk of Tythes — Poor titles &c
— They go off in shower — sit up with the family till
11. & retire

This morng — the Revd Mr Grimshaw & the rev^d
Mr W. A. Ivanson called on me The latter I had met
about 4 years since at Willis's

[358] Thursday, July 15. — Breakfasted with the
Fosters and took leave of them a[t] 1/2 past 8. Flora
at parting gave me a little ms book. Drove in the
Pony car to Bedford — took place in coach — fine
weather & fine road — had a pleasant journey to
town. On the way we met a thin middle aged man on
foot — Who the coachman said walked for his living.
He was of good connexions & decently brought up —
but was Idle & drunken. His brother on dying left
him 30 shillings a week on condition that he was
to have his home in the village about 50 miles from
London and go up to London every week on foot to
receive the money. If he was ever detected mounted
in any vehicle or on any animal he should forfeit the
whole. He has been several years padding the Hoof
& is quite reformed in consequence — He is met as
regularly as the coach — Talks but little & never
admits to the cause of his preferring to walk on foot.
Children annoy him in the village running after him
& calling him the Wandering Jew &c

On arriving at the Boar & Castle I found [359]
Payne waiting for me — Took coach for Mount S^t —
Payne left me married & single to revise. Found
Spencer at home — called at Murrays & got proof

(227)

sheets — called at Newtons — ret^d & dined with Spencer — his son & daughter in law — retired at 10 oclock to my room

Friday, 16. Payne breakfasted with me — Talked over his farce of married & single[1] — called at Davidsons the printers — Then at Miller where I met Price — Perkins & Mr Bull called at Newtons. Then Murrays where I met Mr Hamilton — ret^d home — called with Spencer on Mr Morier (author of Hadji Baba [2]) met there Mr & Mrs Morier — Lord James Stewart Mrs Tyghe — Mrs Cuff — Morier a large, pleasant goodlooking fellow — extremely natural and goodhumoured — Goes to Mexico in a few days

Dined at Newtons — Welles dined there — very pleasant dinner. In Evg went to Miss Whites — met there Moore — Morier [360] Newton, two Mess^r Tighe — Mrs Tighe, Lady Stephens — Mrs Cuff Lady Lestourl, Dr Holland. Introduced to Mr Basil Hall,[3] — a plain looking man — not very entertaining or prepossessing — Moore sang several songs Came away with Moore & Newton. Came home — found Wm Spencer at home & sat & chatted —

Moore told of Currans remark upon a fellow who had a habit of singling out his neighbor in company & boring him with long stories. 'Sir' he has an itch for talking & makes use of you as a scratching post.

---

[1] *Cf.* p. 43.

[2] James J. Morier, *The Adventures of Hajji Baba*, London, 1824.

[3] (1788–1844), naval captain and author. His book on America, which Irving used in preparation for his *A Tour on the Prairies* (1835), was the result of travel several years after this meeting with Irving.

Engaged myself to dine with Lady Lestourl on Sunday.

[361] Saturday 17th July Sat to Newton to alter my portrait — Mr Foster came in — Lake also — Moore, Kenney, Miss Holcroft & Mrs Shelley [1] — came in —

Walked out with Moore — Called on Mr & Mrs Methuen — a handsome couple — Mrs M — beautiful — Invited me to come & see them in Wiltshire — In the course of our mornings ramble we met Mr Martyn — the humane [2] — called at Powers — shop & house & saw the family —

Dined at Mr Moores, near the Park — with Kenney, Moore, Newton & Fitzroy Stanhope — sat long at table — talk about Scroope Davis [Davies [3]] from thence went to Mr Storys to supper all the party dull & heavy — Kenney got lewd with the cushion on which Miss Morier sat — Got home near 2 oclock

[362] Sunday July 18. Got up at 9 — breakfastd exd proof sheets — Sat to Newton — Jones came in — Recd visit this morng — from Mr Morier (Haji Baba) & Mr Maddocks — Lord Dillon was at the Spencers — Went with Moore & Newton to Lord Lestourls to dinner. Met there Mrs Cuff — Mrs   The Knight

---

[1] Mary Wollstonecraft Shelley (1797–1851). The complete story of the relations of Irving and Payne with Mrs. Shelley during the next few years is still unknown. Some account of this curious friendship is given in *The Romance of Mary Wollstonecraft Shelley, John Howard Payne, and Washington Irving*, Boston, 1907.

[2] Richard Martin (1754–1834), "Humanity Martin," so named for his many services to humane causes and societies.

[3] A long account of this dinner occurs in P. M. Irving (*op. cit.*), II, 210.

of King — The two Mr Tighes — Mr Latham — Sat till 11 oclock — an excellent dinner but tedious — afterward — Moore sang for us in the saloon & we returned home

[363] Monday. 19th left Ms: of Ital Banditti [1] at Murrays — fussd a great deal about ascertaining passage to Yorkshire &c —

Dined with Jones. Welles dined there — a very pleasant dinner — passed the evening there till ten — then strolled to Grosvenor square — & parted.

Story of Wm Spencer of a maid of Honor at the Court of Darmstadt — had taken a violent antipathy to the portrait of a Landgrave in the long gallery of Landgraves — could not account for it — was sure her fate was connected with it — whenever she went thro that long gallery she turned away her head — Was found one day stone dead before the picture —

Explanation — there was a stool close by her It was supposed she had got upon it to get near the picture determined to conquer her antipathy — had faltered seized hold of the frame & pulled the picture upon her — a corner [364] of the massy frame had struck her temple & caused her death.

(she used to say How can I be connected with that picture — no relationship — no affinity among my ancestors) — (Moore left London this morng)

Tuesday 20 July — Breakfasted at Newtons called on Murray — gave him Panselts [?] notes on Mexico which he proposes to publish called at Rogers —

---

[1] Part III of *Tales of a Traveller*.

found Kenney and Rogers brother breakfasting with him — sat & chatted till 12 — Kenney accompanied me home where I found letters from P I & Mrs. V. W. Went with Kenney to Leslies — Leslie accompanied us back.

Dined with Rogers tete a tete — He was very critical & censorious on Moore and others — Told a good story of the french abbes Parlez en Anglais [1] — Before the french revolution at the houses of the principal noblemen there would be a plate left for some chance abbe — & the [365] first that arrived took it — about dinner time you would see the abbes — noblemen resigned — picking their way from the top of one stair to another — ringing or rapping at the port cochers [portes cochères] & enquiring y a til de place [2] Non Monsieur — then he would tillup [3] onward. On one occasion at the commencement of the Revolution there was a large party dining — The Cart went by carrying criminals to the Guillotine — all the company ran to the windows. The abbe being a short man tried to peep on tiptoe but in vain so he went down to the port cocher. As the vehicle went by one of the victims who knew the abbe bowed to him — The abbe returned the salutation. What — you are his friend — you are one of them — away with him — The poor abbe was hoisted into the cart & hurried to the guillotine. The company having satisfied their curiosity returned to the [366] table — the Abbes

[1] Apparently an echo from the original tale.
[2] Y-a-t-il de la place?
[3] Canter.

finished dinner — Mais ou est Mons L Abbe — alas the poor Abbe was already headless —

After dinner walked with Rogers in the park — then called at Newtons where I found Jones & went home to supper —— —— [1]

[367] at 1/2 past 9 left London in hackney coach for Blackwall to embark in steam boat for Yorkshire — fare to Black wall — 12/ — breakfast 6 — called & took up travelers — Long dark ride thro London. — Fare to put us on board 2/ hackney 6^d.

The Steamboat James Watt — immense boat — poor accommodations — started at 12 oclock at night — Slept on a sopha or cushioned bench —

Wednesday 21. At sea — Beautiful weather — After breakfast recognize Mr Stewart Nicholson on Deck. Introduce him to Newton — Odd characters on board Auld rooky [2] with faddy face gingerbread cap & spectacles — goes to sleep in corner with book in hand & glass of spirit — old Lady in gingerbread gown & mottled cloak above head — little Roger Dean with parrot face — We run along part of the day in sight of the coast — past Yarmouth at which is a monumental column — stragglers wand[erin]g along the beach —

[368] Dinner — plain joints — no Desert — after tea sit conversing with Stewart Nicholson & Mr

---

[1] The lower half of the page (fifteen lines), written upside down, is illegible, except the last four lines, which are evidently parts of miscellaneous anecdotes: "a man whose whole soul might lie upon your thumb nail & leave an ample margin." "Great God Sir how these men in the cabinet cut us out work in the field."

[2] Irving frequently uses this word, meaning rascal.

McLeod — nephew of Dugald Stewart [1] — Nicholson gives anecdotes of Lord Wellington. The Duke considered himself surprized at Bruxelles. Intended to abandon Bruxelles & fall back upon Antwerp & receive the enemy in the plain before Antwerp but Blucher would not consent —

Wellington was dining at a public dinner at Bordeaux given to him by the authorities when he recᵈ a despatch from Paris informing him of the abdication of Bonaparte — He turned to his aid — Freemantle — "Well" said he in his knowing sportsman tone — "Weve run the fox to his hole at last." "What" — said Freemantle — "Napoleon has abdicated —" Freemantle uttered an exclamation of surprize & delight — Hush — said Wellington not a word — lets have our dinner comfortably —

[369] He laid the letter aside & they went on calmly eating their dinner — when Dinner was over — "There" said he to Lynch the Mayor of Bordeaux — "Theres something that may please you" The Mayor looked at the letter — In an instant he was on the table & announced the news — The saloon rung with acclamations for several minutes — The Mayor then begged leave to give a toast — Wellington — the liberator of France (*Loud acclamations*) — The Spanish rose & begged leave to give a toast — Wellington the liberator of France (*loud acclamations*) The Portuguese did the same — Lynch saw that the thing was going too far — He got up & gave Wellington

[1] See *A Tour in Scotland* (*op. cit.*), pp. 32, 33.

the liberator of Europe — Wellington who had sat picking his teeth, now rose — made one of his knowing cool bows to the company round — Jack said he turng to Freemantle — "lets have coffee."

[370] Freemantle had once come with a flag to Soult[1] Was about departing when Soult — said Mons le   If you will stop here a few minutes I will present you to the Duke of W. How Monsr Oh we know he is to be at such a place by such a time & are prepared to surprize him — Freemantles heart was in his throat — he knew the Duke was to be there. He accompd Soult to a rising ground — they saw the duke riding quietly along — accompd only by

On coming to a certain place He saw a number of Dragoons sallying forth from ambush & approaching him. He turned & spurred his horse in another direction — Another body made its appearance — He was between two bodies — He & his aid tried the speed of their horses. This wont do said W coolly we must head start two foxes & divide the Hunters. Do you take that direction I will this — away they went — Wellington escaped. He was in blue frock — His [371] aid in a scarlet uniform. The greater part of the Horsemen took after the latter — He was well mounted on an English Hunter. They came to a broad deep stream — He put spurs to his horse & cleared it at a leap the Horsemen not being prepared for such a thing nor their horses accustomed to it — were brot to a stand — he took his cap off knowingly made

---

[1] Nicolas Jean de Dieu Soult (1769–1852), statesman and Marshal of France.

them a sportsmans salutation & gallopped [*sic*] easily along to the camp — Freemantle who saw it took off his hat & waved it with a cheer of exultation —

These anecdotes Nicholson had from Freemantle —

Wellington was once while at dinner accosted by one of his officers letting him know that   was recconnoitering the camp — & requested he might fire on him we can hit him easily — No said W. let him look — the more he looks at them the less he'll like them. [372] Walked the Deck till 12 — talking with the Captain — Moon rose about twelve — a large red crescent rising thro a cloud —

Floating light in which 4 men take turns to live quarterly —

At 12 — laid down on cushioned benches in the dining cabin —

Thursday 22 July — passed last night on the benches in dining cabin. This morning we were off the high chalky cliffs of Flamborough head — with thousands of white sea gulls speckling the sea before it — before 9 we were off Scarborough — a picturesque little place with old ruined castle on a rocky height. We were landed there paid 3/6 for landing each of us with luggage — Went to the Hotel — breakfasted in the public room with company. The usual people are seen at all water[in]g places a fat old Lady & fat old gent talking common place — at the [373] other end a pretty warm eyed brunette in green making friends with a young country Squire a dandy by feeding his dog —

Go up to the fragment of old castle on the Hill —

below it an old church with a populous church yard —
Old outer gate way of the castle thro the Arch way of
which we had a fine look down upon Scarboro —

Leave Scarboro at 11. In post chaise — after riding over high bare land we come upon a broad rich
landscape — a variegated valley — ride through very
fine little landscapes — Noble & beautifully shaped
trees along the road — pass thro Wykeham change
horses at Malton — Old bridge & causeway at entering the town — fine mellow landscape after leaving it
— (in which it lies) Malton is a long straggling town
or rather two towns — new & old Malton. It is in
northern Wapentake [1] in the confines of north & east
riding.

Beautiful drive to Castle Howard the seat of Lord
Carlisle — the latter part [374] thro his lordships
property — pass thro a neat little village on his
property — Stop at the Castle Inn — built by the
family — order dinner & go to the castle — are shewn
it by a comely old Housekeeper — Fine painting of
the three Marys —

Spacious Saloons &c

Dine at the Castle Inn — & then take chaise for
York — Beautiful view from a hill over the vast rich
plain from which the towers of York Cathedral rise
like the dome of St Peters from the Campagna —
arrive between 8 & 9 put up at the   Inn take tea —
Stroll by dark to the Cathedral beautiful look of the
vast magnificent pile in the dark of Evg.

[1] In ancient times the chief administrative division of the counties of
Lincoln, York, Leicester, Nottingham, Derby, and Rutland.

Return home & go to bed by 11 —

[375] Friday 23 July — Attend morning service in the cathedral — where we are locked in by one of the vergers — Fine organ service finely performed — (vide mem: book) take walk round the town — Monks bar a fine old gateway — beautiful walk along the Ouse — Old town at junction of the Ouse & Foss — take lunch & leave York in coach for Leeds — from thence by coach to Wakefield — thence in chaise to Pontefract thence in chaise 3 miles to Ferry Bridge — just out of Pontefract pass the fine ruins of a church — Sleep at Ferry bridge — an excellent Inn

Saturday 24 July.   rise early — fine morng — Breakfast at 6 with passengers of a coach just arrived. Newton breakfasts previous to his departure for York. We are surprised by the entrance of Rogers of Baltimore — just from Hotham — going to Edinburgh — but intends to stop at York for a day or two being unwell — Part with Newton — ramble after breakfast along the river by a fine bridge over the Ayre [Aire] to a pretty little [376] country church, at least prettily situated — visit the grounds of a Mr Mills — at 9 — set off for London on top of mail coach — fine   day — pass   through   Doncaster — a neat place — on the race course were squadrons of Yeomanry mounted — Before coming to Doncaster pass by the Robin Hood Inn — (for various minutes of the days journey, vide little green mem. book [1] —) Dine at Newark on the trent — The Trent a smooth

[1] This notebook has been lost.

stream — Old castle of Newark of blackish stone near the bridge — a picturesque object — Newark a neat town — at dinner an excellent dish of Eels.

take tea at Stamford Rutlandsh^r — a very picturesque little place — old gothic churches — gothic houses — a bridge over a beautiful river — country seats & parks in neighborhood — among others the Marquis of Exeters —

[377] *Sunday July 25* travel all night — In morng — pass through Ware (a pleasant country) Edmonton — Islington — & enter London — Stop at Bull & Mouth Inn — breakfast there in large dingy coffee room — vile breakfast — after Breakfast go to Mount S^t N° 4 on the way stop at Newtons & get a letter from Peter — Having dressed I take coach for Greenwich — then a run to Woolwich — call at Major Cockburns — at the Arsenal — John not at home nor the Col. find the boys — Mrs. Cockburn & two ladies one a pretty interesting girl — look over Johns Drawgs —

Walk to Lea — Call at Brandrams. — not at home — walk to the Crown & Sceptre Greenwich — dine on whitebait & veal cutlet — both excellent — walk thro Greenwich — take coach return to town — half asleep on top of the coach — at home — fall asleep in my chair & sleep [378] a couple of hours — go to bed at a little past 10 — & sleep soundly & heavily all night —

Monday July 26. Rise at 7 after breakfast write to Sulivan and Mrs V. W. Call at Murrays. Correct proof sheets till near 3. Mr D'Israeli comes in —

about going to Germany—Call at Davidsons—find them all aback in consequence of Murrays objecting to the arrang^t of the work. Call at Murrays & get proof sheets to revise — call at Andrews who gives me an order for the English opera — receive parcel & letter from V W. Dine at Blue posts — beefsteak, cheese & ale — 2/8 — go to English opera & see Der Freischutz a wretched translation, badly played. Sat next to Smith author of Rejected Addresses. He said Braham was a Brummagem [1] Macbeth — Ret^d home at 11.

[379] Tuesday. 27. Write all the morning at Buckthorne — adding several pages to fill up the volume — vile Book work [2] — Dine at Blue posts — alone — return home and write until time to dress for the opera — go to see the opera of Tancredi (call previously at Mrs Holloways [3]) The opera well performed. Pasta — Rienzi[?] de Beynes[?] — Curioni [4] &c — At Opera meet Mrs Brannagan, just from Moores — and Mr Edghill — walk home with the latter. The Ballet kept us till 12 oclock — (*Page inconstant* [5])

Wednesday 28 July. Breakfasted with Mr Brandram. Albany E. 5. Talked over old travelling anec-

[1] Counterfeit, showy. Irving often uses the word in *Salmagundi*, and other early writings.

[2] This haste and revision, to satisfy Murray's "elbow-critics," was one cause of the failure of *Tales of a Traveller*. This Journal shows Irving inventing and altering until the very appearance of the book.

[3] At Mrs. Holloway's lodgings Irving wrote, in 1817, the early numbers of *The Sketch Book*.

[4] Alberico Curioni (*c.* 1790–?), a famous tenor.

[5] *Le Page inconstant, ou honi soit qui mal y pense.*

dotes. After breakfast went to Newtons and get 10 demijohns — returned home & found Mr & Mrs Sulivan — prevailed on him to stay a day or two in town — wrote all the morng at additions to Buckthorne — Dined with Mr & Mrs [380] Sulivan — Chapel plan Vere St Walked afterwards to Leslies & looked at his pictures — He was not at home — returned took tea with the Sulivans & ret^d home about ½ past 10.

Thursday 29 July. Leslie called on me this morng — went to Murrays found there would be much wantg to 2^d vol. Try to devise a new story. Sulivan with me part of the day. Sketched commencement of adventure of Polish count & his daughter.[1] Dined at Sulivans — Leslie there — In Evg. — went with Leslie to the opera. Romeo & Juliet. Pasta. Renzi de Beynes & Garcia sang finely — returned & supped at Sullivans. ret^d home ½ past 12 —

Friday 30. Wrote this morng at story of Polish Count. Major Cockburn & his daughter called — rec^d letter from Mrs V W. which I answered — finished sketch of story — dressed & called at Leslies — Mr Harding & Mr Beaumont there — Dined [381] at Mr Storys — present Capt Lane — Mr Vaughan & nephew Sir   & Miss Gore — Heavy dinner — talk about racing & Boxing — after dinner go to Vauxhall. A tedious place of amusement — return home ½ past 1.

Saturday 31.st Rewrote story of Polish Count & daughter — rec^d letter from the Storrows — & another from Ewing (Phila^d which I sent to Miller) Did

[1] See "The Belated Travellers," in *Tales of a Traveller*, pp. 333–355.

not go out till 4. Dined at Leslies; with him & his sister—In the Evg—the Miss Stones came in. Came away at a little after 9 — and returned home —

Sunday. Aug. 1. Corrected & rewrote Polish Story. Leslie called at 5 oclock. Walked with him to Ettys, who was not at home. Called on Mrs Brannagan but she had left town — Called at Millers — all out — Dined alone at the Mitre, a place where I used to dine 19 years since when first in London. House much changed different people in it. Dinner salmon, Roast Mutton ale & ½ pint port & cheese 4/6 Called at Paynes but he was not at home. At Kenneys — ditto — Ret^d home found cards from Mr Seabright — Edgill — & Mr Jones — called on the latter not home — retd home at 8 oclock & passed the Evg in my room

[382] Monday Aug 2. Wrote at story of belated travellers — sent it to Printers.

Dined this day at Brandrams — see — Blackheath his brother & Mr   Dined there — In the Evg a dance — Old Capt (now Col) Campbell there — 97 years old — Captain under Wolf[e] at the siege of Quebec, used to be called Handsome Bob — fine looking old gentleman — still walks to town occasionally. Mr Williams — Mr   governor of Greenwich Hospital — Mr Heath, an Italian Merchant (&c — in the italian trade) — Son of Mr Heath formerly of Genoa — born infirm — was fag to Lord Byron at Harrow — says he was mutinous — His story of Byron & the little bust of Napoleon which the little boys were shying at Brandram sister Mrs

[383] Tuesday 3 — before breakfast walked round the grounds with Brandram returned to town by coach — corrected Ms; & sent proof sheets to E I. Called on Jones — Payne called on me —

Dined with Jones at Mr Williams — Mr Harding there — In Evg to Opera — visit Box where was Mrs Story & Mr & Mrs Mc Leod — Opera La Donna del Lago — House oppressively hot ret^d home after opera

Wednesday 5. Wrote introduction to work called at Murrays — met with White there & had long talk. Called at Smiths and got passport signed. Called on Lenox — not in town — bought clothes in Bond S^t returng home found letter from Murray with objections of Gifford [1] to various passages of my work. Go to Jones' & dine in company with Dr Armstrong. Return home go to work & wrote till near 2 Oclock — altering my work. Insert sketch of clergyman

Receive letter from Mrs Foster.

[384] Thursday 6. Write all this morng at alterations write a letter to Murray — Call on him in the course of the day & find him much gratified by my letter — receive letter to day Van Wart. Conclude alterations & go to dine with Jones tete a tete. Evg to opera Semiramis, but too weary & sleepy to enjoy it

---

[1] William Gifford (1756–1826), first editor of the *Quarterly Review*. At an earlier meeting Gifford thus appeared to Irving: ". . . a small, shrivelled, deformed man of about sixty, with something of a humped back, eyes that diverge, and a large mouth." Irving to J. K. Paulding, London, May 27, 1820, quoted by P. M. Irving (*op. cit.*), I, 455.

Friday. 7. After breakfast go to Leslies find a Miss Ross there taking his sisters likeness in Miniature — Shew Leslie the Buckthorne family which he advises me to publish — return home — Bradish calls—then Payne — call at Whites — look over German books. Dine at John a Gaunts — call at Jones — Walk with him to Leslies — Leslie returns home with me and looks over proof sheets

[385] Saturday. 8 Aug. After breakfast, go down to Mr Davidsons. Find a man there whom I suspect to be Tegg — who was busy with Davidson about a book which I see to be Salmagundi — Takes up the book in confusion Sit there all the morng & correct proofs. Call at Millers & sit some time — return home, Dine with Jones — sit part of the Evg with him return home read Peter Schelmel[1] till near 2 oclock.

Sunday 9 Aug. Sleep but 4 — 5 hours last night. After breakfast call at Mills — sat some time with him — return home Bradish & Mills call —

Dine with Mr & Mrs Miller en famille — return home at 10.

[386] Monday, Aug 9.[2] After breakfast Kenney calls — order breakfast for him — talks abt his new piece which is coming out tomorrow Evg — Gives me order. Work all the morng at alterations in Buckthorne — Marring the story in compliance with critique of Gifford — come to a conclusion per force. Call at Rogers —

---

[1] *Peter Schlemihl* (1814), by Adelbert von Chamisso (1781–1838).

[2] August 10. Irving at this point dated his entries incorrectly.

Dine at Mr Mills — Dine 8 oclock. present Charles — John & Frank Mills — Lord Darnley — Hon Mr Byng — Mr   Mr Bing talkes much ab^t Sandwich Islanders —

Came home at 12 —

Tuesday. 10th Kenney breakfasted with me. In good spirits anticipating the success of his piece this Evg — Leslie called on me. Left card for Miss Barton — called at Leslies — Dined tete a tete with Mills. Went to Haymarket—Private Box with Miss Holcroft — Mrs Shelley Mrs Linton — Crossed [387] to opposite private Box with the Storeys — Went with Kenney to the Green room — Actresses assembled painted up — Mr Keten [?] Mrs Gibbs — Mr Farrar &c

Kenneys piece went off bravely —

Wednesday 11th Kenney came to my room after breakfast Looked pale thin & nervous — worried about his piece. Went down into the city worrying about getting proof sheets to the Galignanis —

At 3 oclock Frank Mills called for me in Mr Byngs carriage — Mrs Byng with him — drive to foreign office for Mr Byng — Went in there — large arm chairs — newspapers — Haunt of Visitors

Drove to Greenwich & dined on [388] white bait &c at Crown & Sceptre 16/3. Went afterward to Surr[e]y theatre & saw some wretched mummery — Very Sleepy — got home about 11 [1]

[1] The continuation of Irving's Journal, dated August 13, 1824, may be found in *The Journals of Washington Irving* (*op. cit.*), II, 7 ff.

WILLIAM THE CONQUEROR

FALAISE [1]

It was at a late hour of the night when we entered the old town of Falaise and stopped at the little Inn. As is usual in Normandy, we entered the Kitchen, in one corner of which is the comptoir [2] where mine hostess sits & keeps her accounts. Before the fire place was assembled a group of gossips — among whom I remarked an old fellow with a dusky red face an iron grey beard and his hair tied behind with a small piece of leather that left him the brush of a fox. A kitchen in a small Norman Inn is the general gathering place of all the household; and indeed throughout france, a man never considers himself as stooping from his dignity in entering the Kitchen. I looked round at this chamber, illumined by the flashes and blazes of a large fire of wood and brush — On making enquiries about the old castle of Falaise, famous for being the birth place of William the Conqueror, the old gentleman in [of?] the dusky face immediately took up the parole and began a long history of the castle and its events.

[1] Twenty pages of manuscript form this incomplete essay or chapter on William the Conqueror, written by Irving in Paris in 1824 (*cf.* p. 127). Irving conceived the idea of this essay during a tour in Normandy, from August 18 to November 19, 1820. Notes made at Falaise on November 18, were evidently the genesis of the fragment (*Journal, 1820,* in the New York Public Library). His plan was apparently to expand these by an adroit use of Masseville's *Histoire de Normandie* (*cf.* p. 110). The essay, which is in two parts, has not distinguished literary merit; the subject is trite, and the workmanship imperfect. Yet it deserves a place beside "Annette Delarbre," and the other products of these first years of Irving in France. In editing this fragment, I have followed the principles defined on xiii, xiv. The manuscript is at present in the possession of Gabriel Wells, of New York City, who has kindly permitted its publication.

[2] Counter.

The old castle of Falaise was originally built by the father of William, Robert of Normandy, commonly called Robert the Magnificent; though more poetically renowned under the name of Robert the Devil. He was a mad cap warrior, in his younger days, and acquired his name from the wildness and extravagance of his actions. The story of Williams parentage is whimsical and romantic. Robert had returned from the chace in the neighbouring forests, which stretch along the valley of the Bruyere [La Bruère] and was looking out of a window of the castle which commands a view of Falaise and the surrounding country. At the foot of the rock on which the castle stands was a fair pool of water which remains to this day, and is resorted to by all the good dames of Falaise, to wash their linen. At this fountain Robert beheld a beautiful girl busily employed in this humble labour. Her legs and feet were bare, and she was, if we may believe the old chroniclers and poets, of surprising beauty. Her name was Arlette de Verprey, the only daughter of a furrier of Falaise.

Robert appears to have been as ardent & zealous in love as in war, and to have had an amazingly quick eye for beauty; for though the nymph was at the distance of a good bow shot — he was thoroughly smitten with her charms. He demanded her of her parents, but met with unexpected difficulty. The parents would not consent to yield up their daughter but on honourable terms; and the fair Arlette was equally tenacious. Fortunately for Robert she had an uncle, an old hermit, who lived not far from Falaise, and who either secretly tampered with by the lover, or more anxious for the temporal than the spiritual welfare of his niece, prevailed on her to yield to the counts solicitations. Still the damsel surrendered on proud conditions, which shewed a loftiness of spirit, and doubtless enhanced her value in the eyes of her admirer. She insisted on receiving the same honours as if really the spouse of Robert, and her demand was agreed to; on condition that she would suffer herself to be privately brought into the castle, the following night, by the postern gate. To this she peremptorily objected and insisted on being escorted through the great gate of the castle, in open day, by the Knights of Robert. The amorous count had to consent, and the following day the Knights waited on her on foot; but the tenacious beauty refused to accompany them unless they came mounted on their horses. Every thing was at length arranged to her will, and she passed through the town in state, riding on a beautiful horse, surrounded by the chivalry of the castle. The great gate of the castle was flung open; the drawbridge lowered, and she entered amidst the sound of trumpets and the splendour of chivalric pageantry. The same judgement which she displayed in her surrender she maintained in her subsequent conduct, so as to secure the fondness & fidelity of her lover — and from this connection was born William the Conqueror.

Such was the anecdote related by the old gentleman in very rhetorical language, though I have sadly marred it in the repetition — It was listened to with great interest by the assemblage round the fire, and I found by their conversation that the good people of Falaise prided themselves not a little on their towns being the birth place of the Conqueror.

We were accompanied the next morning in our visit to the castle by the old gentleman in [of?] the dusky face, who I found to be an inhabitant of a neighbouring village, and withal a poet. The castle stands on an eminence above the town, and one part of it — the great Donjon or Keep is on the brow of a rocky precipice. The walls are prodigiously thick, and have stood the buffettings of many ages; but all the interior is in ruins. Still the window was pointed out to us from whence Robert saw the beautiful Arlette, and far below, at the foot of the precipice, was the basin in which she was washing, and which at the time I looked down, was surrounded by busy housewives, making a prodigious clattering with the batons with which they beat their clothes, and chattering at the same time like an assemblage of parrots. Nothing can be more picturesque than the shape & situation of this castle. The Donjon or Keep is a great square tower, with windows in what in England is called the Saxon Gothic The whole beautifully coloured by time Immediately beside the Donjon is a lofty round tower of the finest proportions, built by Talbot, in the reign of

There are the remains of the Hall within the Donjon, with the spacious fire place — from this a flight of steps lead to the chapel. From hence there was a communication with the Talbot tower, and the passage was shewn us; still existing, with the groove in which was an iron door.

This tower was also the prison house of the unfortunate prince Arthur when confined by his treacherous uncle King John. The Falasians record with exultation that the King could not find an inhabitant of the place wicked enough to execute the attrocious [sic] murder of his nephew. Here was the scene which Shakespeare has supposed between the prince and Hubert his gaoler. There is in the very looks of this tower something to kill hope and shut out consolation. The walls are of prodigious thickness — underneath one of the chambers of the tower is a dungeon where the prisoners were confined — a circular hole in the centre of the apartment was the place by which the unfortunate captive was let down into his inextricable prison, a small aperture gave him a feeble ray of light, and lest even this should flatter him with the hopes of escape, the aperture opened within the loop hole of the upper chamber — I looked with shuddering down into this pit of oblivion and despair — which seemed contrived, with such horrible ingenuity, to be the very grave of the Soul.

The interior of this tower is like a well, and the staircases wind about it in the thickness of the walls. When we reached the summit we had a lovely prospect on one side the little town & the distant country. On the other the valley and rocks of La Bruyere, once the scene of druidical rites, and, if popular superstition may be credited, the haunt of fairies. My friend the poet told me that a saying or legend had prevailed among the common people that beneath one of the steps of the tower was buried a sum of money enough for the ransom of a prince; many had therefore visited the castle by stealth and groped among the ruins — Several of the steps had been removed, but no treasure as yet has been found. When on the summit of the tower a place was pointed out where Henry the fourth had made a great breach in the wall, and I was shewn the spot where he had erected his battery.

It is singular that the tradition about the buried treasure should be given as coming from the Tower of London. So at least says a worthy priest who has written a little volume upon the antiquities of Falaise. How the report could have come from the tower, and whether hatched there by those grave and robustious personages the Beefeaters, in their gossippings at the little tap room, knowingly called the Stone Kitchen, I leave for those who are nearer at hand to enquire. My friend the poet seemed to have very little opinion of the historian; and treated the legend with a contempt that rather surprised me, since legendary lore is the very aliment of his craft. But I found in a little while that he was entirely a classical poet — Dealing only in ancient lawes & grecian mythology and looking upon the gothic ages and all the rabble rout of chivalry — with fairies, enchanters, ghosts, & goblins with perfect contempt.

ANECDOTE OF
WILLIAM THE CONQUEROR

When William of Normandy had attained a proper age he undertook to govern his province himself

Among those who sought to dispossess him was Guy count of Brion[n]e, son of Renaldo Count of Burgundy. His claim appeared the more reasonable or sustainable since he was the son of Alice, the eldest daughter of Rich^d II and legitimate sister of the two last dukes. To support him in his pretensions he drew into his party the principal nobles of Normandy such as Renaud Count of Bessin Neel de S[aint] Sauveur Vicomte de Côtantin [Cotentin], Haimon Seigneur de Thorigny [Thorigné] & Gremault [Grimoud] Seigneur du Plessis. They assembled at Bayeux to arrange their plan of operations, and after much deliberation it was determined to assassinate William at Valogne [Valognes], where he then was.

In a corner of the chamber at Bayeux where this precious conspiracy was conducted sat a certain particoloured elf — a fool or Buffoon, a kind of privileged vagabond, sometimes in the Service of these nobles sometimes in that of William. He was considered a stupid dolt, and wandered about at will; the nobles sometimes treated him with sportive kindness — sometimes kicked him aside like a worthless hound. Probably the Duke who was young was more to his taste & treated him with kindness — certain it is he manifested a fidelity to him in a most important crisis — Without seeming to attend to the consultation of the confederates he heard and noted every word. The instant he had informed himself of their plans he slipped out and set forth at full speed for Valogne. There was no time to lose; the assassins were to perpetrate their murder that very night, and would be well mounted. Zeal seems some times to lend wings, and an inspired fool can almost effect prodigies — With incredible quickness he made his way to Valogne, but it was already late at night and all were asleep at the quarters of the Duke. The fool thundered at the gate but had nearly received at the hand of the porter the treatment of a dog who disturbs the house by his impertinent vigilance. The Fool was not to be repulsed; he made his way by clamour and main force and bolted into the bed chamber of the Duke who had been awakened by the uproar — "Save yourself Monseigneur! cried he, in breathless accents, save yourself! fly this instant or you will be murdered in your bed!" The Duke demanded an explanation — the fool gave it in an agony of trepidation but with a truth & simplicity that left no doubt — The Duke sprang from his bed — gave himself no time to dress, but wrapping himself in a mantle and threw himself on a horse to escape to upper Normandy. He fled forth without attendants, trusting to the swiftness of his steed & the suddenness and singleness of his flight for safety. The night was dark — In the confusion and gloom he lost his way, and instead of taking the road which led to upper Normandy, gallopped furiously along the highway to Bayeux. He came to the mouth of the river Vire, where a deep inlet of the sea called the grand Vay, interrupts the road and is only fordable at low tide. Fortunately the tide was out; he traversed it in safety and got to the opposite side (into the county of Bessin) before day break. He continued to urge on his steed when he heard a troop of horse approaching. He had just time to hide himself behind a hedge when they reached the spot. They were his enemies going in quest of him to Valogne. Escaped from this imminent peril he abandoned the high road and took to the fields on the side towards the Sea; but his faithful steed was exhausted & he was obliged to dismount. In this disasterous [*sic*] plight he met with a gentleman named Robert de Ry who recognized him and was surprised to find his prince thus wandering on foot, without attendants or even apparel. He entreated him to disclose by what strange account he had been reduced to this deplorable state — The Duke related his adventure, and intimated that if he assisted him in his escape he should one day or other remember it. The chevalier was a vassal of the count de Bessin; but that was not sufficient to shake the fidelity which he owed to his sovereign. He ordered his sons to attend upon the Duke and never to quit him until he was in a place of safety. They accompanied the Duke made good his escape to his native castle at Falaise, and from thence he proceeded to Rouen.

The Enemies of William were furious when they found that he had escaped — they flew to arms and ravaged all the country. The Duke, not having as yet sufficient troops to make head against them hastened to Paris to claim succour of King Henry. For this once the King shewed himself the true protector of his vassal. He received the Duke with great humanity and far from seeking to profit from the feebleness of an oppressed prince, resolved to assist him with all his forces. He put himself at the head of an army and penetrated to the middle of the province, before the factions The Duke joined this army with troops which he had caused to be levied in the païs de Caux, de Vexin, de Rouennois[?] & d'Auge, and in the neighborhood of the cities of Lisieux, of Bernay, Conches and Argentan. On the other hand the army of the factions was augmented by auxiliary troops of Brittany Maine and Anjou.

These two powerful armies encountered each other near to Argences,* at a place called the valley of the Dunes (or Douns) [Val-des-Dunes]. The royalists were the first to assault and the battle was extremely bloody. The chiefs engaged with implacable fury against each other. The King singled out the Viscount de Côtantin and the Duke the count de Bessin. Guillesen, brother of the Viscount cut his way through the throng to come to his assistance, and attacking the King with his lance unhorsed him. The King was instantly relieved by the Count de S' Paul and the Seigneur de Châtillon: Guillesen was slain on the spot, as was likewise Hamon de Thorigny, in a similar attack upon the King. The duke, on his side, pushed the Count de Bessin with so much vigour, and made such great carnage among those who surrounded him that he at length routed him. The Viscount de Cotantin endeavoured in vain to reassure the count and to rally his troops, all took to flight and he was obliged to join in it himself. Thus did the Duke gain a complete victory † by the generous assistance of the King. Guy of Burgundy who was wounded, fled to the castle of Briône where he made show of resistance; but the Duke besieged him and pressed him so close that he obliged him to surrender, and to resign his counties of Vernon and Briône, insomuch that this unfortunate prince had no other resource but to return to his possessions in Burgundy. The other chiefs of the Factions disposed of themselves in different ways. The Viscount retired into Brittany; some

* Argences a place not far from Caen on the road to Lisieux [Irving's note].

† 1042 or 47 [Irving's note].

sued for grace of the Duke, who granted it; several went to the Kingdom of Naples to establish themselves with their countrymen. Grimoult de Plessis who remained in Normandy with evil designs was taken, and executed in prison.

Hist de Normandie.

Par le Sr de Masseville
imprimee a Rouen 1698.

INDEX

INDEX

(264)

Mansfield, Mrs., 126, 135, 136, 139, 142, 155, 156, 159, 160, 162, 165, 167, 176, 178, 187

Mantes, 45, 188

Mardin, Mr., 221, 222, 224

Marianne, 64, 64 n, 95, 97, 125, 185, 213, 214, 226

Marie Antoinette, 160

Marmont, A. F. L. V. de, 182, 182 n

Married and Single, 43, 43 n, 44, 54, 227, 228

Mars, A. F.-H. B. M., 28, 28 n, 44, 104

Marsh, Mr., 50, 155

Marsh, Mrs., 155

Martin, Richard, 229, 229 n

Martyr of Antioch, The, 157 n

Masseville, Louis Le Vavaseur de, 110 n

Mathews, Charles, 197, 197 n

Matsys, Quinten, 24, 24 n

Max, Prince, 84

Mays, Mr., 116, 127, 141, 165

Medwin, Capt. Thomas, 99, 99–100, 99 n, 114–17, 122, 126–29, 132, 133, 139–43, 149, 151, 152, 155–64, 166, 169–72, 174, 176

Méhul, Étienne Henri, 174, 174 n

Meissen, 4

Mémoires sur la vie privée de Marie-Antoinette, 49 n

Memoirs of Captain Rock . . . , 190, 190 n

Merinden, Mrs., 214

Merseburg, 6

Meschede, 17

Metastasio, P. B., 107, 107 n

Methuen, Mr., 229

Methuen, Mrs., 229

Micali, Giuseppe, 143

Mildmay, Lady, 84, 158

Mildmay, Sir Henry, 151, 162, 165, 167, 169, 169–70, 179, 185

Millbrook, 225–26

Miller, Mrs., 243

Miller, John, 37, 43, 43 n, 58, 68, 143, 147, 152, 161, 194, 220, 228, 240, 241, 243

Mills, Charles, 193, 195, 217, 244

Mills, Frank, 120, 120 n, 133, 141, 142, 145, 149, 151, 152, 154–65, 167–74, 176–79, 184–87, 190, 192, 193, 195, 198, 216, 243, 244; his trip to England with Irving, 187–90; his visit to Mr. Compton with Irving, 198–206

Mills, John, 195, 244

Milman, Lady, 115, 159

Milman, Henry Hart, 157, 157 n

Milner, Henry M., 219 n

Miltown, Lord, 86, 87, 115

Mohawk, R., 188, 188 n

Molière, 29, 74, 148, 159

Mons, 25

Montaigne, Michel de, 74

Montelli, 172

Montucci, Mr., 43, 43 n

Moore, Mrs., 190–91, 208, 209, 211

Moore, Thomas, viii, ix, xii, 27 n, 62, 67 n, 73 n, 80–81, 80 n, 151, 170, 186, 190–95, 207–10, 210 n, 213 n, 228–31, 239; Irving's visit to his cottage, 210–11

Morier, Miss, 229

Morier, Mrs. D. R., 122

Morier, Mrs. James J., 228

Morier, David Richard, 61, 61 n, 62, 66, 83, 84, 92, 122, 123, 123 n, 133, 149, 172, 173, 173 n, 178, 197

Morier, James Justinian, 123 n, 124, 131, 166, 167, 171, 228, 228 n, 229

Morier, John Philip, 61 n, 118

Morpeth, Lady, 197

Morton, Mr., 148, 150, 156, 168, 169, 170, 175

Paulding, James K., 116, 116 n, 126, 175, 219, 242 n
Payne, John Howard, viii, xi, 29, 29 n, 32 n, 34, 59, 59 n, 81 n, 177, 179, 190; his correspondence with Irving, 64, 66, 67, 69, 71, 72, 73, 73 n, 74, 76, 88, 89, 93, 94, 98, 114, 115, 116, 127, 150, 155, 167, 176, 185, 201, 203, 205, 221, 226; his financial affairs, 5, 8, 60, 93, 95–98, 105, 116, 118, 119, 120, 122, 167, 198; Irving collaborates with, ix, x, 20 n, 36, 36 n, 41, 41 n, 42, 54, 57, 57 n, 76, 190 n, 193, 194, 194 n, 195, 221, 227, 228 (*see also Azendai*; *Charles II*; *Married and Single*; *Richelieu*); Irving's social contacts with, 29–35, 37–39, 41–44, 52, 53, 56, 192, 197, 218, 219, 227, 229 n, 241, 242, 243; shares lodgings with Irving, x, 32 n, 52, 64 n, 105, 185
Payton, Miss, 226–27
Payton, Mr., 226–27
Peter III, 163 n
"Peter Parley," 116 n
Peter Schlemihl, 243, 243 n
Petrarch, Francesco, 116
Philips, Mr., 85, 86, 87, 194
Philips, Mrs., 85, 86, 88
Phillips, Henry, 208, 208 n
Pilot, The, 147, 147 n, 162
Poissy, 188
Polke, Mr., 105
Poll, Old, 202
Pollard, Miss, 99, 105, 125
Poniatowski, Joseph-Antoine, 5, 5 n
Ponsonby, Miss, 50
Ponsonby, Lady Barbara, 196
Pont-de-l'Arche, 45, 188
Pontefract, 237
"Poor-Devil Author, The," x, 39,

41, 82, 82 n, 113, 113 n, 146, 147, 150, 214
Popkins, Mrs., 114, 114 n, 115
Powell, Peter, 92, 92 n, 104, 192, 192 n
Powers, Mr., 229
Price, Stephen, 141, 143, 143 n, 194, 228
Procter, Bryan Waller, 191, 191 n

Quandt, Mme. de, 98, 100–1, 102, 103, 113
Quedlinburgh, 12
Quilleboeuf, 47

Rabelais, François, 121, 206
Racine, Jean, 107, 148
Raguet, Mr., 57
Rancliff, Lady, 67, 149, 155, 158, 163
Randolph, John, 213, 213 n
Raymond, Mr., 43, 44
Reed, Mr., 93, 96, 165
Rees, 18
Rejected Addresses, 105 n, 239
Remarks on Forest Scenery, 206 n
Rennik, Mrs., 176
Reynolds, C. F., 179 n
Rhine, R., 18, 19, 22
Rice, Mr., 85
Richards, Mr., 87, 109, 128, 140
Richards, Hope, 212
Richardson, Mr., 43
Richelieu, Cardinal, 136
Richelieu, 39, 39 n, 41, 41 n, 42, 54, 56
Ringwood, 201, 202
Ritchie, Mr., 59
Robber Tales, 135, 140, 161, 163–64, 165, 185, 226
Robertson, General, 110
Robertson, Mrs., 110, 112
Robertson, Colin, 109, 113
Robinson, Mr., 85

(273)

(274)